THE WAR BEHIND THE WIRE

THE WAR BEHIND THE WIRE

EXPERIENCES IN CAPTIVITY
DURING THE SECOND WORLD WAR

by

Patrick Wilson

Research by Miranda Ingrams

Accompanies the BBC TV documentary

Pen & Sword Books Limited
47 Church Street, Barnsley
LEO COOPER

First published in 2000 by
LEO COOPER
an imprint of
Pen & Sword Books Ltd
47 Church Street
Barnsley
South Yorkshire
S70 2AS

A CIP record for this book is available from the British Library

ISBN 0 85052 745 7

Printed in Great Britain by Bookcraft Ltd., Midsomer Norton

CONTENTS

British soldiers of the Eighth Army surrender under the cover of a white flag in the Western Desert. Behind them is a knocked-out Grant tank.

ACKNOWLEDGEMENTS

This book could never have got off the ground had it not been for the men featured within it. Their agreement to have a book written about their remarkable experiences made the entire project possible. It was an honour to hear and read the recollections of Michael Alexander, Squadron Leader Bill Armitage, Tony Bethell, Lieutenant General Sir Chandos Blair, Alex Cassie, Major Jack Comyn, Brigadier Michael Dauncey, The Earl Haig, The Earl of Harewood, Alfred Heinrich, Squadron Leader Jimmy James, Gordon Laming, Walter Morison, Wing Commander Ken Rees and Colonel Bob Walker-Brown, and I am extremely grateful for their help throughout. Each man has an extraordinary story to tell and a number have recorded these in print. These titles are referred to in the Bibliography on page 216.

Photographs form a key element of this book and, in addition to the private collections of interviewees, we gratefully acknowledge contributions and permissions from Mrs Barnett; British Red Cross Society; Colditz Museum, Germany; Hartswood Films; Imperial War Museum, London; Manfred Knochenmuss, Colditz; Steve Martin POW Archives, Canada; Museum of Martyrology for Allied POWs, Żagan, Poland; Pen & Sword Books Library; Taylor Library, Barnsley and the Special Collections Branch of the USAF Academy Library.

I must say a big thank you to Beryl Vertue of Hartswood Films for providing me with the opportunity to write the book to accompany the excellent BBC documentary series and to Michael Davies, Writer and Director of the series from whose interviews this book is taken. In particular, I owe Miranda Ingrams a huge debt of gratitude for her research. Her sound words of advice, her massive help with the material and the photographs, her liaison with the veterans and her excellent company have proved invaluable.

Charles Hewitt and the publishing team at Pen & Sword deserve a special mention for all their efforts. Tom Hartman's expert editorial suggestions and Roni Wilkinson's work with the photographs have been much appreciated. I am also very grateful to George Chamier, Head of History at Bradfield College, for his help and encouragement. Finally, I would like to express my thanks to my father for his excellent advice and constant support throughout this project.

PATRICK WILSON
Bradfield
September 2000

PREFACE

I grew up with films like *The Great Escape* and vividly remember the BBC Television series *Colditz*. These works of fiction based on fact made a lasting impression, and I recall more than once trying to emulate Steve McQueens dramatic escape on my own motorbike, albeit with limited success. But I never imagined that I would ever meet the remarkable men who were the inspiration for these classic stories of escape.

It was whilst making a film about the Chelsea Pensioners, with producer Beryl Vertue, that I heard at first hand what it was really like to be captured, to be a prisoner of war and to attempt to escape. I realised that all was not as portrayed in the movies; that *fact* was indeed stranger than *fiction*. It was hearing these stories that gave me the idea for the television documentary series *The War Behind The Wire* and set me on a path that ultimately lead to a forlorn looking forest in Poland, where I discovered the base of the stove that had covered the entrance to *Harry*, the 360 foot long tunnel that was used in the ill-fated Great Escape.

The first cut of the television series *The War Behind The Wire* ran for nearly ten hours, which would have been fine but for the fact that I was only commissioned to make two one hour films! This book, based on the series, does not suffer from the same time constraints and includes many of the extraordinary stories that regrettably had to be left out: stories of hope, of despair of loss and, occasionally against all the odds, of triumph.

MICHAEL DAVIES
Writer and Director of the Hartwood Films Series
The War Behind the Wire for BBC TV.

VOCABULARY

A

APPELL:- (noun.) Roll-call. Called Roll-call by the Ger-
-mans so that P.O.Ws can understand. Called Appell by P.O.
Ws so that Germans can understand. (adj.) e.g. A-time, or
A-goon:- a goon concerned with roll-call (see GOON).

B.

BASH:- (noun) A large meal. (verb) to bash:- to eat, to
make, to do, e.g.- B-the pit, (see pit) B-tin, B-circuits, (see circuit)
BEND:- Round the :- Mad.
BREW:- (noun) Tea, coffee or cocoa. Raisin Brew:- alcohol-
-ic drink made by fermenting raisins (verboten).

C.

CIRCUIT:- (noun) The perimeter track of the compound.
COOLER:- (noun) Detention cells for the unruly.

D

DHOBI :- (noun) A washing of clothes, hence DHOBI-STICK,
an implement used for pummeling clothes. May have some
Phallic significance.
DIENST:- (noun) A job. e.g. dhobi-D , cooking-Dienst.

F

FERRET:- (noun) A goon employed in snooping.

G

GASH:- (adj.) Extra, unwanted. e.g. G-glop (see glop.)
GLOP:- (noun) A slushy mess of food, esp. as provided by
the cookhouse.
GOD:- (noun). Padre. Hence G-box, church, G-botherer,
one who goes regularly to Church Services.
GOON:- (noun) A German. (adj) German, e.g. G-Aircraft.
Also GOONISH:- of Germanic type.
GOON-BOX:- (noun). Armed watch tower for German sentries
GOON-SKIN:- (noun). German uniform.
GOONIQUE:- (noun). The official German Military Communique

K

KEIN TRINKWASSER:- (noun). Zinc water jug.
KRIEGIE:- (noun.) P.O.W.

P

PIT:- (noun). Bed or Bunk. Hence, P-basher, one who is
perpetually in bed. EMPITTED:- (adj), well settled in bed.
PRANGER:- (noun) Any substitute for a hammer.
PURGE:- (noun) A consignment of Kriegies to or from a camp.
(verb), To send Kriegies to another Camp. PURGEE, a member
of a purge. P-gen:- News from home supplied by new purge.

S

SACK:- (noun). Bed or Bunk (see PIT). S-artist, a pit-
basher.
STOOGE:- (noun). One who does the dirty work - usually
applied to dish-washing. (verb):- To do the dirty work,
to wander about aimlessly.

SUPPLEMENT, NOT IN ALPHABETICAL ORDER.

RACKET:- (noun) Derogatory term used by the
indolent to describe enterprise on the part of the
go ahead.

8

Glossary of terms used by POWs reproduced from Alex Cassie's Wartime Log.

INTRODUCTION

Few servicemen ever considered they might be captured. Hours earlier they may have been sipping tea in the mess or relaxing on an airfield in Southern England. Some were to find themselves behind the wire for virtually the entire war. Thousands, for example, were captured in the first few weeks of the blitzkrieg attack on France in the summer months of 1940. The miracle of Dunkirk came too late for them. Others were captured during the reverses in North Africa soon after, while a number were imprisoned much later. It is easy now to view the war with the benefit of hindsight, but for the men enclosed in a barbed-wire compound their future was far from certain. None could accurately predict how long the war could last, nor did they know what its outcome would mean for them.

From their point of capture the only thing that every soldier, sailor and airman could be sure of was that for the time being their war was over. Another war, however, was just beginning. This new war, the war behind the wire, was no less challenging. It would be waged against boredom, hunger, despair and sometimes brutality. For some it was a battle of survival, for others a battle to escape. It marked a new dawn.

Reactions varied from prisoner to prisoner and were often determined by the varied conditions. Life in a camp in Italy, for example, was markedly different to one in Germany. Loneliness at being away indefinitely from loved ones, irritability at being confined with too many captives in too little space, injustice at being imprisoned, having committed no apparent crime, were but a few of the

These British soldiers were captured north of the French town of Cassel during the withdrawal of the British Expeditionary Force towards Dunkirk in May 1940.

British and French soldiers, with their backs to the Channel and nowhere left to go, surrender to elements of the 7th Panzer Division.

emotions that prisoners had to try and overcome. But many also fostered hope: hope that the war would soon be over, hope that they could hatch a successful escape, hope that their families were safe.

Weaponless against a fully armed captor, it was a war in which their destiny was far from in their own hands. Winston Churchill, who had himself been a prisoner in the Boer War in 1899, wrote, 'You are in the power of your enemy. You owe your life to his humanity and your daily bread to his compassion. You must obey his orders, go where he tells you, stay where you are bid, await his pleasure, possess your soul in patience.'

Periods of boredom might suddenly be broken by extraordinary events that they often had little power in determining. Prisoners in Italy, for example, were confronted on 3 September 1943 with the news that the country they were being imprisoned in had surrendered. Some prisoners found themselves victims of allied bombing. Others were suddenly moved from one camp to another. Nothing was certain as long as you were behind the wire. Yet some inmates were determined to force the pace of change. Escaping was a popular but dangerous pastime. Bravery, skill, improvisation and dedication were all necessary ingredients for a successful breakout. Secrecy and teamwork were also essential. Remarkably few succeeded. Even if a prisoner did manage to get out of the camp, his journey to freedom was in its infancy. The next stage was perhaps the most difficult of all, for he would then have to make the hazardous journey back to 'Blighty' over alien territory, often without the necessary language skills. If he was very lucky he might establish contact with an underground organization. However, civilian contact spelt danger and most tried to avoid the risk.

For the first time in history international rules governed the treatment of military prisoners, on paper, at least. The Geneva Convention was the result of work by the Swiss government, working hand in hand with the International

10

Major-General Victor Fortune, Commander of the 51st Division, surrenders to Major-General Erwin Rommel at St Valery-en-Caux, June 1940.

Committee of the Red Cross. In July 1929, forty-seven nations, including all Second World War belligerents except the USSR, agreed to follow a number of principles and guidelines concerning the treatment of POWs.

The Convention dictated that a prisoner 'must at all times be humanely treated' and spelled out in considerable detail the rights of the captive and the obligations of the captor. The terms only applied to uniform-wearing members of a regular military unit. As such, guerrillas, spies and commandos were not

British prisoners captured after the 'fight to the finish' of 30 Brigade at Calais in May 1940.

officially POWs as defined in the Convention. Among the terms was one that a prisoner's food, clothing and shelter were to be equal to that of the captor's own troops and he must be allowed to communicate with his own family. In practice, however, the application of the terms was unpredictable and depended less upon the provisions made by the Convention than upon the customs and attitudes of the captor. Germany tended to abide by it in its treatment of prisoners from France, the United States and Britain on its Western Front, whilst ignoring it on the Eastern Front. By the testimony of its own official records, Germany killed no fewer than 473,000 Russian POWs during the war. It is estimated that of the 15,000,000 prisoners of all nationalities at least 6,000,000 did not survive to return home. Many of these died under the Japanese. This book does not, however, cover the appalling experiences of POWs who suffered in the Far East. It is solely based on the experiences of British servicemen imprisoned in Italian and German camps. The majority of these were not subjected to such horrors.

For the most part, British prisoners were held in camps run by the Wehrmacht or Luftwaffe, who made considerable attempts to follow the terms laid down by the Geneva Convention.

Thus British POWs avoided, on the whole, the appaling atrocities that many Eastern European and Jewish peoples suffered under the Nazis. The danger for escaping prisoners and, particularly for British commandos and spies, was that they would find themselves in the hands of the Gestapo and SS whose code of conduct all too often resulted in torture and death. There are numerous references to the Luftwaffe and Wehrmacht doing their best to keep captured escapees under their own jurisdiction, but sometimes they failed. The shooting of fifty Allied prisoners who had taken part in the 'Great Escape' is one such example.

British and French prisoners marching off to five years of captivity.

'For You the War is Over'

'For you the war is over' were words heard by tens of thousands of Allied servicemen between 1939-45 at their time of capture. They signalled a frightening journey into the unknown. A moment of complacency or misfortune, an overpowering enemy, an act of betrayal, a poor command, a simple mistake were often all it took to find oneself facing the rest of the war behind the wire. Every POW has his own story of how he was taken. Some were shot down over enemy territory, others were simply overwhelmed in the field. Fate had conspired against them, no matter what the cause of their capture had been. They were combatants trained to fight in their own field and few had ever envisaged, let alone prepared for, captivity. It is hard to imagine the sinking realization they must have felt as they were led away for interrogation and a new life within the enclosed confines of an enemy camp. Their war had taken a drastic turn.

Walter Morison
1944

> ## Walter Morison, Flight Lieutenant, 103 Bomber Squadron. Captured 6 June 1942, aged 22.

WALTER MORISON was an undergraduate at Cambridge when the war broke out.

'I felt an urgency to join something but I didn't know what. The idea of being in the army wasn't appealing. The First World War was very recent and barbed wire and machine guns didn't sound very nice. I didn't know anything about the sea so that ruled out the Navy. I was, however, a trained glider pilot and I thought if a grateful government is prepared to provide me with a wonderful toy then I'll join the RAF. There's no mud in the sky. In truth it was a case of "Fly now – die later", but fortunately not in my case.'

Walter Morison
1999

Morison had initially planned to fly Spitfires, but was posted to a Bomber Command Operational Training unit, where he became a staff pilot flying trainee navigators around the north of Scotland and, later, training pilots to fly Wellingtons. His next posting was to 103 Bomber Squadron, stationed in Lincolnshire, at a time when Air Marshal Harris was ordering 1000 bomber raids over Germany. He made two operational flights as Second Pilot with his flight commander, the first being a raid on Cologne. A few days later, 6 June 1942, he took part in a bombing raid on an aero-engine factory in Paris.

'It had to be a bright, clear night as it was a very small target near the

A Wellington Mk.1A of Bomber Command receives its bomb load prior to a raid over enemy territory that night.

Seine and we didn't want to hit Frenchmen. Paris was lightly defended and we dropped the bombs with little difficulty. The Captain then swung the aircraft round, flew across the centre of Paris and said, "Know Paris well, Morison? Beautiful city! Look down, there's the Arc de Triomphe. Over there, that's the Eiffel Tower!" "What on earth is he going on about?"I thought to myself. All I wanted to do was go home whilst the going was still good. I think he was trying to give me a lesson in keeping calm over the target area! Anyway, we got home safely.'

His next trip was as Captain. The Squadron was to be involved in a mass bombing raid on Essen in the Ruhr. Essen was the centre of the German armaments industry and, as such, came in for special attention from the RAF.

'As the aircraft gathered speed down the runway there came a chorus over the intercom from the crew, "Good luck, skipper". We knew we needed it. After making our way across the North Sea and over the Dutch coast, we could see what was evidently the target in the distance. Flak was bursting all around, and searchlights and fires lit up the sky. After a little alteration of course, a call came over the intercom, "Aircraft to port, skipper!"At that point a Wellington bomber flashed across us. The message came too late and we hit it with an almighty crash. Aircraft didn't burn lights in those days unless they wanted to be sitting ducks for night fighters.

'The plane immediately went out of control. There was nothing I could do but give the order, "Abandon aircraft" and then bale out. The pilot is in the happy position of sitting on his parachute and having the escape hatch straight above his head. The fact is that, apart from the tail gunner who should be able to get out pretty easily, anyone in the centre of the aircraft stood no chance of baling out of an aircraft that was out of control. You are not on a very good pitch trying to find your parachutes in such circumstances. They were all killed.

'I was dragged out of the plane by the slipstream and must have hit my head on the tail or something, because I was very much worse for wear. Thankfully I came to in time to open the parachute and floated down. It wasn't long before I was crashing through some trees and landing in Germany. The whole thing was a fairly traumatic experience.'

Morison found himself suspended from the trees, but fortunately was only a few inches above the ground. Having unstrapped himself, he went to a little hayfield nearby to lie down and take stock of the situation. There was little cause for optimism. He had lost his heavy flying boots baling out, his head was bleeding and he was unable to move his right arm. More importantly, whilst hoping he was in Holland, he was afraid he probably wasn't.

'I was in considerable pain and I lay down to think about what my next course of action should be. It was too painful when I finally tried to get up and, being rather lacking in courage, I just lay there waiting for something to happen while above me I could hear the bombers returning home for bacon and eggs in the mess.'

Dawn finally came and an old peasant with his cart started mowing the hay. He saw the wounded pilot and they had a brief conversation which confirmed Morison's well-grounded fears that he was in Germany. The peasant had a little girl with him and he sent her off.

'Eventually a couple of policemen arrived on the scene and said, "Get up – *Aufstehen*!" "I can't," I replied. I thought I couldn't but soon discovered that their guns acted as a very quick painkiller. I stood up without delay and they took me to a local hospital, where I was put in a room with some very alarmist French prisoners of war. "Whatever you do – don't let them anaesthetize you. They'll cut off your arms and legs!" I took no notice as I really wasn't accustomed to people being beastly to one. I was also very encouraged when an elderly nurse came to take me to the operating theatre. I got stretched out on a table and she ran her fingers through my blood-caked hair. I think she must have fancied me! "*Schon, nicht wahr*!? – Beautiful isn't he?" she said. And then the doctor, with a degree of tact, stuck a needle into my arm and I passed out. They didn't cut off my arms and legs, but did manage to put my shoulder back in place. Soon after, I came round and was immediately ordered to dress, whereupon I was taken off with an escort to a hospital in Dusseldorf.

'Here there was a fellow young pilot who had dislocated his knees and was in a pretty bad way. We talked about escaping. It was a relatively easy place to break out from as it was barely guarded. But both of us were worse for wear and our chances of successfully evading capture wandering around Dusseldorf in RAF uniform with no money or papers were slight to say the least.'

Before Morison was anywhere fit enough to try an escape, he was taken off to the Luftwaffe transit camp, Dulag Luft, near Munich, and placed in solitary confinement, where he faced an interrogation.

'After a while a Luftwaffe officer came in to ask questions. A number of feeble ploys were used to try and gain information such as the notorious false Red Cross forms which he produced and asked me to fill in. It started with your name, rank and number and then went on to ask a whole lot of military questions. I filled in my name and crossed the rest out. The interrogator looked pained and was further irritated when he witnessed my reaction to some alleged telegrams from the Air Ministry. These asked for information about Sergeant so-and-so of such-and-such squadron, shot down on such-and-such date. They were manifestly false. "Anyone can use a typewriter," I said. He reacted angrily. "You accuse me, a Luftwaffe Officer, of fraud?". I denied this, "That's not what I said." "C'est le tone qui fait la musique! Do you speak French?" he replied, and he was quite right. My tone was offensive and it was intended to be. So that got me stuck in the place without very much to eat for a while.'

A few weeks later Walter Morison was 'purged' from Dulag Luft and, along with a hundred and fifty fellow Kriegies was taken to the main Luftwaffe camp at Sagan – Stalag Luft III.

Michael Alexander 1942

Michael Alexander, Lieutenant (temporary Captain), Scots Guards attached to Special Boat Service. Captured 17 August 1942, aged 21.

Michael Alexander 1999

MICHAEL ALEXANDER was stationed in Alexandria with the Special Boat Service, a unit whose role was primarily to raid behind enemy lines.

'We were a sort of SAS but by the sea rather than by land, using motor torpedo boats, submarines or whatever to take us to our destination, where we would then try and do a little bit of damage. For the most part we just lived rather a good life in Alexandria, which was a very social and fun place in those days. I had just come off the tennis court when I got a phone call from my commander, Mike Keeley. We had been on a mission to blow up some ammunition dumps behind the lines the night before but had landed in the wrong place. He told me we were going to have a second attempt on the same job that evening. I whizzed back to the hotel and did a quick change before duly setting off to the harbour. It was all a bit of a rush and I wasn't even in my uniform – just silk shirt, gabardine trousers and a Russian Circassian hat. Not very military looking, but I wouldn't have stood out among the Italians.

'We took the motor torpedo boat and went out under naval command to our intended landing destination. It was only about thirty or forty miles from Alexandria. I remember quite a big moon and we came in slowly towards the shore, then got into rubber boats and pulled up at the beach. Then, almost as we were landing, everything suddenly woke up. It appeared we'd landed right in the middle of an army unit. Lights went on, dogs barked and machine guns went off. I discovered later that we had landed in the headquarters of the 90th Light Division, which was a crack unit of the Africa Korps. There were twenty of us and it was now a question of what to do. The majority decided to return to the boat. A marine corporal, Peter Gurney, and myself thought otherwise and stayed behind. Our units hadn't had much success and our reputations were getting a bit tarnished through lack of activity.'

Typical German positions in the Western Desert protected by barbed wire and mine fields.

Alexander and Gurney, now alone, lay low in a sand dune waiting for the commotion to die down before pushing on through the enemy headquarters under the cover of vehicles and tents.

'We had a bag of bombs with a time pencil in them, which, when you nipped it, went off about an hour or so later. They were powerful weapons. My thinking was that we might not find the ammo dump but we could at least do some damage. So I put two of these bombs on a tank transporter, which might not sound all that interesting but is in fact equal to two tanks. If you don't have a tank transporter then when they break down or need to be taken somewhere they can't be moved.'

After placing some bombs around the transporter, the two men moved off in search of their original target.

'As we crossed the road, there in front of us was this great ammunition dump with a wire round it and one guard patrolling it. I suppose the correct commando training would have been to stick a knife in his back but I felt a bit more surreptitious about it. Anyway, we managed to place half a dozen of these bombs around it and moved off rather quickly as it was getting latish. There was no chance of us getting back for our rendezvous, so we decided to walk back. Unfortunately we found the sun came up rather quickly. We had no supplies because we had left all the stuff in the sand dunes. I didn't even have my water bottle, which was extremely stupid of me. So we sat under a tree and a while later some Arabs arrived. They didn't like Italians, so we pretended we were Germans. "We need somewhere to spend the day", we told them. They duly found us a cave in

A German encampment in the Western Desert.

the desert which wasn't very comfortable and assured us they would come back at night or early evening with some supplies so that we could walk back.'

The Arabs never returned and, by the time they left the cave, Alexander and Gurney had lost some valuable hours of night cover. Nevertheless, they embarked on their night walk with the hope of reaching British-occupied territory by daybreak. Things, however, did not go according to plan.

'As the sun came up we found ourselves surrounded by tents all over place. It was the German rear line, which we should have got through had we had another two hours. We approached a large tent and I went in with my pistol. I ordered the men inside to put their hands up in German, which they did. There were six of them. We then proceeded to take their breakfast which was spaghetti bolognese and washed this down with some coffee. I was keen to take a Luger or two, as us Brits rather liked the Luger pistol, so I took a belt and stuck three into it. I also stupidly took one of their Afrika Korps hats – not so much to disguise myself but to keep the sun off. Gurney tied them up. One of them had fainted and I told Gurney to go easy on him. I can't think why I said that, because the very same soldier managed to untie himself and sound the alarm as soon as we had left the tent. We should have killed the lot! Anyway, as we set off to pinch a lorry we began to get shot at by people. There was no escape. We were prisoners. Of course, I was caught in this embarrassing situation with my German hat on and no marks of distinction as a British officer.'

To make matters worse, Alexander was informed that he was on a murder charge. The bomb he had placed in the tank transporter had gone off and killed some German soldiers sleeping inside it.

18

'Quite a nice Oxford-educated German officer brought me a document with all these charges. "You're in trouble because the Führer has given an order that anyone caught playing commando games is to be shot." "Well," I said, "do you think I am going to be shot?" He said I probably would be. At this point Gurney rather cunningly let it out that I was related to General Harold Alexander, who had just come out and who they all knew about. I think they quite respected Alexander, like we respected Rommel. So gradually I began to admit that I was a relation. In fact I made out he was my uncle as that sounded rather more impressive. A few hours later, Rommel himself came to have a look at me as did General Westphal. A decision was then taken that they wouldn't shoot me in the field, and Gurney and myself were flown back to Germany.'

General Alexander (left) arrived to take charge in North Africa. General Mongomery (right) took over command of the the Eighth Army. Michael Alexander's claim that the C-in-C was his uncle undoubtedly saved him from execution under Hitler's directive that commandos were to be shot on capture.

Both men were imprisoned in a civilian jail called the Tagel in Berlin. Later, Michael Alexander was sent to Colditz. What happened to Peter Gurney remains a mystery. 'I've written to the marines headquarters asking for information about him and I haven't had an answer. I don't like to think quite honestly that he might have been disposed of at that time. It's one of those things that slightly haunts me. I've just never heard from him.'

Bill Armitage 1940

> ### Dennis (Bill) Armitage, Squadron Leader, 129 Squadron. Captured 21 September 1941, aged 29.

BILL ARMITAGE was an experienced Spitfire pilot who had fought in the Battle of Britain with 266 Squadron. Soon after, he formed 129 Squadron. Their job was to do fighter sweeps over France, a job that Bill was far from happy with.

'We seemed to be asking for trouble and not doing any good. Our job was really just to show the flag. It was supposed to boost French morale by seeing us fly over, but I think I can safely say we lost as many pilots as we knocked down. During the Battle of Britain you were fighting for your own ground and that was the difference.

'On the day I bolted we were tootling around somewhere over France when suddenly we were jumped on by a load of Messerschmitt 109s. Someone got under my tail. I was the squadron leader and I think that

Bill Armitage 1999

Bill Armitage in the cockpit of a Spitfire when he was serving with 266 Squadron, November 1939 – May 1941. During this period he fought in the Battle of Britain.

makes you marginally more vulnerable than the rest because you were always keeping an eye on how things were going or attempting to keep the lads together.

'My plane got hit and I was slightly wounded in one hand but I thought we were going to be all right. The plane was still flying perfectly and I was about to round on the chap who had attacked me when the damn thing caught fire. The incendiary bullets seemed to have a slow-acting effect and it actually took about thirty seconds, or possibly even a minute, before she caught fire. The problem was that in a Spitfire you have the tank in front over your knees and when the tank went off the whole cockpit soon became engulfed in flames. My oxygen caught fire too. From that point one's only objective is to get out, and to get out quick. I was in a panic and couldn't undo my strap, so I desperately tried to pull myself out but that was no good. Then I pulled myself together a bit and managed to sort the strap out. My next problem was that the perspex hood didn't slide back. I actually went straight through. To compound my errors, the final stupid thing I did was to pull my parachute cord much too soon. One is meant to drop for a while before pulling the cord, but it is rather tense wondering if the parachute is going to open, so I pulled it at about 20,000 feet and took a dickens of a time to float down.

'As I was descending a Messerschmitt came flying around me. I remembered a story I had heard of a chap who was seen bailing out quite successfully but whose body was full of holes when he landed. In many ways this wasn't such a surprising event as there were more Spitfires than there were pilots. Anyway thankfully he didn't shoot me up. Nevertheless, by the time I had at last landed there were lots of little Germans in their nasty green uniforms waiting for me. Their greeting was the standard "For you the war is over". They all tried to get souvenirs and were keen on persuading you to give them your watch, but there was no trouble.'

As he was slightly wounded, he was taken to a makeshift hospital near Boulogne where he stayed for a few weeks.

'There was little to do and I became very worried then about the idea that I wouldn't be home for God knows how long. I'd never even given a thought to the fact that I might become a prisoner of war before. I just wondered what the hell was going to happen next.'

On recovering from his wound Bill Armitage was taken to a transit camp in Lübeck in Germany, before being moved to another camp near Hanover. He spent his final years in captivity at Stalag Luft III.

Jack Comyn
1939

John (Jack) Comyn, Lieutenant, 8th King's Royal Irish Hussars. Captured 10 December 1940, aged 25.

JACK COMYN was given command of a troop of three light tanks the day before General O'Connor began a large-scale attack on six Italian divisions. The battle began well for the British and a line of about thirty miles was penetrated:

'We knew there was an Italian Division on a ridge which ran back to the frontier with Libya. It was presumed they must have retreated when they saw the rest of their divisions being driven back. I was suddenly sent for by the Squadron Leader and told to take my troop and reconnoitre this ridge in order to ascertain whether the Italians were still there. I set off with my three tanks amidst a tremendous sandstorm. We hadn't gone very far when a few shells landed around us – not particularly near. At this moment one of our tanks broke down. In those days the treads used to come off very easily. We left it and I went on with the other tanks.'

Jack Comyn
2000

Suddenly the sandstorm lifted and Comyn saw in the distance, some thousand yards away, a line of stone sangars (little low stone walls that the Italians used as a semi-fortification). Behind it he could make out the tops of lorries. Realizing that the Italians were still there, he tried to make contact with his Squadron Headquarters on the wireless.

'Unfortunately, I found that I could only contact the tank behind me so I ordered the corporal in the tank to tell the Squadron Leader the news. I received a message back again through the other tank saying "Count numbers of men and vehicles". This was a pretty impossible thing to do as they were all concealed. The Squadron Leader must have thought I'd seen a column on the move. Anyway, I was keen to impress on my first day as a troop leader and so I decided to try and get a bit closer.

'We moved forward, but, even using field glasses with my head out of the turret, could still count nothing! Suddenly an anti-tank shell slammed through our tank right opposite the driver. I hope it killed him straight away. The blast from the shell had gone through the driver and up the little aperture between the front of the tank and the gunner/wireless operator who was down on my left. I pulled open his turret but found the poor fellow couldn't get out. I don't know how I did it but I managed to get down under his arms and pull him out. It was then that I realized that one of his legs was completely blown off, poor fellow. The tank was now on fire and I got him onto the ground and dragged the poor chap towards the other tank. The awful thing was that when I asked him how he was feeling, he replied that he had a pain in his toe. The fact was that he didn't have a leg at all. Suddenly a whole lot of Italians on foot came out and surrounded us. The best thing to do was to surrender. They were very good and they got him straight off into some field hospital but

Three-man crew of a Vickers Light Tank Mk.VI scour the desert landscape for signs of troop movements. A British large-scale raid was turning into an all-out attack as the Italian army began to disintegrate.

unfortunately he died that night. I gesticulated to the Italian Lieutenant that my driver was still in the tank, but we both realized that we could never get at him. He was battened down, locked down in front, and the tank was now blazing away.

'I was rather surprised the Italians didn't finish me off. I was certainly at their mercy and they had made quite a reputation for themselves in Abyssinia for their heartlessness. However, I must say that the war in the desert – whether with the Italians or the Germans – was almost always conducted in a sort of chivalrous manner.

'The next thing I knew was that I was being interrogated by an English-speaking intelligence officer. He only really asked me the conventional questions, name, rank and number, before ordering that I be searched. At this point I suddenly remembered that I had a little list of code names and thought, "Oh my God, I'm going to give away a huge amount of information". So I pulled it out and stuffed it in my mouth. Some seven or eight Italian soldiers fell on me but were too late to prevent the damage. A little later I had my scratches and bruises seen to by an Italian medical officer who said, much to my surprise, "Lieutenant, you have done what any Italian officer would have done in those circumstances".

The day after, Comyn was driven to a camp on the Sofafi Ridge. Down below, the desert stretched towards the Mediterranean and he could clearly see battle in the distance.

'I was taken to a cave, with two armed sentries placed outside it. To my amazement a table, a chair, and even a mess waiter were provided and I settled down to a delicious meal. As I ate it I looked out to the north where there was nothing but fires, smoke and noise. From this high vantage point one could witness the battle unfold. I don't say I saw every tank, but you could certainly see a good deal of the fighting going on. I was treated extraordinarily well and an Italian officer even apologized for not being able to find a pillowslip that evening for me. Despite the hospitality, that evening my predicament dawned on me, but I remained optimistic that I would be recaptured soon after. Otherwise I think I would have become very depressed. Of course, more than anything, I felt terrible sadness at the death of my driver and gunner.

'I didn't get much sleep that evening. In the middle of the night I was roughly awoken by four Italian military police and hustled into the back of a truck where I found myself in the midst of a lot of very soft bodies. There were little feminine noises and curses, and it became clear these were the ladies of the Italian camp brothel. They were obviously fed up of the war and were making cutting throat gestures all the time about Mussolini. Thankfully, they viewed me as a fellow sufferer in this awful débâcle and were terribly nice to me. The thought did cross my mind that if my regiment surrounded this lot what the hell was I going to say to them! I resolved to jump out should any tanks appear, as my life wouldn't have been worth living!'

Jack Comyn was driven to Tripoli, where he was placed on the liner, *Conte Rosso*, and sailed to Naples.

'There were only four officer prisoners in Italian hands at the time and, after a couple of weeks, we were all put on board an old Lloyd Triestino liner, where some stewards took us to a very pleasant cabin. They then offered us some food the like of which we had not seen for months – white bread, very good coffee, jam and everything. Throughout the journey we were looked after us like kings. Ironically, the only danger came from British submarines! We were even allowed to go on the promenade deck, which was full of pretty little Italian wives who'd been evacuated from Tripoli because the war was going badly for them. The Carabinieri did, however, object when we began conversing with them, but, instead of moving us, they moved the girls!'

On reaching Italy he was taken to an Italian prisoner of war camp at Mont Albo. He escaped at the time of the Italian Armistice but was recaptured by the Germans after a four-hundred-mile journey down towards the south of Italy. His new captors sent him back to Germany where he was imprisoned at Moosberg camp, near Munich.

The Earl Haig 1941

The Earl Haig, Second Lieutenant, Royal Scots Greys. Captured 22 July 1942, aged 24.

The Earl Haig 1999

THE EARL HAIG, son of the Commander-in-Chief of the British Expeditionary Force in the First World War, was an officer in the Scots Greys in North Africa. By the beginning of July 1941 Rommel's drive towards the Delta had been halted and the situation at El Alamein became more stable. With the Germans now consolidating their positions and reorganizing their arms, weapons and supplies, General Auchinleck decided to mount a series of infantry night attacks before the enemy was ready to move on to invade the Nile. Lord Haig was made Liaison Officer between the 22nd Armoured Brigade and the New Zealand Brigade in one such attack.

Haig's Crusader tank was equipped with a wireless set with which he could communicate with the 22nd Armoured Brigade, which was ready to come up in support of the New Zealanders at first light the following morning. At around 2000 hours the New Zealanders went into their attack through the minefields. As it grew dark Haig moved slowly towards the point of the wedge which had been driven into the enemy line. Enemy fire was still intense.

'I remember getting out of my tank to pee and getting back in again fairly smartly as bullets whizzed past my nose. Next morning at first light we found ourselves trapped in a saucer. The New Zealand infantrymen were lying in slit trenches which they had dug during the night. German

24

tanks armed with 88mm guns were firing at us from the ridge in front and the situation was serious as the British tanks which should have come to our support were not there. I have read since that Brigadier Fisher commanding 22nd Armoured Brigade got his map references wrong and did not appear in the right place. I had been unable to get in touch with Armoured Brigade Headquarters since the beginning of the attack, due to the jamming of our wireless by the Germans.

'Shells were now landing all round us. I saw a New Zealander, dreadfully wounded below the waist, crawl pitifully towards the tank. The tank itself was in a very exposed position. We were a sitting duck. I wanted to move it but there was a danger of running the New Zealanders over in their trenches, so I decided to stay still, despite knowing it couldn't really contribute to the battle. Our little 2-pounder gun was absolutely useless against the enemy tanks drawn up along the ridge. It was like a peashooter

Lord Haig, at his easel in the Western Desert, finds a curious audience among the local Arabs. He would soon have sufficient time on his hands to develop his hobby. This photograph was taken shortly before his capture

A German 88mm anti-aircraft tank gun is being brought into action by its crew and is still in transport mode (the fixed mounting stabilizers have not been secured). This gun was to prove a formidable weapon throughout the war.

at that range. We had a few shots but that didn't do much good. Legging it back to our lines wasn't a possibility as we would have probably been picked off, and it wouldn't have gone down too well amongst the New Zealanders if the British presence in the form of the Crusader tank had just disappeared at that critical stage.'

The enemy scored a direct hit on the Crusader soon after. Smoke and flames began engulfing the machine and Haig and his crew of three were left with little option but to bale out, thankful to be alive and not wounded. While he jumped for cover into the nearest slit trench, two of his crew attempted to escape but were killed trying to get away on a Bren carrier. After some time the enemy closed in for the kill.

'Our Brigade was surrounded and forced to surrender. Brigadier Clifton, having taken off his badges of rank, acted as a stretcher-bearer and later escaped back to our lines, where I subsequently learnt that he reported me dead. As the German tanks rolled past us, we rose from our trenches with arms raised in surrender and were gradually collected into groups, formed up and marched back several miles towards El Daba. There, we were given water and some food and were then forced to lie down in the fierce heat. Some of the New Zealanders were desperately thirsty, having had little to drink since the night operation. Towards evening we were taken on to Daba where we were handed over to the

The British Crusader tank was fast and handy but mounted an inadequate 2-pounder gun and consequently was out-ranged by the German Mk IIIs and IVs. Also, since the shell of the 2-pounder lacked a piecing cap, it often broke up on impact with the heavy armour of enemy tanks.

Italians. Several of the Germans were envious of our situation. "For you the war is over," they said as they left us to return to the front line.'

The day after his capture Haig and his fellow captives were taken past Ma'aten Bagush to Matruh where they were put in a wire cage. There was no shade and little food or water. The conditions were all the worse for Haig as he had been suffering from dysentery for several days. After a time a truck arrived and his name was called out. He was taken back east to Ma'aten Bagush where he was to be interrogated by an Italian officer in an armoured command vehicle.

'Behind him were some boxing gloves, an epee and a silk dressing gown. He knew who I was and introduced himself as an Italian count who had frequented the world of London society before the war. He asked me some questions, which I refused to answer except to say my name, rank and number. When I remained silent the officer looked harsh. He said he would give me ten minutes to think things over. A while later I was brought back but remained silent. He looked grim. He said he admired me but that I must face the consequences. Thoughts of torture flashed across my mind. In fact I was taken by the guard into a dugout and the door was then locked. Inside it was cool and an old camouflage net was on the ground. Still weak and debilitated, I lay down on it. I was later given some excellent risotto in a mess tin and felt better.

'Some time later the door was opened and a dark-skinned officer dressed in RAF uniform came in. I sensed he was an Italian sent to live beside me as a stooge. His tale sounded plausible. He had made a forced landing ferrying a plane from England. He talked of London and told me who had won the Derby. In fact we got on quite well together. Next day after lunch I was taken into the officers' mess and given coffee and a liqueur. The Italians tried to break down my reserve but I managed to keep off all military topics. Whenever my stooge friend tried to discuss the war, I excused myself on the grounds that there might be a dictaphone hidden behind the wall. Apart from information about our forces and equipment there was nothing I could have divulged anyway as I had spent the war far from the corridors of power. I knew nothing of the Russian situation, nor of our plans for a Middle East offensive.

'After about three days, when they had given up all hope of getting information out of me, I was put in the truck again. As I bade goodbye to my original captors, the stooge told me that there had in fact been a dictaphone in the dugout. For a moment I wondered to myself if I had been discreet, but then I felt confident that I had not given any information which could be useful to the enemy.'

A month later Lord Haig was flown back to Italy, to a transit camp near Bari, and soon after was taken by train across central Italy to a camp in Sulmona, near Rome.

Alex Cassie, Pilot Officer, 77 Squadron. Captured 3 September 1942, aged 25.

*Alex Cassie
1937*

*Alex Cassie
1999*

ALEX CASSIE'S squadron of Whitleys was loaned to coastal command during the summer of 1942. Their task was to do anti-U-boat patrols over the Bay of Biscay. This involved searching for submarines, which would then be targeted with depth charges. Cassie found these daylight flying sorties long and tedious, and would have preferred bombing raids. However, his thirteenth mission was different. His task was to attack an armed tanker in the early morning, which was believed to be anchored near La Rochelle, using armoured-piercing bombs rather than the usual depth charges.

'Our intelligence people couldn't give us any information about the tanker. I remember asking at the briefing about what height the side of the tanker would be. Nobody could tell me. I also felt a little uncomfortable because I didn't have entirely my own crew. My regular navigator was off on leave and my new second pilot, who I had only flown once with before, didn't like me and I didn't like him. At least I had my own tail gunner who was a wonderfully alert, cheerful and observant cockney, as well as a fellow Scot as a radio operator.'

Their first problem was that they were supposed not to attack after the sun had risen, but, on reaching the French coast, they found themselves in brilliant daylight. To make matters worse, as they flew along the miles and miles of

An Armstrong Whitley bomber of Bomber Command.

featureless coast they began to struggle with their orientation.

'We realized we had no idea as to whether we were north of La Rochelle or south of it. Eventually I decided to abandon the mission as we had been ordered not stay longer than 6.30. On our way back my tail gunner spotted a U-boat. So we went down to attack. Normally these submarines try to submerge, but this one didn't play by the rules. It stayed on the surface and we found ourselves having a wonderful view of it as we went straight towards our target at some fifty feet. A couple of U-boat gunners were firing the light machine gun – or whatever it was they had on the deck. We laughed and said, "He's trying to shoot us down". Then suddenly these tracers started going past us very quickly and pop, pop, pop, our starboard engine was out of action. It was now clear we would have to ditch the plane as we were far too far from home to consider making it back. So I gave ditching orders and everyone leapt into action and, as was procedure, everyone apart from me went back into the centre of the aircraft to take crash-landing positions with their backs against a bulwark.

German U-Boat caught on the surface. In Alex Cassie's case the U-Boat Captain decided to put up a fight rather than submerge.

'I felt very lonely having to handle this thing and tried hard to remember all I had been taught about the dangers of ditching a Whitley. Thankfully, I noticed a French fishing boat in sight and decided to attempt to come down near it. I strapped in extra tightly and desperately tried to keep the plane steady. As soon as I felt the thing bite, I put my hands up over my face. There was a tremendous high-pitched splintering noise and the next I knew was that I was tasting salt water. I clambered out of the hatch and went on top, waiting for the crew to emerge. There were noises from inside but no one came out. To my horror, it became clear that someone had panicked and pulled the release cord to the inflatable dinghy inside. They couldn't push it out and were effectively trapped. There was a very real danger that the plane was about to sink and so I crawled along it and punctured the dinghy with a knife I was carrying in my pocket.

'Once all were out, being the skipper, I said, "Right then, one of you swim over to that boat and get them to come and pick us up." There was silence. None of them could swim so I had to go. My crew have since told me that I was very methodical in my preparation for this venture. Apparently I took my shoes off and put them side by side on the roof of the plane, then took my trousers off and hung them up with the pleats in the right position over the aerial and set off into the water. I swam very hard for a while and thought that I must be nearly there, turned round and realized that I had got little further than the wing tip.

Alex Cassie sho[w]
before he was brou[ght]
down by the U-Bo[at]

'The sea was pretty rough and it was all proving rather difficult. I disposed of my Mae West and with it came my dress jacket so I was literally in my shirt and socks ... and underpants of course. In the distance I could see men climbing out of the fishing boat into a rowing boat and soon after must have lost consciousness because the next thing I remember was being hauled on board. I think I stammered, "*quatre hommes*", which was about all the French I knew. They understood and eventually all the other members of the crew were brought on board.

'I remember thinking that this French crew would find it rather difficult to hang on to us without the Germans finding out, as I knew that they were pretty closely monitored. Sure enough as we reached Concarneau harbour we were greeted by a small German officer – a perfectly nice chap – on the quayside. There was nothing officious about him.'

The German officer marched the party off to where the local army unit was stationed. They were shown into a room and several mattresses were thrown down for them to rest on. Cassie collapsed exhausted, but was awoken soon after and told that their chief wanted to see him.

'He was a caricature of all that's cruel and vicious in the popular conception of the German army officer. A typical bullet head – a really nasty looking thug – and I was terrified that he might try and give me a real nasty blow. However, before he had any time to ask me any questions, I think I must have fainted because the next thing I knew was that I was falling over. He caught me and held me up, and to my surprise said, "Oh, poor chap". He was actually terribly nice. I never saw him again and the next day we were entrained to Dulag Luft, where I was placed in a solitary cell. Treatment was pretty good and I even remember asking for a cigarette and being given one by my guard. Indeed I was also given a First World

30

War Polish army tunic and was intrigued to discover there were three cigarettes, which someone had placed in the pocket. It was a rather nice gesture, I thought.

'Later a German officer came in and said, "Good morning, Mr Cassie. Another loss for 77 Squadron, hey?". How he knew I don't know but we had been warned they tried various tricks to find out more information than just name, rank and number, which was all that the Geneva Convention said was required. "Your Commanding Officer, Wing Commander Embling, must be missing you by now," he continued. He realized he was going to get nothing out of me and said, "All you people do this. It's so silly; you know it won't help you. If you let us know the information we're after, we'll pass this on to your relatives right away. Don't you want them to know?". I don't remember being scared at all. I think we had faith in what we had been told by the RAF which was that the Germans seemed to be observing the Geneva Convention pretty well.'

Cassie was later interrogated at Dulag Luft and from there was imprisoned at Stalag Luft III.

*Tony Bethell
1942*

*Tony Bethell
1999*

> ### Richard (Tony) Bethell, Pilot Officer (RAF Volunteer Reserve), 268 Squadron. Captured 7 December 1942, aged 20.

TONY BETHELL, a Mustang pilot, whose missions mostly involved intruder work – flying up and down the Dutch coast and harassing German convoys, as well as attacking other enemy targets.

'Mustangs had a long range and as such they were the first fighters into Germany. One used to fly across the North Sea and when the Dutch coast came in sight on the horizon that's when I, and I'm sure a lot of others, started being frightened. The Germans mounted some very accurate and heavy flack along that coast.'

One day Bethell and three other pilots were put on a mission to go to the Dorklands Canal in Germany and any target of opportunity along the way. They

The North American Mustang built in the United States to British Air Ministry specification.

Extract from Tony Bethell's Wartime Log *in which he recorded his crash-landing and capture.*

flew from Snailwool near Newmarket, where they were stationed, up to the coast at Cotteshall. There they filled up with petrol and set off at around ten o'clock that evening.

'After a slow flight over the North Sea in order to conserve petrol, we reached the Dutch coast and were met by heavy flack. I was hit in the engine and the tail and soon discovered that I didn't have any lateral control. Meanwhile, the other three planes went their various ways. My engine sounded like an old washing-machine and I knew that I was in trouble.

'I cut back on the engine, jettisoned the hood and since I was only some twenty feet off the ground realized that I would have to land. I skidded across a field and ended up in the nose of the dike. The engine was smoking but thankfully didn't burst into flames so I was able to get out relatively easily. I instantly tore up my map and stuffed it in the tail wheel hole. Then to my surprise I looked up and there, before my amazed gaze, were these German air force anti-aircraft gunners some hundred and fifty yards away and hopping across the field in my direction. They reached me, armed to the teeth with rifles and loads of hand grenades in their belts, with the greeting, "For you, the war is over".

'I was feeling pretty shaken up and somewhat bewildered. I'd certainly jarred my back but wasn't seriously wounded. I had never contemplated

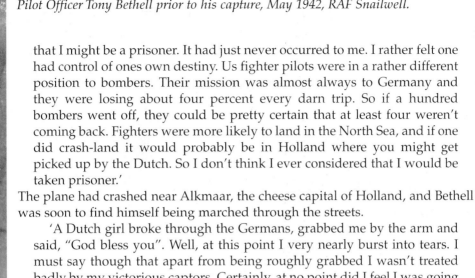

Pilot Officer Tony Bethell prior to his capture, May 1942, RAF Snailwell.

that I might be a prisoner. It had just never occurred to me. I rather felt one had control of ones own destiny. Us fighter pilots were in a rather different position to bombers. Their mission was almost always to Germany and they were losing about four percent every darn trip. So if a hundred bombers went off, they could be pretty certain that at least four weren't coming back. Fighters were more likely to land in the North Sea, and if one did crash-land it would probably be in Holland where you might get picked up by the Dutch. So I don't think I ever considered that I would be taken prisoner.'

The plane had crashed near Alkmaar, the cheese capital of Holland, and Bethell was soon to find himself being marched through the streets.

'A Dutch girl broke through the Germans, grabbed me by the arm and said, "God bless you". Well, at this point I very nearly burst into tears. I must say though that apart from being roughly grabbed I wasn't treated badly by my victorious captors. Certainly, at no point did I feel I was going to be mown down.

'I spent my first night as a prisoner in an Amsterdam prison – a real Hollywood jail with bars all around. My feelings were one of loneliness and of course one couldn't help wondering what would happen next, but for the most part I just felt very, very alone. The lavatory facilities in this place were in a compound outside the cellblock, and I was marched out

The official 'Missing in Action' telegram received by Tony Bethell's mother – note the wrong spellings.

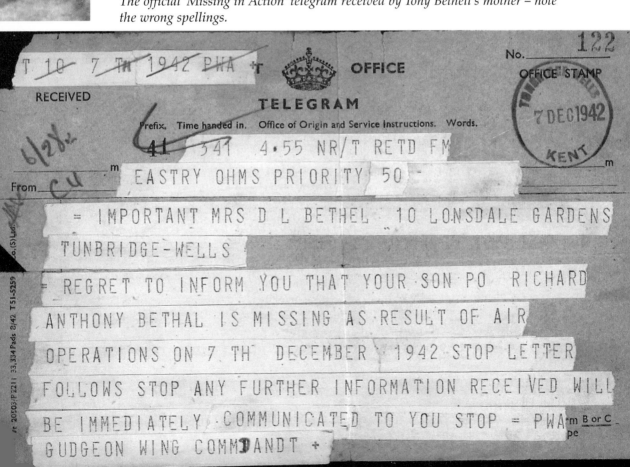

once a day it transpired by a German guard. While I was sitting on the can my first day, I looked around and there was a sort of trap door on the roof. The next day I made a further investigation and discovered it lifted, and the following day the first thing I did was to jump on the loo, shove the trap door open and pull myself up there. It was a long loft with windows along it and it struck me that it would be possible to get out of a window, jump over the wire and into the canal that was alongside. So the next morning, equipped with my escape money and map that I had been hiding in my palliasse, I made myself ready for my trip to the loo. But it never happened as unfortunately it proved to be the day that I was to be hustled off to an interrogation centre in Germany.'

Tony Bethell was taken to Dulag Luft where he was placed in solitary confinement.

'The first meal was repulsive and I just didn't eat it. I think it was a sort of combination of neat vinegar and bad cabbage. I was later approached by this immaculately dressed officer who shook hands with me and introduced himself referring to me as "old boy", and with a rather phoney Oxford accent. I soon identified him as a fraud but was prepared to accept his offer of a cigarette. He got my name, rank and number, but that was all, although he tried in vain to address the question of what squadron I was in, what I was doing and so on. The briefings we had had about what to do in the event of being captured were minimal, and I was a twenty-year-old who never thought he would be a prisoner. I really didn't know how to act in this situation except that I should give nothing away. There was never any time when I thought I was going to get roughed up though. After the fourth or fifth time of questioning me for more information, he just grabbed my cigarette, made some rather curt remark and disappeared out of the door. And that was really the end of my interrogation.'

Soon after, he was taken to Stalag Luft III along with six fellow prisoners. He recalls his journey there from the Luftwaffe interrogation centre:

'We were packed into a carriage with two guards inside and another two outside it. I can remember going through Berlin. It had quite an impact on me. This was really my first vision of Germany on the ground. It seemed dark and gloomy, and everybody seemed to be in uniform. The place was packed with lots of policemen, railway porters and men in the Luftwaffe, army and navy. As the train rolled on, it felt like one was disappearing deeper and deeper into this very militaristic, dark and dingy world. It wasn't a nice feeling. From Berlin the train went straight through Frankfurt and on to the camp. Sagan was made up of a number of compounds. The famous North camp did not exist at that time. I was taken to the East camp, which was not a particularly cheerful, prepossessing sight. Much of the wood outside it was all burned out. It was a pretty scruffy bit of country and certainly nothing that you'd write to your mum about.'

*Gordon Laming
April 1941*

Gordon Laming, Private, Royal Army Ordnance Corps. Captured 23 June 1940, on his 21st Birthday.

*Gordon Laming
1999*

GORDON LAMING had never envisaged joining the Army.

'At school I had no inclination to join the O.T.C (Officer Training Corps). This playing at soldiers seemed to me to be a most uninviting voluntary exercise. There was no background of service in the Forces in the Laming family. My father and brothers had worked in power stations which, during the Great War, had been a reserved occupation. Furthermore, there was a strongly pacifist sentiment in the Methodist Church.'

When conscription was introduced at the beginning of 1939, twenty-year-old Laming soon found himself forced to enlist. He joined the Royal Army Ordnance Corps and in March 1940 sailed over to France. In April he and a dozen others were sent to establish a forward RAOC depot in the suburbs of Metz where they would accompany the 51st Highland Division which had taken over a full sector of the Maginot Line.

On 10 May, Laming was awoken by Luftwaffe bombing. The German offensive had begun. Ten days later the Division was pulled out, following the rapid breakthrough by German Forces. Laming and his dozen colleagues were

German troops sweep round the back of the Maginot Line over-flanking the prepared positions of the Allies.

French troops surrendering to German infantry during the Battle for France. Gordon Laming's unit was cut of from the main forces of the BEF and it soon became 'every man for himself'.

left to load stores and equipment. Curiously, the enemy completely by-passed Metz and Laming and the others were unaware of the mayhem going on in the other parts of north-east France. They had no idea that by 4 June 1940 the British Expeditionary Force had evacuated from Dunkirk. They had been completely forgotten in the chaos.

'From 11-13 June we were taken up to a village cemetery some thirty kilometres from the German border to tidy the graves of British soldiers who had been killed in the skirmishing around the Maginot Line. There was a great deal of activity on our return. News had come through to our sector that the Germans were coming our way. It was a curiously unreal sort of war at this time as the mayhem of the fighting had up until now just passed us by. I hadn't even fired my rifle. About a hundred of us British soldiers got on a train and headed south. Progress was very slow. On the journey I recall some wild rumours that, the USSR, Turkey and America had entered the war. After passing Vesoul, the major who was our senior officer left the train and reconnoitred the local village only to discover that the French had asked for an Armistice.

'As a result, he decided that the 100 of us should leave the train and go into some nearby woods to consider what to do. I was on observation duty and nervously watched a stream of German scout cars pass on the road below us. There was little we could do. We were not a fighting force, just a hotchpotch of pioneers and disparate sections.'

By 18 June the major decided that the situation was militarily hopeless. It was every man for himself. He pointed his troops in the general direction of Switzerland and told them to do the best they could to escape. They were instructed to abandon their rifles, after having taken the bolts out. It was a worrying and disorientating time. None of the men even knew about the lines of demarcation that had been drawn up by the Germans and the French and, as such, had no idea that they were in fact only about fifty miles from the unoccupied zone.

'We were left to our own devices and wandered through the villages somewhat aimlessly. None of us had any maps. I went off with five others heading towards Switzerland and taking care to avoid the roads, as there were thousands of Germans going up and down them. It was a curious and bewildering feeling. To be let loose in France was a very novel situation for me. I had never been further than the Isle of Wight before coming over and here I was, with no competence in any foreign language, trying to make good an escape. We really had no idea where to go and just wandered through woods and fields. The local villagers were generous with food but very apprehensive about us. At one point some French soldiers surrendered to us. They had never seen

'Front-Stalag 142 Kr. Gef. 1331'
Gordon Laming's POW identity disc.

Entrance gate of Caserne Vauban, the second prison in which Gordon Laming was held and from where he escaped via the sewer system.

English troops and thought we were Germans. We had to tell them they were all right and that they were free to go.'

After a couple of days walking around Laming and his companions bumped into three other British soldiers and they resolved to stay together. On 21 June they were taken into a house for a few nights. Then on the morning of 23 June, Laming's birthday, the householders came and told them that the Germans were now in the village and that they would have leave quickly.

'We hurriedly left the house amid thanks and misgivings. Our one hope was that apparently the German unit in the village were not taking prisoners but telling troops that they should go to Besançon to surrender. We met some of them in a café and told them that we would go there after breakfast. The ploy seemed a good idea and so we took the road and decided to see how far we could get. The problem was that we just didn't really know where to go. After a while we stopped at another café to get something to eat. It was my twenty-first birthday and I had raging toothache, so there seemed to be at least two excuses for going into this restaurant for a cognac or two. As we did so, a German officer walked in. Well, for him it was one thing seeing a few French soldiers wandering on their own but he was rather uneasy about having British troops going about unescorted. So he arrested us and we were taken by lorry to a French barracks that the Germans were now using as a huge prisoner of war camp, comprising some three thousand Frenchmen and a handful of Englishmen.'

Laming spent the next four months in captivity before escaping from the camp. After a series of adventures, he eventually succeeded in crossing the Pyrenees to freedom.

Ken Rees 1942

Ken Rees 1999

Ken Rees, Acting Flight Lieutenant, 150 Squadron. Captured 23 October 1942, aged 21.

KEN REES was an experienced bomber pilot when he was captured in late 1942. After eight operations from England, he was posted to the Middle East and then on to Malta where he completed a further forty-eight operations. Thinking that he was getting over-confident, his commanding officer posted him back to England where he became an instructor. He got married in October 1942 and soon after was detailed for a special operation in Norway laying mines.

'They told us this was not going to be a difficult mission from the flak point of view, but did require an element of special expertise so special crews were picked. I gathered my great friend Gwyn Martin as navigator, Jim Wiley, who was another good chum of mine, John Taylor, a Canadian, as rear gunner, and an Australian who volunteered to join us. We were briefed by a naval officer on what it involved and told that we

Vickers Wellington – the main stay of RAF Bomber Command in the early years of the war

were to go in at about three hundred feet and at a speed of 150 mph.

'It was a brilliant moonlit night and all was going according to plan. Suddenly, as I was turning to make my run, all hell broke loose. The oil tank was hit immediately, all lights went out, the intercom had gone, one engine was hit and the propeller came off. I was thinking that this was

The Norwegian lake where Ken Rees put his stricken Wellington bomber down. The crash site is ringed.

getting quite nasty when the wireless operator came rushing in. His face was all blackened and he had been quite badly burned. He lifted up my helmet and shouted, "We've bloody had it," and then shot off again. I knew he was right and I now had to think about somehow landing the plane. All I could do was just point towards the water, throttle back with one engine and hope. Luckily we made it and splashed down into the lake.

'The next thing I remember was that all was still and that I was alive and in the water. My navigator started to call out, so I swam across to him and hauled him onto the wing. The wireless operator had also survived, but was badly burnt. Thankfully our dinghy had inflated automatically and we clambered aboard and soon after found the front gunner floating nearby in a very bad condition. He was completely unconscious, but we managed to get him on board. There were no signs of the rear gunner. As the fuselage was on fire he had either baled out, been hit by shrapnel, or had burned. We knew something had happened because he had been firing away madly and then suddenly it had all stopped. It was clear we now had to get to the shore, which was probably only about forty yards way, but the dinghy wouldn't move. The crew didn't seem interested in getting in the water. It was freezing and I think they thought that I'd got them into this position so I'd better try and get them out of it. So I jumped over the side and started kicking away. Nothing happened. It was only then that we realized that the dinghy was still attached to the plane by a rope.'

On reaching the shore they laid the front gunner out. There was little they could do for him and, aware that the Germans would be on the scene very quickly, they left him and set off in the direction of Sweden. The journey was made all the more difficult as Rees had lost his shoes in the crash and the navigator only had one.

'We spent the next four hours walking through marshes and climbing up rocks. The navigator was working with the northern star and he pointed in the distance and said, "Sweden's over there. It's a long way and we've got a couple of mountains to climb." Soon after, we passed a house and knocked on the door. Nothing happened for a while but after a few more knocks a head appeared at the window. "What do you want?", he asked in English. We explained that we were survivors from an aircraft. He then pointed us to another house some five hundred metres away. There we stripped most of our clothes off and I told everybody to burn anything incriminating. I then tried to tend to the wireless operator who had a lot of burnt skin hanging off his hands and face, and put some disinfectant on these areas. We were all exhausted. Gwyn Martin, the navigator, had almost passed out on a bench and Jim Wiley was barely conscious. I was in the process of trying to talk to our Norwegian host when the front door smashed open and what appeared to be half the German army, navy and air force along with some Gestapo in civilian clothes burst into the room with machine guns and revolvers. I almost pushed my hands through the

Gwyn Martin, navigator, (left) and Ken Rees, pilot, re-visit the crash site at the Langevatnet, Norway in 1969. They are holding parts of the wreckage of Wellington BK309 including a CO_2 bottle which had lain beneath the water for twenty-seven years.

ceiling as they came out with those familiar words, "For you the war is over".'

Rees and his surviving crew were driven by convoy to a place called Haugensund, where they were taken to the German Headquarters, formerly a guesthouse in the town.

'We sat around here for a while and then a huge major general came along. He was shouting like mad and I couldn't help but start laughing. I found the whole scenario very funny. The guard then, much to my annoyance, hit me over the head with his revolver, but I was powerless to do anything about it. We then had a slight interrogation, and my interrogator informed me that a battle had started at Alamein. "I am afraid you British have left it too late," he said. "No," I replied, "we have been waiting for this. This is the turning point." The truth was that I had never even heard of Alamein, but I pretended I had. Little did I know how prophetic my words were to be.'

Soon after, they were taken by train, bus and aircraft via Amsterdam to Berlin and then on to Dulag Luft, an interrogation centre for all new air force prisoners.

'I was put in a single cell with only a white table, a bed and a chair. You couldn't see out at all. First of all a nice chap came along to ask me to fill out forms, false Red Cross forms. I just only gave them my name, rank and number. Day after day they followed the same procedure. They would leave you until the evening and then a nice interrogator came in, followed later by a more serious one. It was a most peculiar feeling just sitting there and saying, "I am afraid I can only give you my name, number and rank." They kept on saying that they could tell our next of kin that we were safe if we would just fill in a form with details of our squadron and everything else. One had to reply that one's next of kin would just have to wait. The fact was that we really only knew about how to fly Wellingtons and so there wasn't anything we could have told them that would have been of any use anyway.

'The interrogation went on for about seven days. Eventually they came in with a folder saying, "You are a very experienced pilot. You must have done about fifty operations. You were on a squadron as a sergeant pilot, you were at Malta with 38 and 40 Squadrons and you have been shot down with 150 Squadron." I think my mouth must have been hanging open, amazed that he seemed to have more information about me in this folder than I knew about. I assume that their embassies must have got information from the flight magazines that was available in neutral countries, and from people who were unaware of the significance of what they were saying, and then slowly pieced together bits of information. Their knowledge astounded me. I later found out that a lot of people had the same experience.'

After his seven-day interrogation at Dulag Luft, Ken Rees was sent to Stalag Luft III.

*Mike Dauncey
1944*

*Mike Dauncey
2000*

MIKE DAUNCEY knew from an early age that he wanted to be a soldier.

'When I was aged four I went round to see a friend of my father's who showed me a gas mask, a revolver, his medals and his tin hat which he had worn in World War One. From that point on I never wanted to do anything else.' He joined up in September 1940 and, after five months of officer cadet training in Droitwich, became a second lieutenant in the 5th Battalion the Cheshire Regiment, who were at the time stationed in Northern Ireland. The battalion was later given the task of training people in England.

'I was becoming a little bit worried about my part in the army. I didn't want to be a trainer for all my army life, and so in late 1943 I volunteered to join the glider pilot regiment and went to an operational squadron in January 1944. Our prime job was to get air landing troops to the battlefield and, having hopefully landed the glider in the right place and at the right time, we would either be withdrawn in order to be used again or would find ourselves employed fighting alongside the airborne soldiers. Colonel Chatterton, our Commanding Officer, used to call us total soldiers as we had to be able to do everything.'

To his considerable regret he did not go to Normandy in June, where his battalion excelled, and had to wait until September that year before he had his first brush with the enemy at Arnhem.

'We were all thrilled at hearing the news that we were about to take part in what was clearly going to be quite a special operation. The whole thing

A Stirling bomber tows off a Horsa glider during the Arnhem operation.

One of the Landing Zones at some ten miles to the west of Arnhem.

was kept terribly secret and our first briefing was on the Saturday before we set off. This informed us that our mission involved going to Holland, west of a town called Arnhem. A few maps were shown to us and I was given a little photo showing exactly where I was to land. On one side there was a farm with a little triangular copse in the middle of it and to the east of that was the local lunatic asylum.'

Dauncey's glider was taken to the spot by a Stirling bomber. The green light then flashed up and the glider pulled off, so that they were no longer being towed. Dauncey landed the glider with no problems. Once successfully on the ground, the glider pilots had to fulfil a new function. Their order was to stay and protect the gunners.

'We were now infantry soldiers and our job was to act as a kind of screen to the men in the Royal Artillery. It was envisaged that we would later be withdrawn and sent back to England again ready for the next operation.

'I felt very excited. At last I might see a little bit of action. The odd burst of gunfire could be heard in the distance. No one came close to us that evening, and so we began digging slit trenches around the gunners to give them some sort of protection. We had clearly taken the enemy by surprise. For most of the evening the only people we saw were those from the lunatic asylum, who were extraordinarily friendly. They all came out wearing white nightshirts and kept shouting, "Hello Tommy", which I thought was very endearing.

'Later that evening, when it got dark, we had our first serious casualty. A voice was heard shouting, "Hello Tommy" and we assumed it was our friends from the asylum. In fact it was a German who must have heard these cries earlier that day. Someone shouted back a reply and a German threw a stick grenade straight into his trench. It didn't kill him but he was badly wounded, and it certainly had the effect of sharpening us up a little. In fact, it was a long first night. I couldn't sleep at all.'

When morning did eventually come, the force moved to Oosterbeek, a town some six or so miles west of Arnhem. Here the gunners would be in a position to support the first airborne division, whose main task was to seize the river bridge at Arnhem. Dauncey and his fellow glider pilots were once again to stay with the gunners and act as their support and shield.

'We received a wonderful welcome on arrival at Oosterbeek. It was great as we were the first friendly troops that the Dutch had seen for many years. Everyone wanted to give us apples and things like that. There was little time to savour the moment though, as the gunners soon began digging places for their guns and we began occupying a number of little houses around to give them protection. There were no signs of the enemy, but later that day a report arrived that a German had been spotted in a house some two miles away, and I was sent off to pick the poor chap up. I succeeded. He was absolutely terrified and thought we were going to kill him. Anyway we took him back in great triumph and he apparently provided the local intelligence people with some very useful information.'

The next few days were relatively incident-free and much of his time was spent checking various houses where known pro-Nazi Dutch people had lived. Most had long since gone.

'Probably our toughest job comprised trying to stop the telephone exchange from working. Then gradually the first signs of the battle began to emerge, and one or two soldiers started appearing from the direction of Arnhem. When this happened, some of the senior officers began forming these soldiers into defensive positions that would later be known as the perimeter. Eventually the perimeter stretched right round the whole division, with the gunners inside it. It was a very strong point and needed to be because as the week wore on the bridge was retaken by the enemy. The Germans soon began turning their attention on us. They were very good at using their 88mm anti-tank gun, which would literally make your position disappear if it hit it. To make matters worse the RAF bombers, not for want of trying, were having trouble dropping supplies for us and many didn't reach us. They couldn't have done more – they flew over us at 500 feet, absolutely straight and level. Unfortunately they came across fierce resistance. On the Thursday afternoon, for example, 190 Squadron in Fairford lost lost seven of its ten aircraft.'

The battle at Arnhem warmed up from day to day and began to reach a crescendo some three days after his arrival.

'That day someone took a pot shot at me. The bullet went through my beret and cut my skin a bit. I was elated that I had survived and my luck continued until the next Saturday when I was looking for a sniper near the village school. I returned there with a parachutist, after an initial first search had borne no fruit, and thought I saw something move. Suddenly I was shot at. Unfortunately he had spotted me first. His bullet hit a pipe beside me and a sharp splinter from the pipe went into my eye, which slowly became enveloped by a sort of red film. My partner saw the splinter and did his best to get it out using a couple of matches from his pocket, but to no avail.

'The wound didn't really stop me and, as the enemy were clearly going to make a major thrust, we busied ourselves on our defences. As the morning wore on, the ominous squeak of enemy tanks began to get louder and louder. One of the parachutists gave me a gammon bomb and armed with this I went up the road accompanied by another airborne soldier to await the tanks' arrival. Eventually a tank came into sight and I ran

Weverstraat, west of Arnhem, where Mike Dauncey fought his prolonged battle from the house on the left. This photograph was taken some months after the battle.

forward and threw the bomb. Nothing happened for a long time and I began to wonder if it was ever going to explode. Then suddenly there was an enormous blast. Dust was everywhere. The tank didn't move. I just hoped and prayed it had done enough damage. Certainly it stayed stationary. When I looked around, though, my comrade had gone. As I didn't feel I could do very much more with only a German Luger pistol in my hand, I made my way back to a group of soldiers a little behind me and we formed a place to stop the enemy infantry.

'More tanks soon began to roll into the vicinity. We threw a few grenades in their direction and they threw one or two at us. Slowly but surely the enemy crept towards us and I was hit in the thigh by a bullet that fortunately just went straight in and out. It certainly made me fall but it didn't break my leg. The time had now come to seek refuge in a slit trench. Wandering around the battlefield had become a very bad idea. On taking shelter, I suddenly heard a noise on my left and looked down to see a German stick grenade beside me. It went off and broke my jaw in two place. Amazingly I could still think all right, but I couldn't very easily speak and my face was a mess.'

Dauncey began to feel the effects of the wound and, realizing he was in no position to contribute to the battle, he was led away by two airborne soldiers to a house called the Old Rectory inside the perimeter, which was being used as a regimental aid post.

'The house was full of people. There were hundreds of wounded men strewn around inside it, and some fifty-seven dead in the garden. It was so full that my two comrades laid me on the lawn and went back to the battle. I instantly fell asleep.

'During the afternoon it started to rain and I woke up soaking and finding myself beside a dead soldier. I felt rather ashamed but, anyway I pulled the blanket off the poor dead chap next to me and put it over me to keep myself a bit dry. Later in the evening the battle died down. We still held the perimeter. Someone opened the door of the house and I made enough noise to let the person know I was there. To my relief, he pulled me in to the hall. It was somewhat perilous just lying on the lawn in the middle of the battle with mortar and artillery fire all around you.'

Later that night the news came round that the division was about to withdraw. It had also been decided that, if the evacuation was to succeed, the wounded would have to stay behind. The next morning, as Dauncey lay in the hall, the Germans arrived.

'The first thing they did was take my watch, much to my annoyance, but I couldn't do much about it. Things from now on were going to be different. After a few hours I was taken to a nearby house manned by nuns. Nothing happened in the way of treatment, and the following day we were taken further afield to a little known town called Apeldoorn, about ten miles away. I was with about thirty other British officers in a room there when a German intelligence officer came in and told us he was very

The fighting at Arnhem is over and British airborne troops are rounded up by the Germans.

worried about the fact that there were wounded British soldiers who had yet to be found, and he wanted to know where they were. It is hard to forget the silence that greeted him. Not a word was said by anyone.

'By this stage I still hadn't had any treatment for my wounds, and my condition was fast deteriorating. There was a hole in the lower part of my face and every time I drank anything the liquid just came out. It was an extraordinary sensation. Fortunately, our regimental padre happened to come in and saw me. To my delight I was sent to a local Dutch hospital, which gave me marvellous treatment.'

After his operation, it was agreed that he and five other airborne soldiers should be sent to an eye hospital in Utrecht, some forty miles away.

'We were a motley bunch and only had four good eyes out of six people. Our reception at the Dutch eye hospital was absolutely incredible. The Dutch, instead of blaming us for spoiling their lovely towns and villages with our bombs and artillery, were

British wounded at the Battle of Arnhem.

remarkably grateful for our efforts. They said it gave them heart because they had had such a bitter time over the years. The care and concern of the nurses and the skill of the doctors was almost unbearable. I had two operations on my eye and they told me that it could remain but that it would be what he called a 'reserve' eye. In fact it survived remarkably well and it was only in 1998 that they had to remove it.

'I raised the question of whether I should slip off with the head doctor who ran the place. "You must do what you think is right but you must realize that the hospital could possibly at worst be closed, or they might send the doctors to prison. The worst scenario would be that someone might be shot," he replied. From that point on I didn't contemplate escape. It would have been a very poor response to the kindness and help that we had received from this Dutch eye hospital. I had to take my chance later. That moment would come when it was time for me to leave and go to a German prison hospital in Utrecht, where we were properly guarded.'

Dauncey was to seize his chance there and successfully managed to escape, with the aid of the Dutch underground, back to England.

*George Lascelles
1944*

*The Earl of
Harewood
(formerly
George
Lascelles)
1999*

> **George Lascelles, Lieutenant, Grenadier Guards.
> Captured 18 June 1944, aged 24.**

GEORGE LASCELLES was a reluctant soldier. 'A month after my nineteenth birthday I joined my father's old regiment, the Grenadiers. Enthusiasm was perhaps not uppermost in my mind, and my diary rather plaintively marks the day with the entry, "End of Civilisation".' After completing his training at Catterick and latterly at Sandhurst, Lascelles was sent to Africa and in January 1944 arrived in Italy.

'It wasn't long before we went into the front line. It was mostly shadow boxing – we were holding a line and occasionally pushing it, and the Germans were holding a line and occasionally retreating from it. I was going on what was considered to be a safe patrol in the middle of June 1944. I got unlucky.'

His job was to escort a sapper up a road to see if it had been mined. They were supposed to be stopped by the furthest advanced British troops.

'It was two o'clock in the morning and we had got about as far as we could go. Then, instead of hearing a British sentry ask, "Halt, who goes there?" which would have signified the end of our mission, a voice shouted out, "*Halt! Wer da?*", and we realized we had bumped into the German line.

'We felt rather exposed on the top of the road and needed a diversion to get across to the other side of the road. I thought to put my rather rudimentary knowledge of the use of the hand grenade into practice, so I

Allied armour in Italy drives north towards Rome after breaking through the Gustav Line.

pulled one out of my pocket and extracted the pin. I was lying in a puddle and promptly dropped the pin in it by mistake. The grenade was primed to go off in five seconds, and without the pin I therefore decided the best thing I could do would be to lob it as far as I could. There followed a tremendous explosion a few seconds later. It seemed to land in a rubbish dump full of tins, which showered the neighbourhood and struck me at the time as irresistibly comic. Less funny was the reception the sapper and I got when we ran across the road. I was peppered with bullets – totally knocked flat. The sapper came to my aid but I told him to go. He refused. The truth is that I thought I was going to die. Anyway he was terribly encouraging and applied some first aid dressing. As it was pitch black most of the bandaging was put in the wrong place, but I am sure it did some good. I had absolutely no idea where exactly I had been hit. I thought it had gone through my stomach and that I would probably be on rice puddings for the rest of my life which was not a prospect I relished. I had been hit in the legs as well. It was only the next morning that I discovered that I had an enormous internal wound of about eighteen inches running from just over my heart – which the bullet missed – inside my ribs and through my hip.'

George Lascelles was captured by the Germans next morning. However, a barrage of artillery fire forced them to fall back leaving behind the injured Lascelles. The barrage was a cover and soon after an allied armoured vehicle arrived.

'By one of those pieces of ill luck, a corporal stretcher-bearer decided, after a quick diagnosis on the evidence of the hole apparently just over my heart, that I was too badly wounded. After six to eight hours of bleeding the wound had saturated my bandage and gave the impression of a rather severe body wound. He insisted that we stay under cover in a nearby farmhouse until a better means of transport could be brought up. Quite soon Italian partisans appeared and offered help, but we stayed there too long; the Germans started to return. By this time most of my blood-soaked battledress had been cut away and my various holes bandaged up. Three Guardsmen and the corporal were captured along with me, but thankfully the sapper officer, who had so bravely tended to my wounds the night before, had got away before the Germans arrived.

'When captured, I was stark naked except for my boots, beret, watch and bandages, and feeling much the worse for wear. It was in that rather startling garb that I was carried out of the farmhouse on a stretcher and into captivity, amidst a volley of language as by then I was in quite a lot of pain and every jolt hurt. Fortunately they couldn't understand me. The fear was that they might not think you worth taking prisoner, or that they were retreating too fast, and that they would find it easier just to bump you off. Thankfully I was taken to a proper hospital, where I lay amongst a number of wounded Germans. Of course at that point one felt an element of fellow feeling towards each other. The German soldiers tended not to be the kind of savage brutes that they were depicted in cartoons in English newspapers. They were perfectly decent people who like me were in a rather awkward position.'

Coincidentally, he was taken prisoner on the anniversary of the Battle of Waterloo, in which one of his ancestors was wounded; his father had also been wounded on 18 June 1915, precisely a hundred years after Waterloo; and he had been wounded on 18 June 1944.

The Germans were retreating fast and George Lascelles soon found himself being moved from one hospital to another.

'One hospital, near Verona, was within a quarter of a mile of a strategic bridge. My one consolation was that this hospital had a great red cross on it and so I assumed that if American bombers targeted the bridge they would miss us. A very ill American airman in the same ward had less confidence. He explained that Americans did day-bombing from about 40,000 feet up, which made precision bombing, let alone reading a red cross painted on a hospital roof, very hard. He knew because he'd done it. His pessimism was understandable as he'd had a terrible war. Shot down and taken prisoner, he had managed to escape half-way down Italy, following the Badoglio Armistice in September 1943, when he was challenged by a young local chap with a gun. Despite putting his hands up, he'd been shot twice in the middle and taken to a hospital. Whilst recovering, he was in a ward on the top floor when it was bombed, ironically by Americans, and he fell through to the bottom. As a result, he was in a very bad way and died while I was there.

'On the third day in hospital I had an interesting interrogation. I still couldn't get out of bed and was propped up by pillows when an officer came in and said, "I've been sent by the General to see how you are. He was worried about your wounds and wondered if there was anything you needed." I was amazed as he spoke with an immaculate English accent. I learnt he had been to British schools. He then went on to ask some questions which I refused to answer, before asking if there was anything I wanted. "Well, I would very much like a toothbrush," I replied. He agreed.'

George Lascelles was sent to an officers' camp at Spangenberg Castle, near Kassel, before being imprisoned at Colditz in the latter stages of the war.

Colditz Castle during its use as a prison camp..

CHAPTER TWO

A Kriegie's Life

REACTIONS TO CAPTIVITY

Shame, frustration, anger, betrayal, relief were just a few of the differing emotions POWs experienced in their moment of capture. No man was the same. Much depended on your enemy. The commandant and his guards to a large extent set the tone of the camp. There were other factors, such as age. For a young man cut off in his prime from the outside world, life behind the wire was no doubt hard to come to terms with. Similarly, captivity was a huge burden for a married man. Prisoners, beyond the use of illegal radios and conversations with guards, would have had little or no idea about what was happening in the war that they had become victims of. Some were to spend as long as five years away from their loved ones. Indeed if the Russians were becoming impatient as to when the Allies would invade Nazi-occupied France, so too must the men captured in early 1940.

From being active participants they were now spectators in a war the course of which they were powerless to determine. Many found this fact hard to cope with. An RAF pilot, used to the exhilaration and freedom that flying afforded, had to come to terms with having his wings clipped. Few servicemen avoided, at some point in their captivity, what Churchill referred to as the 'melancholy state'. Yet in time the majority of British servicemen did manage to adjust to life behind the wire.

A fate not many were mentally prepared for – capture by the enemy. British prisoners are led off after capture in France in 1940.

JACK COMYN, the commander of the tank troop captured by an Italian Division on the Libyan frontier, took time to come to terms with the fact that he was now a POW.

'I could hardly believe I was a prisoner. There were prisoners taken in the first war but it never occurred to us young men that it might happen to us. We could be wounded, we could be killed, but being a prisoner didn't cross our minds.

'I remember feeling very anxious to know what my parents were going to hear. Only years after did I know that they received a telegram from the Under Secretary of State for War stating that he was sorry to report that I was missing. I don't think it said, "believed killed" though. I had been captured just before Christmas and they must have had a pretty miserable time. Thankfully, later they got a message from the Vatican, who were very good at this POW thing, saying that I had been taken prisoner and was neither missing nor dead. Also my regiment ran over the place where my tank had been blown up, saw the wreck of it but thankfully also met an Italian priest who said that he had seen me and that I was a POW, but was unwounded. But it was a long time before I heard anything from my parents and that obviously worried me. Nevertheless, I was young and I think was pretty optimistic even though the war was going pretty badly for the British Empire at the time. It wasn't until 1941 when Russia and America joined us that we began to feel more confident.'

MICHAEL ALEXANDER, captured in Egypt on a commando mission which had killed some German soldiers, had more reason than most to be pleased to be sent to Colditz, having been informed earlier that he would be likely to face the ultimate penalty.

'Personally, I saw the whole thing as a bit of an adventure. I had already been under the threat of death and had spent some time in solitary so Colditz had to be an improvement in lifestyle. I was young and hadn't left anybody behind to be seduced by Americans or anything like that. I didn't have to worry about a wife or a girlfriend, which must have been very serious for some people. Consequently I didn't suffer emotionally at all. In fact, I remember thinking as I entered the courtyard at Colditz, "Well, if it's good enough for Saxon kings, it's good enough for me".'

LORD HAIG, the young Scots Greys officer captured by the Germans in the desert in 1941, was handed over to the Italians who flew him back to a transit camp near Bari.

'The prisoner of war's first reaction after the battle is probably one of thankfulness to be alive and of having survived. As he leaves the noise of gunfire behind, he begins to think in terms of peace. Although he is a prisoner and has lost his freedom he feels nevertheless a sense of liberation coming over him. Perhaps the realities of the battlefield have shown him the limitation of his courage. The awareness of the horrors of war are uppermost in his mind. During the battle he has carried out his duties to the best of his abilities with the help of such training as has been given to him during the preceding months. Now fate has stepped in and his life has suddenly and unexpectedly taken a different turn. He can now honourably retire from the battlefield, retire into the privacy of his own being and start to cultivate the hidden resources of the mind. He will meet new people with whom he will share sufferings and during the period of his captivity will learn a new kind of gregariousness whilst cultivating his own individuality.

'For myself I was able to shed the burden of the responsibility of living up to my father's great reputation as a soldier. Now suddenly fate had liberated me. However, as I lay down to sleep I thought of the gulf that lay between home and myself, and wondered how long news would take to reach them that I was not dead but a prisoner. I knew that under the rules of the Geneva Convention they would have to be told. There was nothing I could do now but submit, follow the instructions of the Italian guards and accept the new tempo of life.'

BILL ARMITAGE, the Spitfire pilot shot down in a dogfight over France on 21 September 1941, remembers his emotions as he entered through the wooden barbed wire gates of Stalag Luft III:

'It was a sort of feeling of hopelessness – wondering what the hell was going to happen and how long it would take. We tended to be on the optimistic side as regards the length of the war. I don't think any of us ever doubted that we would win in the end. Most thought it would be over in a year or two. It ended up being three and a half years in my case. I was

Officers and Senior NCOs of 266 Squadron, June 1940. Bill Armitage is seated, second from left.

also worried about my family and about how they were coping. In particular I thought about my mother because she was living in a big house almost by herself. Another concern was the family mills, which had been run by an uncle of mine and myself before the war. He had died just before I was shot down and I had just had time to appoint someone to take over, but I was obviously worried about how it was all going.'

KEN REES was 'honoured' when news of his capture, after being shot down laying mines in Norway, was broadcast to this country on the German propaganda radio. He recalls:

'My first worry on being captured was for my wife Mary and my family. They would not know what had happened to me. There was little I could do though, as the first letters wouldn't arrive for another three or four months. As it happened my mother had been informed by a neighbour that I had become a prisoner when they heard my name mentioned by Lord "Haw Haw". The next day, the Air Ministry informed her that my name had been mentioned on the German radio, but that they were waiting for official confirmation through the Red Cross. This came about three or four days later. All in all they had to wait about three or four weeks before they knew for certain that I was safe. But of course at the time I didn't know this and it was a worry thinking about them.

'It was all quite strange for me during the first few months. All the men in my room were experienced prisoners of war. One of the first things they would do was to chat to you in order to try and establish whether you really were a true British flyer and not a spy that had been put in by the Germans. This was soon established because several prisoners on the camp knew me from days gone by.

'Lack of alcohol was one of the big differences between life on the camp and life at our airbase. I used to get a bit depressed thinking that I should have managed to escape in Norway. We also had a radio and the news about events in North Africa and on the Russian Front was good. I felt that I was missing out.'

GEORGE LASCELLES, the Grenadier Guards officer who had so unexpectedly been wounded and taken prisoner near Naples in June 1944 whilst on a mine patrol, arrived at Spangenberg Castle shocked at his captivity but hopeful that it would not last long.

'I had never anticipated being a prisoner and so it was a pretty bewildering experience. When you go into battle, you have to expect that you might be wounded or even killed but one never anticipated being taken prisoner. My first worry was whether my captors were going to keep to the Geneva Convention. I was not too disillusioned with my plight as I was captured about a week after the D-day landings. They had clearly been successful and I naturally presumed the war would be over by the winter.'

PRISON CAMP DIET

While conditions in camps varied, one common memory among all the prisoners of war was the constant hunger they felt through their time in captivity. Rations were often supplemented by Red Cross parcels of food sanctioned by the Geneva Convention and distributed under the auspices of the International Red Cross. These parcels, weighing about 11 lbs, proved to be the prisoners' most treasured possession and were vital in supplementing their starvation diet. A parcel would typically contain such staples as dried fruits, canned meat and fish, crackers, cheese, margarine, dried milk and extras like jam, chocolate, cigarettes and soap. At best prisoners might receive one a week, but in reality they were considerably less frequent. Indeed, towards the end of the war prisoners in Germany often did not receive any for months.

A general view of Stalag Luft III. Tree stumps are in evidence indicating the wooded area felled to construct the prisoner of war camp. These stumps would eventually be taken up and used by the prisoners as fuel towards the end of the war.

SPECIAL COLLECTIONS BRANCH OF THE USAF ACADEMY LIBRARY

Jimmy James shortly after capture June 1940

Bertram (Jimmy) James, Pilot Officer, 9 Squadron. Captured 6 June 1940, aged 25.

Jimmy James 1999

JIMMY JAMES was flying Hurricanes when he was shot down over Holland. In addition to being forcibly grounded, he felt that his career was shattered and that he was of no further use to the war effort. But now his immediate concerns were of a more basic nature.

'We subsisted on the German ration for a non-working civilian: a cup of Ersatz coffee, made from acorns, in the morning, a bowl of soup, usually Sauerkraut, with a few potatoes at midday, and one fifth of a loaf of black bread with a pat of margarine and a small piece of sausage or cheese in the evening, supplied on a room basis and divided up by the room "stooge" for the day. The bread was a heavy, soggy mixture of rather questionable ingredients. The sour taste at first offended the palate but there was little else to eat, and it could be improved by toasting when there was fuel. These rations amounted to barely 800 calories a day, less than half the minimum required for an adult human being. The pangs of hunger were ever present.'

Things did, however, improve when in the spring of 1941 Red Cross parcels began arriving.

'The parcels made a tremendous difference to our well-being. They were the difference between near-starvation and an adequate diet. I well remember the meal in our room after the first parcel issue. It seemed we ate solidly for some hours. Amongst the goodies produced from the various tins were cheese, corned beef, stew, biscuits (hard tack), prunes, even cocoa, and best of all, tea. We were careful to eat slowly; a man in another camp died after bolting the entire contents of his first Red Cross parcel too quickly. '

KEN REES could scarcely believe how little he and his fellow prisoners received at Stalag Luft III.

'I was amazed at the first meal I ate in the camp. I thought, "God, We've got to live on this." Indeed the first couple of months were spent thinking about what one was going to eat tomorrow. You were hungry the whole time. After a few months, though, your stomach shrinks and although you still feel famished you don't worry about food so much. Also at the beginning one was inevitably short of cigarettes as well as shaving and washing facilities, but the other prisoners were well established and handed you over razor blades and the rest. Your first Red Cross parcel tended to take about five or six months. Once that happened you were set. In one's first parcel you hoped for clothes, after that you wished they'd send you fewer clothes but lots of goodies like chocolate.

'Our daily food ration worked out at around 1,500 calories. You would

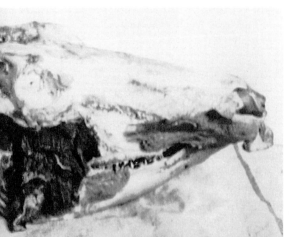

What a Kriegie could expect on the menu: Some form of vegetables; a loaf of fortified bread; thin soup known as 'green death' sometimes made with ox head, sometimes weed; and cabbage. Food was a major preoccupation with prisoners. SPECIAL COLLECTIONS BRANCH OF THE USAF ACADEMY LIBRARY

get three slices of bread a day, and some potatoes and soup at lunch time. In the evening you might perhaps get a couple of pieces of bread and a little jam. The Red Cross parcels were the things that really saved our lives. I became the cook in our room and that was quite a job. We used to keep the potatoes from lunchtime and we tried to make a meal with spam or something in the evening. You would soak some biscuits in klim milk and put some currants in it as a sweet, and that would make a reasonable meal and meant you could have some bread in the morning. When I was dishing out the evening meal, if there was the odd piece of carrot or three or four peas left over, the cards came out. The first jack got them. Everything had to be very fair. One would always be looking over at the next person's plate to make sure he didn't have any more than you. It was all a big laugh really but in some ways we were quite serious. You had to be terribly careful dishing it out.'

BILL ARMITAGE, the Spitfire pilot shot down over Boulogne, remembers how food became an obsession in his prisoner of war camp at Lübeck.

'I found myself in a room with six majors in the army. We each got one and two-fifths of a loaf of bread every day, which then had to be divided up between us. Amongst the seven of us, there was a recognized breadcutter. He was regarded as the best bread-cutter in the room and he divided it up every day without fail. Once he had divided it up, we had a rota for choosing who had first choice and second and third and so on. This was great daily entertainment and certainly gave us something to do. One of the chaps had a small six-inch measure and the chap who was at the top of the rota would then measure up all the pieces and decide which one he wanted. The middle cuts were easy enough to compare but the end cuts were much more difficult because the corners were rounded off. As well as having a rota, we also kept a log of the times people took to choose their piece of bread. I remember the average time that it took the first chap to choose, which was of course the longest, (it was easy when you got down to the last two pieces) was forty-seven minutes.

'We were also given turnip soup every day, which was boiled in a great big cauldron. It wasn't awfully good but it helped, I suppose. The other thing that we had was spisal fat, very similar to the stuff we used for greasing the wheels on old motor cars. It was a sort of grease, which was supposed to be used instead of margarine. Not very nice to eat but it did lubricate the bread just a little bit. I never liked it but it later proved useful because it was just solid enough to make a sort of nightlight out of, once you had found something for a wick. We could therefore light tunnels using it, but the snag was that it used up a lot of oxygen

'We also used to bribe the guards for some yeast. This was mixed up mostly with sugar to make hooch. We had a distillation plant made of *Klim* tins and run by a spisal fat lamp, which would gradually get our mixture to boiling point and then the magic liquid started dripping from out of one end. It might take months to make a decent lot of it and it didn't taste very nice so we mixed it with some of the dried fruit provided by Red Cross parcels. It was really good strong stuff and occasionally we had a party. It was amazing how happy it got us and how we forgot all our worries! Some people would be standing and talking quite merrily one minute and the next they just flopped on their backs. There was one occasion when a chap slept for over two days after sampling our concoction and we began to get quite worried so we sent for a doctor. He took his pulse and told everybody not to worry and just to let him be. Sure enough after another half a day he did wake.'

JACK COMYN recalls how food in his camp in Brunswick got progressively worse as the war went on:

'The last few months of being a prisoner of war were the worst. There were

A welcome addition to the POW diet – typical contents of a Red Cross parcel.

SPECIAL COLLECTIONS BRANCH OF THE USAF ACADEMY LIBRARY

three reasons for this. One was that we were desperately short of food. German rations had never been lavish but they got steadily worse. We really only got three boiled potatoes a day and some millet soup. They dished out a loaf of rather good black German bread once a week, but that had to last, along with the ersatz butter. It got even worse when the Russians came on and overran the eastern parts of Germany, which had been the great producer of food. We were very cold and very hungry. A cigarette in a funny way sort of filled your tummy and there were some people who would actually barter a bit of bread for a cigarette if they could arrange it. Hunger did have the effect of making us inactive and for the most part we did rather tend just to lie on our wooden bunks and really just do nothing.'

ACTIVITIES

Boredom was a prisoner's worst enemy. It was vital for the inmates' mental and physical health that they should try and keep themselves preoccupied as much as possible. Every prisoner had different means of breaking the monotony of life behind the wire. The Germans also saw the importance maintaining the general mental welfare of the prisoners. They tended to support religious and educational pursuits. Some camps had libraries, as a result of prisoners gathering books sent by relief agencies. A number of prisoners took the opportunity to further their education. Jimmy James, for example, when he was not escaping took the Royal Society of Arts Intermediate Certificates for German and Russian in Stalag Luft III. Sport was played by those with sufficient energy.

JIMMY JAMES describes the problems faced by inmates:

'War has been defined as "long periods of boredom interspersed with short periods of tension and terror". Life as a prisoner was a minor extension of war. There seemed no end to the boredom which stretched out endlessly into the grey future. We were all young men cut off in our prime from normal life, and forced to live a spartan, closely knit, communal existence, hemmed in by barbed wire, guard boxes, machine guns, patrolling sentries and dogs.'

James soon found escaping the best means of keeping himself occupied.

Jimmy James entertaining room-mates in Stalag Luft I.

LORD HAIG discovered that it was vital to keep oneself occupied with a hobby. Here he recalls how he and his fellow inmates managed to do this:

'Soon after my arrival at the transit camp in Bari I found some scraps of paper and a pencil on and began to draw the sprawling bodies of my fellow prisoners lying almost naked in the sun. I remembered Humphrey Guinness's description of a friend who had been captured in the First World War. Apparently the man had bounced a tennis ball against a wall with a stick and later came home a Wimbledon player. I decided to do the same kind of thing with drawing. This helped to pass the time and helped pick up morale. At Sulmona I was able to buy some watercolours through the Italian blackmarket – in pans, because tubes would have been confiscated due to the possibility of tiny maps being hidden inside them – with which I managed to escape for hours, painting studies of the camp and of my fellow prisoners. Later when I was at Colditz there was never any shortage of paints, even at the end of the war. Not surprisingly my less artistic companions got rather irritated when parcels of oils, brushes and canvas boards sent by the Red Cross continued to arrive at a time when our supply of food and tobacco dried up.

'Prisoners of war roughly divided themselves into five categories; escapers, creators, administrators, the students and the sleepers. Many individuals combined two or more of these approaches in their system of dealing with captivity. I adopted the second and fourth lines of activity.

Dawyck Haig's sketch of Sulmona hut-life captures the tedium of the inmates' existence.

Whiling away the hours in captivity. Haig's illustration.

The escapers plotted in dark corners and dug tunnels and, as a regular soldier, I should have joined them.

'The administrators' way of life was to provide all the necessary aids to our material wellbeing. They were the housekeepers, the dolers out of Red Cross parcels from the stores. They organized rations and meals, and cooked when there was anything to cook. In Sulmona, where there was scope for initiative because of the blackmarket and superfluity of lire in the officers' pockets, the administrators managed to provide not only a reasonable diet but a weekly ration of wine. The task of dealing with the Italian camp authorities involved much patience and persuasion, since the word '*domani*' was often used and had to be taken at face value. We found later that the Germans were, by comparison, more co-operative and more reliable in this respect, though they were more conscious of the rules and regulations.

'The students were the thirsters after knowledge who attended lectures on almost every subject known to man. Their interests included education, art, science, agriculture, politics and the law. Many of us welcomed the opportunity to learn about matters which had evaded us in peacetime. Some of us were able to develop a talent which might flower after the war. I valued my time reading and absorbed many books, mostly modern English literature and books on art. There were quite a few who seemed to do little more than lie about, think of the past, and who were unable to find any outlets except perhaps playing bridge or volleyball. I remember the latter was rather precarious at Hadamar camp in that when the ball went out of court it was apt to roll towards the wire. Once it had reached the inner wire it was beyond recall and anyone trying to collect it did so at his peril. One day an unfortunate South African did this at a time when the guard who happened to be on duty in the tower was an ardent and hysterical Nazi. Several shots were fired and the South African fell wounded to the ground. This attempt at cold-blooded murder in the middle of the afternoon came as a great shock to everyone present.'

BILL ARMITAGE spent the war in a number of different prisoner of war camps.

'One's first thought was how to overcome the boredom. What the dickens could you do with yourself? We eventually started getting books, which were supplied to us by the YMCA and our library became quite extensive. But you couldn't read novels all day and many of us ended up studying something. Some people actually took degrees. The Law was a subject that naturally lent itself to camp studies as it is a matter of learning something that could easily be written down.

Exhibition of prisoner of war art at Stalag Luft III, 1944.

Bill Armitage, second from right, keeping score on sports day at Stalag Luft III, Sagan, Poland.

'Some chaps thoroughly enjoyed the activities that prisoner of war camps provided. Szchubin was a terrible camp – for example, if you wanted to wash, there was a stone trough to use and you literally had to break the ice in order to get to the water. We went to bed fully clothed. I used to wake up at Szchubin with my beard frozen to the wall. The temperature got down to about minus fifty-five degrees. Altogether it was a pretty ghastly hole although there was this one chap who clearly enjoyed it and hoped the war would go on. He loved it for two reasons. Firstly he could play bridge every afternoon for hours and, secondly, because he never saw his wife. He thought it was a wonderful life.'

Things picked up for Bill Armitage when he was taken off to Stalag Luft III. Here he found himself in improved conditions and there were more ways to fill his time. He recalls how a lack of resources meant that prisoners were forced to rely on their own ingenuity to keep themselves amused.

'One of the things that the YMCA sent us was golf clubs but for some reason they never sent us any golf balls so we had to make some for ourselves. Using a razor blade, we used to shave off strands of rubber, as thin as you could make them, from gym shoes. We would then find a small round pebble and the rubber strands were then spun round it as tight as was possible. You could finally finish it off with a bit of leather that was stitched around it. It was a very skilled job, and took around about a week to a fortnight to complete.

'In these camps most people had a skill of some sort. Some could make radio receivers from various bits and pieces. For example condensers were made out of the silver paper you got in cigarette packages. The only thing we couldn't produce which we needed was valves. It was therefore necessary to bribe the goons. Our chief bribe was tinned coffee from our Red Cross parcels. They would risk their lives for our coffee.

'Later on we got our receiver sets sent to us. We used to get Players cigarettes in twenty packets, ten cartons in a packet. If they had the magic mark on them, you knew that there was a complete receiver set inside. Listening was a tricky business though and had to be carefully organized. If people were seen gathering around listening to something there would have been trouble straight away. What happened was that, when the news came through, a shorthand typist would take it down and there would then be a meeting in another hut where a representative from each hut would gather to hear the shorthand chap. They would then memorize it and go back to their huts and disperse it to the occupants.'

TONY BETHELL, in Stalag Luft III, recalls letter-writing, although the limited numbers the inmates were allowed to send home meant it took up little time:

'We were only allowed to write three or four letters a month. They were form letters and were heavily censored. I wouldn't tend to be too negative,

The standard letter form issued to British prisoners by the Germans for communicating with home.

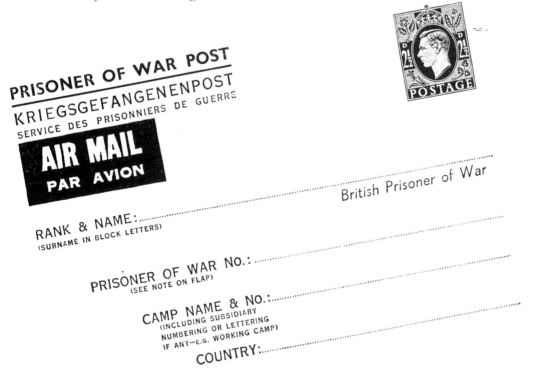

because I obviously couldn't hurt my mother's feelings. I have since read them though and found that one did express disappointment at the lack of food frequently. On the whole, though, I think one used to write in a cheerful way. My mother had two sons who were prisoners of war, as Drew, my eldest brother, was wounded and captured as a gunner supporting the Irish Guards in North Africa. He ended up in a camp in North Italy, before later escaping by walking all around the spine of Italy, a five-hundred-mile walk. Another brother was in Canada, so my mother had her problems and I think one didn't want to make her any more unhappy.'

THEATRICALS

WALTER MORISON remembers some other ways people kept occupied:

'Stalag Luft III was a miserable, daunting place but I soon discovered you could make a very good life for yourself. There was plenty to do – we had books and music. People had guitars and there was even a piano. You could play chess, football and other games, and so there was no reason why you should be bored. You could fret, complain and feel injured about why you had been imprisoned, but most didn't. There were too many things to do. With limited resources, things like keeping clean, feeding yourself and so on, all took time. The only thing that could be really tiresome is if you found yourself in a room with people you didn't get on with. It happened to me on one occasion – I didn't lose my temper, but I did tell two people in no uncertain terms that I thought they were better off in another room somewhere.

'I involved myself with some acting and, because I was a pretty boy, I played the female lead, Diana, in *French Without Tears*. I enjoyed it very much but, as a result, got rather typecast. This was fortunate as far as the goons were concerned. German officers used to come and watch these productions. They were certainly better that anything that was available in Sagan, and I found that it paid to be known as 'Diana' as they thought that butter wouldn't melt in my mouth. I remember on one happy occasion a senior ferret looked in at the window of my room and I was doing something I shouldn't have been, but he just said, "Ah, Herr Morison, I was just checking up, but I know you wouldn't do anything wrong, would you?" I'm sure he was thinking of me as Diana. Being typecast as such might lead to the question of whether homosexuality was rife in prison camps. As far as I noticed it wasn't. I certainly don't recall any overt example of homosexuality.

'We hired costumes for our performances from Berlin and other places, and other such facilities were made available to us. The reason was that the Geneva Convention actually states the captor should make adequate provision for intellectual activity. Another reason was that, in the eyes of

Walter Morison, second from the left, as the female lead 'Diana' in the Stalag Luft III production of French Without Tears.

the goons, a happy *Kriegie* would be less anxious to escape or cause any sort of trouble.'

JIMMY JAMES, like Morison, was also held captive at Stalag Luft III. He recalls the depth of thespian talent within the confines of the wire:

'Surprisingly, the Germans allowed us to build a theatre in the North Compound. We had an architect in the camp called Callwell who designed it and many people helped with the building. It was actually a very fine theatre, with an excellent stage. The auditorium could hold something like two or three hundred.

'Some very good plays were produced, including all the latest West End hits like *Rookery Nook*, *Blithe Spirit* and *Arsenic and Old Lace*, and of course there were a number of Shakespeare plays put on too. I remember somebody had a ticket to see *Arsenic and Old Lace* in London but got shot down before he could go. He arrived with the ticket and someone said,

"Oh that's all right old boy, you can come and see it here.

'Amongst the prisoners there was some fine talent including Rupert Davis of *Maigret* fame, Peter Butterworth of the *Carry On* series, Polly Rothwell who actually wrote the *Carry On* series, John Casson who was son of Sybil Thorndyke and so on.'

The stage play **Blithe Spirit** *put on at Stalag Luft III. Note the high standard of costume and props. The performances (largely because of unlimited rehearsal time) were of professional standard and enjoyed by all, including the German guards.*

Alex Cassie, far left, in the finale of the successful production, Turn Back the Clock. **Originally** **captioned:** *Myself, Roy Wilkins, Nick Page, 'Fairy' Fairbank, 'Hank' Martin, 'Pud' Davis, Tom Kirby-Green (killed March '44), Bobby Laumans, Hardy de Forrest, 'Fumph' Watson, 'Snowflake' Biers, 'Gaspipe' Gaston.*

The production Hewers of Coal. *On the right is Peter Butterworth, who would go on to make a successful career as a film actor after the war.*

ALEX CASSIE in Stalag Luft III did his best to keep himself busy:

'A lot of people were extremely bored. I was fortunate as I could be pretty self-sufficient. I had always been a fairly enthusiastic artist before the war and had been the principal illustrator of our various university rag week magazines and so art provided me with a focus. I managed by the grace of the camp organization to acquire a fairly large sketchbook and with it made as full a record of camp life as I was capable of. One picture for example was an aerial record of the Stalag in which I simply projected myself mentally into a hot air balloon. I look back at some of them now and think, my goodness, I could draw quite well then. Certainly anyone who could draw was always in demand for portrait painting and I filled the days doing a number of these. Other things such as the homemade theatre kept people busy holding productions, and latterly we were able to get hold of films.'

Whilst in the camp Alex discovered a new talent.

'I didn't appear in the theatre very much, but did sometimes get involved. At University I had done quite a lot of dramatics and let it be known that I would like to do some acting. The theatre in the original

The Royal Raviolas acrobatic team perform their 'Final Pyramid' – no doubt to tumultuous applause, appreciative whistles, hoots and cries for 'encore'. Alex Cassie sits on the shoulders of Nellie Nelson. Left to right, S/Ldr Murray, Wally Parsell, Tony Gordon, Desmond Plunket.

compound was simply two bedrooms knocked into one – a very crude theatre but later on we were moved to the North Compound, which had a purpose-built theatre. There were some very impressive performances there and some of the chaps produced some magnificent scenery in very limited conditions. Of course one problem was that there were no women for female roles and so those with smooth skin, sparkling eyes and so on found themselves cast in those roles!

'On one occasion in the camp, I was asked if I'd like to join a group called the Royal Raviolas, which was a skit on a rather tatty, ageing acrobatic team. Being the smallest in the team, I was the one who was hoisted to the top. We were aided by a co-operative German who had actually been a stage acrobat before the war and he managed to provide the equipment such as a big reinforced belt with a metal plate in the back and a big hook so I could be hoisted up on old lengths of piano wire. I didn't enjoy this much, not least because in the first rehearsal the group hoisted too hard and I damn near hit the ceiling. Anyway the wire enabled me to appear to do some quite magnificent acrobatics, although it actually snapped one night. Fortunately Blanket, the strong man in the Raviolas, caught me.'

THE WILL TO ESCAPE

Of all activities escaping was the most exciting and many spent their days consumed by the desire to break out of the wire. Not only was it enthralling but it required ingenuity and daring. Indeed, while some were driven by duty, others simply viewed it as a remedy to the frustration and boredom of camp life. The Geneva Convention decreed that officers should be excluded from manual labour. The result was that they had a considerable amount of time on their hands and were desperate for action of any kind. Importantly, escaping provided men with the feeling they were still involved in the war. A number were ambitious and desperate to avoid the career stagnation that resulted from prison life. There were no medals or promotion for a POW. The contrast between being liberated by allied armies or being the hero who evaded the Nazi peril and successfully returned to fight another day was stark. It was a bonding, adrenalin-fuelled occupation which led to the ultimate goal – freedom. At the beginning escaping was all the more appealing in that their Wehrmacht and Luftwaffe captors were unlikely to punish the perpetrators with anything more than a few weeks in solitary confinement. Later the Gestapo and SS became more involved and that spelt much more serious trouble for escapers.

The desire to forge escapes was not, however, universal. Only a few were prepared to take the risk. All too often movies and books concentrate on the escapers without acknowledging that the majority of POWs preferred to come to terms with their captivity rather than constantly fight it.

Escape attempts were sometimes even resented. A tunnel, for instance, meant considerable disturbance for the prisoners within its vicinity. Some inmates no doubt believed they had faced enough trouble as it was without attracting more on themselves.

WALTER MORISON on escaping:

'It was the great game. It could occupy you for twenty-four hours a day. We liked to say it was our duty to escape and in a sense it was, but it was also a wonderful occupation and technically fascinating trying to devise a way of getting out. I always rather likened it to a British field sport: you play strictly to the rules, which are simple and well understood on both sides: Don't use violence. Don't engage in sabotage or espionage. Don't wear German uniform. And if caught, return to square one and spend a couple of weeks in the cooler. There was no serious penalty, unless of course you found yourself in the hands of the Gestapo, who could be distinctly dangerous. The Luftwaffe though would move heaven and earth to get you back if they knew you were there. I don't wish to belittle those people who passionately believed that this was something they had an absolute, overriding duty to do, as some people became literally obsessed. Sadly, I remember one who was shot and killed because he flipped and ran

Alex Cassie's drawing of perimeter fence with goon box, Stalag Luft III.

for it when he had no conceivable chance to get away. But for most people it was just a first-class occupation which could be a lot of fun. It was like the National Lottery. The odds of winning were very slight but it was a great daydream picturing the amount of free beer you'd get in the mess and all that sort of thing.'

BILL ARMITAGE was also keen to escape and noted why a number of officers were so inclined.

'Escaping was the number one activity. It was really the duty of an officer to try to escape and a fair percentage of us had a go. Other ranks were made to work and I think they had a better time in captivity as a result, because working on the land was considerably more pleasant than being cooped up as we were.'

Robert Walker Brown 1942

Robert (Bob) Walker-Brown, Acting Captain, 2nd Battalion Highland Light Infantry. Captured 5 June 1942, aged 23.

Robert Walker Brown 2000

BOB WALKER-BROWN, serving with the 2nd Battalion Highlanders, had been captured in the Western Desert in 1942 by the Germans and handed over to the Italians. He recalls his motives:

'From the moment I arrived at the camp I had one thought only – to escape. I felt a considerable amount of shame at being made prisoner, because I knew I was not the slightest use to anybody. I felt I had let my regiment down and was desperate to rejoin them. Moreover, I believe it is the duty of every British officer and British soldier to attempt to escape.'

TONY BETHELL discovered on his arrival at Stalag Luft III that not everybody was enthusiastic about escaping.

'When I first arrived at the East Camp I was allocated a room where about nine other chaps were living. It transpired pretty quickly that they had no interest in escaping. I don't think it would be unfair to say that they felt they had done their bit and they probably had – certainly there was one DFC in there. I wasn't interested in learning Greek or anything. I just wanted to get out. Anyway the occupants in the room discouraged any

An aerial view of North Camp, Stalag Luft III, drawn by Alex Cassie.

Summer 1944, 122 Block, Cricket 1st XI – winners of Compound Competition. Back row: Dakene; Lang; Self (Tony Bethell); Jarvis; Dyer; Bacon. Front row: Fordham; Murray; Wimbaley; Willis; Haydon. Original caption from Wartime Log.

such thoughts, which I found enormously depressing. I was quite unhappy until thankfully we moved over to the North Camp and I found myself in another room.

'Why did one want to escape? I think it was a mixture of sentiments really. There was a bit of a feeling that it was your duty to escape, but boredom also played a part. I was a fairly physical sort of person and games were always my main interest at school. I suppose attempting to escape provided some therapy to the inertia.'

JIMMY JAMES spent much of his time behind the wire hatching escape plans. He too remembers that escaping was not everyone's ambition:

'Of the 1,500 in the north compound at Stalag Luft III only about six hundred were in the Escape Organization. The others weren't interested. I would say about a third of the prisoners were, like myself, hard-core escapers. Of the others, some had been very keen in the early days but now thought it wasn't worth it, and the rest were either against it or just didn't think it was worthwhile.

'My motivation was simply freedom. Being behind the wire is not a thing to be recommended. Churchill, who had experienced being a prisoner in the Boer War, talked about the hours crawling by like paralytic centipedes. You're just shut away in a little world of your own. You feel out of it. You are useless. One fantasised about life outside the wire – the life you'd left, a girlfriend you'd left and so on. Naturally you thought about your village pub, where you could just go and have a pint of beer when you wanted it.'

GUARDS

The Commandant and his guards set the tone of the camp. Commandants were usually elderly, retired, ex-senior army officers recalled back to the colours. Some, like Oberst Lindeiner-Wildau at Stalag Luft III, were respected by their inmates, whilst others were objects of vilification. Guards differed according to the country you were imprisoned in. In Italy many were poorly trained conscripts whose actions were unpredictable. In Germany the guards were often men who had seen active service and been drafted into camps as a result of a partial disability or age, and they were under considerably more pressure to follow the rules. The Punishment Company awaited any German guard who neglected his duties and that meant almost certain death. Liaison between prisoners and their guards was thus considerably more dangerous for the latter.

'Goons' and 'Ferrets' conferring at Stalag Luft III. For the most part they were amiable enough. Both guards and prisoners had to combat a common enemy – boredom.

On the whole British POWs were held by units of the Wehrmacht or Luftwaffe and were as a result considerably better treated than Jews, Eastern Europeans and gypsies, who tended to be under the violent and cruel regime of the SS and Gestapo.

If imprisonment was boring for the prisoners, it was little better for the men who guarded them as they looked over the camp from their watch towers and patrolled the perimeter. POWs at least had social contact with their fellow inmates, something a sentry didn't when he was on duty. Guards were also victims of jokes and teasing. Indeed, it seems that for many POWs this was an outlet for their frustration as well as a reminder that they were still in the war.

A fun rapport was sometimes established with the German guards. Indeed the inmates and their captors played a number of jokes on each other.

Kommandant of Stalag Luft III Oberst Friedrich von Lindeiner-Wildau. He was well respected by his prisoners.

ALEX CASSIE, imprisoned in Stalag Luft III, recalls one guard in particular:

'Sergeant Hermann Glimnitz was the camp's chief ferret, an anti-escape specialist. Although he was responsible for unearthing more than a hundred tunnels, he possessed a sense of humour and was respected by the inmates. On a rainy day his favourite line was, "It is bad weather to be above the ground, isn't it?".

Oberfeldwebel Hermann Glimnitz.

'Glimnitz was quite a character. He sometimes played tough and used to swagger into the reception block to greet a new purge arriving at the Stalag looking all tough and ugly, saying, "Good morning gentlemen. Velcome to Stalag Luft 3. Here you will find that the beer is piss poor but the gin is shit hot." A colourful character certainly, and we used to play jokes on him. Our buildings were all raised some 18 inches off the ground so that tunnelling out of them would be easily spotted. One day Glimnitz was secretly checking under our huts so all the occupants decided they'd wash the floors. The morning was spent clearing the floors of everything, lifting chairs onto tables, carrying buckets of water and emptying them on the floor. The result was that wherever Glimnitz went there was no shelter from the dripping water. He finally emerged from his checks looking very cross and disgruntled and saying, "I'll have you buggers". But with a twinkle in his eye.'

LORD HAIG was in an Italian prisoner of war camp when his guards unexpectedly joined in the inmates' party.

'Christmas at Sulmona was a monumental feast. For weeks our buying officer had arranged for the ration cart to wend its way up the valley with special black market supplies hidden under the straw. In addition to turkeys and wine, there were bottles of *Grappa* and also of *Ardente* described on the label as *Superiore al Whisky*. When the big night came, a bar had been installed in one of the huts. We had an agreement with the Italians that there should be a temporary armistice, the equivalent of parole, and some of the Italian guards joined our celebrations. The result was that the Italian orderly officer became so drunk he had to be carried to bed, and two of the guards were totally inebriated and incapable of doing their jobs. They handed their uniforms to two Australian officers, who finished the job for them and even went on to the guard tower. It was the most enormous blow-out and we were all quite merry for several days running.'

GEORGE LASCELLES was surprised to discover that not all guards were devout followers of the Nazi creed:

'On arrival at Spangenberg concentration camp I was informed of the Hitler Plot by a German sentry, whose delight at hearing that Hitler was dead was unbounded. He knew the war would end soon and was quite open about his pleasure at hearing the news. Two or three hours later the news came through that Hitler was in fact still alive. The plot had failed.

'The Wehrmacht's attitude to prisoners was a lot more correct than the Gestapo or SS. I remember that after the Hitler Plot our guards were ordered to do a Nazi salute rather than the German salute. They hated doing it and I suspect many of them were not very keen Nazis. This did not stop us doing our best to torment and bait them. For instance, we all mocked and jeered when they did the Nazi salute, which must have been very painful for them. We hoped it was, anyhow. Another thing that used to annoy them was by making it difficult for them to count us at roll call. If you were skilled, you could get them to count you twice. This was terrribly tiresome for them, but was a bit of a double-edged weapon as it meant we had to stay out in the cold until he got it right.'

Some guards were sympathetic to their captives' plight.

'I recall one guard, a sergeant, in particular. He had been a well-treated prisoner in the First War and was very pro-English. This chap was given the job of leading a group of guards who were escorting me from Spangenberg to Colditz. I found him particularly friendly and agreeable. I

Some of Jimmy James's fellow POWs at Barth, Stalag Luft I, 1941. Standing: Palmer; Torrens; Russell; Tyrie; Ritchie; Wilson; Long; Morgan. Front: Shore; Goodwin.

think he must have realized the war was lost. On the journey he even gave me part of his rations. We arrived at Munich and had to go through the town by tram as the city had been bombed very badly and the railway was damaged. I was herded down one end of the tram and a group of Germans manifested their anger by spitting at me. The German sergeant was furious and thought this was quite wrong.'

JIMMY JAMES particularly remembers one misguided act of generosity by his Commandant at Stalag Luft I in Barth:

'The camp staff were all members of the Luftwaffe and behaved, for the most part, in a civilized manner towards the prisoners. In the early days, particularly, our relations with the Germans were good, provided that Higher Authority and the Nazi Party were kept at a distance. Major Von Stachelski, the Kommandant at Barth, was a humane and thoughtful man. He was imbibing one evening in the Mess bar, as was his custom, when he fell to thinking about the poor British locked up in their compound with nothing to drink but water and Ersatz coffee. The more he drank the more he dwelt on their sad state. Then he could stand it no longer. He gave orders that some boxes were to be filled with a good quality of bottled beer and ensured they were delivered to the compound where they were received with due gratitude and joy by the inmates. Unfortunately, the incident was reported to Higher Authority and the Kommandant was relieved of his post immediately.'

Such incidents of such generosity were rare, although sometimes the inmates themselves might offer their captors a cup of tea or an English cigarette, both of which the Germans regarded as delicacies. Occasionally they were given something stronger.

'At Christmas time we were in the habit of brewing up a hooch of some sort made from prunes or whatever dried fruits we could get, which we then fermented into wine. It was double or triple distilled by our home-made brewery. The result was a bit horrifying but it nevertheless kept us warm and we drank it. At Christmas in 1943 a guard came round with a couple of dogs and was shutting a window of a room when he was handed a bottle of this home-made hooch, which he drank on the spot and promptly collapsed. His two dogs dragged their master to the gate. It's not known what happened to him but he was never seen again. On another occasion somebody threw a bottle of this hooch at a guard in the guard tower. He also drank it in one go and seconds later fell out of the guard tower.'

'Goon baiting' was common. James remembers how he and his friends treated the guards at Stalag Luft I:

'The guards were conscripts from all walks of life and they seemed ill at ease in their helmets and new military uniforms. They were an obvious target for our youthful exuberance. We called them "goons" and often whistled a popular ditty like the *Wizard of Oz* in time to their marching when they went off after *appel*. This caused so much irritation that the SBO soon put a stop to it. Nevertheless, the popular sport of "goon baiting" was often irresistible to the younger prisoners and continued in one form or another for most of the war.'

'Appels' or roll calls were the most common opportunity to annoy and tease the guards. **BILL ARMITAGE** recalls one such incident.

'We used to have two *appels* a day. The guards normally only counted us but they became increasingly hot under the collar about people staying in

Appel at Stalag Luft III. SPECIAL COLLECTIONS BRANCH OF THE USAF ACADEMY LIBRARY

bed and arriving late for the nine o'clock in the morning *appel*. On one occasion they decided to take the matter in hand and several goons, as we called them, began to take down the names and numbers of the latecomers. Our boys however just gave them silly names, such as "Hastings 1066" and so on, which the Germans solemnly took down. It was only later when they presented the list to the Kommandant that it was discovered what a load of rubbish had been put down. That was the only time they tried to take our names!'

The *kriegies'* treatment of the guards differed from camp to camp. Some prisoners were discourteous, while others befriended them.

WALTER MORISON:

'Colditz was a different world to Sagan. For example the *kriegies* there had a tradition of bleating like sheep to the German guards, which we would have regarded as discourteous at Stalag Luft III!'

MICHAEL ALEXANDER also found some of the behaviour of his fellow inmates towards guards at Colditz rude.

'Some friends and colleagues rather took it into their heads to tease the Germans about the fact that the war was turning. Increased allied bombing and Russian victories in the east provided the butt of much of this, and some of the lads used to pretend to be bombers. They made noises and threw water bombs down on the guards. I thought that was very bad manners actually. It was done by "men of spirit" but some of us formed a slightly negative attitude towards this "bull baiting" as they called it. Okay, go and bait the *Schutzstaffel* man in jackboots but don't bait the old Bavarian guard.'

BOB WALKER-BROWN in a prisoner of war camp in Chieti recalls that his Italian guards needed to be treated with caution. Despite this, inmates still played games on them.

'Every month or so a new company of Italian troops would be brought in to guard the camp. Some were *Alpini*, who were good, but most were from ordinary infantry regiments, normally low-category men who were very, very trigger-happy. They were prepared to cock the rifle, fire a round and ask questions later.

'Everyone was confined to huts from about 5 o'clock in the evening and any movement outside would be fired on. We once amused ourselves by stringing together Red Cross tins between barrack blocks, which made a hell of a lot of noise. We thought that the sentry on the left-hand wall would open fire and hit his opposite number. It didn't work. They fired a lot of bullets but no one was killed.'

CHAPTER THREE

Break Out!

'And fear not them which kill the body and are not able to kill the soul.'
St. Matthew Chapter 10 verse 28

Thousands of attempts to escape were made by British prisoners during the Second World War. Some, like the 'Great Escape' and the 'Wooden Horse', are well known; most, however, have never been recorded. Many took months and even years to engineer, but a number were spur of the moment opportunities that were gratefully seized upon. The sheer courage of the men who tried to break out is remarkable, but they would be the first to acknowledge that a kriegie was unlikely to make it back home without having luck on his side. Escaping also required ingenuity and resourcefulness. Camps such as Stalag Luft III were specially built to foil escape efforts. Furthermore among the guards were anti-escape specialists known as 'ferrets' whose job combined the duties of guard and detective. The slightest change of routine might provide them with a clue. By 1942, German anti-escape measures included using seismographs which were dug into the soil and used to record earth tremors.

Even if a prisoner did successfully get over, under or through the wire, they

Cramped living conditions, the monotony of camp life and sheer boredom acted as an incentive to some prisoners to seek a way out. SPECIAL COLLECTIONS BRANCH OF THE USAF ACADEMY LIBRARY

were still a long way from making a 'home run'. Breaking out was only the first stage in their quest for freedom. An escaper then had to set out on a long and hazardous journey over alien territory without being discovered. Language problems, lack of adequate maps and passes, hunger and shelter were but a few of the difficulties they might encounter as they crossed borders and evaded road blocks and enemy patrols.

The vast majority of escapes never succeeded. Yet what they did do was not only irritate their captors but also require them to use up considerable amounts of time and manpower to hunt down the escapees. Furthermore, and perhaps most importantly, planning escapes provided many inmates with hope. For some it was a game, for others it was a duty, but for all it was exciting at a time when many were struggling to come to terms with the mundane nature of life behind the wire.

Escaping carried with it many dangers. While the usual penalty was a term in solitary confinement, this could not be counted on. The risk of being shot breaking out was real. In addition, once a serviceman became a prisoner, he lost his status of 'combatant' and became subject to the civil law of the enemy country. If during an escape attempt he killed a guard he committed the civilian crime of murder and expected to pay the penalty. Furthermore, as the war progressed, the Gestapo increasingly tried to take action against escapees and their penalties were considerably more punitive.

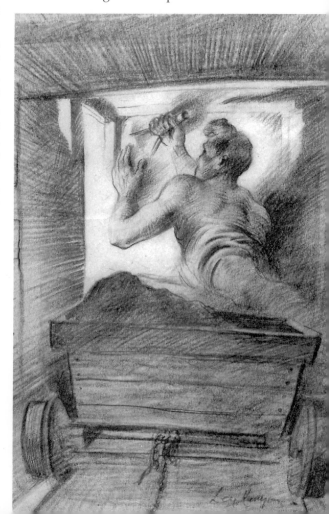

Tunnels were the most popular means by which prisoners tried to break out for a number of reasons. An escaper could chose his own time to leave, thus enabling his departure to be unhurried and well prepared. He could take luggage and food, and could leave ready dressed as a foreign worker, businessmen or whoever he had decided to impersonate. He could seal the exit after him and his absence would not be immediately noticed. Lastly, and most importantly, a considerable number of prisoners could escape at the same time. Yet tunnels were also very dangerous and had a remarkably low level of success. (Of the hundreds dug at Stalag Luft III, only six succeeded.) There was always the ever-present worry that they could cave in. A further problem was that they often involved many people and took a long time to dig. Secrecy was therefore very difficult to maintain, particularly because

Ley Kenyon drawing of the workface of **Harry** *at Stalag Luft III.*

84

diggers often had difficulty disposing of the excavated earth without attracting the attention of the ever-vigilant camp ferrets. Even if a tunnel was successful, the fact that a considerable number of people had escaped normally ensured that an extensive search involving police, troops, Home Guard and Hitler Youth would be carried out. Nevertheless, despite the drawbacks of tunnelling, it was often the only escaping option a prisoner had.

BILL ARMITAGE was involved in a number of tunnels at his camp in Warburg.

'Soon after arriving in the camp, I went along to the Escape Committee and said I wanted to try to get out. The Committee in those days was not really an authoritative body; it was just there to help. For example, you didn't want to find that your tunnel was on top of another. It also provided help with forging papers and general advice about what to do if you got out. So I went along and they said, "Oh, you're just the chap we want. We've got a little Czech chap called Joe Rix who is a great escaper and a terrific digger but we want someone to organize the show. We've got a place for him to dig from too but we just wanted someone to run it." So I took it on.'

The intended run was from one of the huts near the perimeter wire and as such, was a relatively small tunnel.

'It was to be a little rat hole, some thirty feet long - the absolute minimum size required, which we would "scrawl" through. "Scrawling" was where you pulled yourself along on your toes and elbows. Kneeling in it would have been impossible. It was horribly claustrophobic. It needed to be small though as our chief difficulty was disposing of the earth that we dug out. We couldn't just dump it anywhere in the compound because the "goons" in the "goon boxes" would see us. Equally you couldn't carry a box of the stuff, so the way we did it was by making big stockings out of any spare material we could find and hanging them down the inside of our trousers. It was a very laborious task.

'Little Joe was a wonderful digger and within a month we were ready to go. Joe obviously was first in line to escape, but we drew lots as to what order the rest of us should go in. I drew number eight. Joe broke the heathland outside the camp and got out, as did the next chap. We went down in pairs as people liked to travel with another person. The next two went down and they were followed by another couple of lads.'

Once the men had got to the end of the tunnel they had to wait for the right moment to run for it. They were only some fifteen feet beyond the wire and two searchlights continuously swept around the area around the exit hole. The escapees were therefore forced to wait for that moment of darkness when neither spotlight was near them. A further problem was that guards with dogs regularly patrolled the perimeter. Despite these dangers, six got through.

However, just as Armitage was making his way down the tunnel, the breakout was discovered.

'The chap just before me must have lost his nerve and gone too soon, because he was spotted and all hell broke lose – sirens blaring, searchlights blazing and goons shouting all over the place. I had to back out of this nasty, narrow tunnel with a great pack of food and all my escaping equipment attached behind me. It was a hell of a job backing out but thankfully I managed to reach my hut before the goons arrived. We'd arranged for the necessary number of people to sleep in our beds and I managed to get away with hanging my special escaping clothes in amongst the others.'

Undeterred by this, Armitage decided to have another go. This time the tunnel he planned was considerably more ambitious.

'I was living in one of three big huts in the middle of the compound, where most of the earth was put under from the little tunnels around the perimeter. I made a scrutiny check and discovered that there was still ample room for earth from my proposed tunnel. Rather than building another one from the edge of the perimeter, I decided we should dig a 300-foot tunnel from my room in the centre of the camp. The hope was that we would take it some hundred and fifty feet outside the camp so that we wouldn't have to worry about dogs and spotlights. It was a great inconvenience to have somebody digging from your room but the chaps sportingly agreed and two of them joined the team. The great thing about digging from the big hut was that the dispersal of the earth was no problem. It could just be scattered underneath the same building, so there were no people staggering down the steps of the hut carrying loads of earth. Furthermore, when the "ferrets" saw it piling up there, they just went off to blitz one of the huts nearest the perimeter, thinking that it must have come from there.'

Their first job was to cut a trap-door from the floor of the hut. This had to be done with great care. Once completed, they sunk a shaft some fifteen feet deep, with a trap-door – the top of which they covered with a little pile of dry earth on closing it. They then set off toward the wire. Unlike at Stalag Luft III the earth was clay, not sand, so the tunnel didn't need to be shored up.

'The thing worked like clockwork and a railway was built using strips of wood as rails which we stole from a hut that was in the process of being built in the compound. The trolley too was easy enough to make. We would fill it up with earth and then drag it along using a rope, which proved extremely difficult to acquire. Lighting was a problem because we had ten people working in pairs underground and each group needed a light point. Spisal fat lamps were a damn nuisance because they used up too much precious oxygen. We scratched our heads about this for a while. In the end the wire from the loudspeakers around the camp, used to make us listen to Lord "Haw Haw", the chap who broadcast over Germany in English, provided our solution. Three volunteers armed with makeshift

Bill Armitage (right) with three fellow prisoners at Stalag Luft III, Sagan, Poland.

cutters shinned up the telegraph poles and managed to cut the wires down in about three minutes dead. The result was that we had 600 yards of wire, which we were able to rig up to lights taken from our room. The wire wasn't very well insulated but thankfully the voltage was about one hundred and fifteen volts so if you did get a bite from it that wasn't a problem.'

All was going according to plan and good progress was made throughout June and July. The only thing the tunnellers had neglected to think about was the weather.

'The Westphalian plains are quite notorious for thunderstorms in August. A great pool of about thirty feet wide and some twelve inches deep started forming up against the first hut that we had gone under. Then it broke through into our tunnel and we were forced to bale desperately. The clay was yellow, sort of ochre colour, and this damn water came out coloured with clay. Gradually the baled water began trickling out of the sides of our hut and a yellow mud began forming around it. Then suddenly the "ferrets" cottoned on and they were in like a flash.

'I was making my way toward the shaft when I suddenly saw two Germans climbing down the rope ladder and into the tunnel. There was little I could do but say, "Boo". They jumped out of their skins and one of them actually fell into some four or five feet of water in the well at the bottom. I helped him on his feet and then followed them back up the rope ladder. I didn't have anything on as I used to strip off entirely when tunnelling. So there I was without any clothes at all in a room which was full of about sixteen goons. The Kommandant had also arrived by then and was sitting in the only chair in the room, with all the other Germans spread out in a semi-circle all around him. We stood looking at each other. "You are a fool," he told me, at which point he flung his arms out and caught one of the goons standing beside him in the privates. The whole situation seemed so ludicrous that I couldn't help laughing. Now you have to be very careful about this because a German doesn't like being laughed at. It makes him angry. Fortunately the Kommandant presumed I was laughing at myself for being a naked fool and he laughed too and of course, when the Kommandant laughed all the other goons had to laugh as well. All of us stood there roaring with laughter for about thirty seconds. The Kommandant thought it was getting out of hand and his face suddenly straightened. Everyone instantly stopped laughing. They then stood up and just marched straight out of the room.'

Extraordinarily, no punishments followed. Normally Armitage and the others could have received a few weeks in the cooler at the very least, but they never heard another thing about it.

'All that happened was the goons just filled in the shaft, but nobody received any punishment at all. After that, though, I'd had enough of digging tunnels. We had had this tremendous fall of earth during the rains and that had frightened me. I couldn't help thinking of the possibility that one of the lads might have got mixed up in it. Several of the very keen tunnellers who were in my little batch felt the same and never dug again.'

Not all escape attempts were so meticulously planned.

TONY BETHELL and a friend, Pat Langford, one of the men later shot in the Great Escape, discovered an opportunity to break out with a single night's work.

'The Germans were digging a ten-foot ditch along the perimeter wire. It seemed to us that it would be possible to just hop out of a window at night, scurry across to it and tunnel out. The tunnel only needed to be about six feet long in order to get past the outside wire and we could be away before daylight. It was a golden opportunity and we agreed to seize it. As soon as it was dark we jumped out of the hut. Pat went ahead and was first into the ditch. I was following him. All of a sudden I saw the *Hundmeister* and his dog. It began to bark and I didn't feel capable of taking the two of them on, so I yelled to Pat and took off for our hut. Pat followed and we jumped straight through the open window without touching the sides with the dog behind us with its paws up on the window. In fact I don't think the *Hundmeister* had seen us and approached our building not knowing what

Exercising around the perimeter at Stalag Luft III. Any attempt to step over the thin boundary wire could cause the guards to open fire. <small>Special Collections Branch of the USAF Academy Library</small>

the dog was making such a commotion about.'
Some were not so lucky.

BILL ARMITAGE recalls the layout of his camp near Hanover and one man's desperate attempt to gain freedom by simply climbing over the wire:

'It was a fairly typical prisoner of war camp with lots of barbed wire surrounding it. There were two barbed wire fences, about seven foot high and some six feet apart. In between them were coils of barbed wire. On all four corners of the compound were what we called goon boxes. These were also situated in other areas of the camp where the layout was not exactly straight. The goons in them were armed with machine guns and of course had searchlights. Inside from the fences was a single strand of barbed wire about a foot of the ground, which we called the trip wire, and we were liable to be shot if we went over it.

'One chap lost his cool and charged the perimeter fence. He was able to climb the side of it. It was sort of like climbing a ropeladder really, but he must have got pricked to death, even though he was wearing big gloves. Anyway, he had no difficulty getting to the top, but he then had to get across this massive coil of loose barbed wire in the middle. He soon became hopelessly entangled in it. Inevitably, the goon box nearest to this chap spotted him but the German guard sensibly didn't shoot as it was clear that he had no chance of getting out. He was well and truly stuck in this mesh of wire. Unfortunately another goon nearby was not so generous and riddled him with bullets. It was one thing trying to get under it but to go over it was nigh on impossible.'

JIMMY JAMES was witness to another doomed effort to break out at Stalag Luft III.

'There was a chap called Edwards who hated the camp and was desperate to get out. He got up one day and said, "Well boys, I'm going for a walk round the compound and am going over the wire." He'd said this before but no one had taken much notice. This time, however, he meant what he said and half an hour later began climbing up the fence. A guard shouted at him to come down but he paid no attention. The guard just shot him dead. He fell off the wire like a bird and there was a rather ugly incident, in fact it was a near riot, when he was taken off and they wouldn't allow anyone to go near him.'

Some tried to climb over the wire in a bid to escape, but it proved to be impossible, and became a sure way to find relief in death. The body of this Russian prisoner of war was left hanging as a deterrent.

GORDON LAMING, captured in June 1940, was imprisoned in a French barracks at Besançon that had been converted into a prisoner of war camp by the Germans. It was from there that he made his successful home-run.

'I thought the war wouldn't be over before Christmas 1942, and when you are twenty-one years old two years seems an eternity. That was my motivation. I had considered the idea of just bluffing my way through the front gate with a false pass, but the chances of success were minimal. Invariably most people who escaped did so not so much by planning but opportunism while out in working parties.'

He spent the next four months mulling over how best to make good an escape before learning about a plan to leave through the water sewers under the camp. These had been made inaccessible with barbed wire but some Frenchmen had come in from the outside and cut the wire, thus making it possible to pass through them.

'A mate of mine called Stan and I had been told that these sewers led to a place near the railway track. Four chaps left on the Friday night and I heard that another four were going down them the next evening. We were a little perturbed about a rumour that we were to be shipped off to Germany on Sunday morning so a few of us decided to take a gamble. We asked the person who knew about the entrance if we could use it and he agreed, saying that he would show us where it was and would ensure that the plaque was safely put back once we had gone. I had a map of the town, which I had stolen from the back of the barrack-room door. We also had an

Gordon Laming, in 1993, standing on the manhole cover through which he made his successful escape from inside Caserne Vauban in 1940.

address of some people who might help. So we were all set.'

The original group left at around six o'clock. Stan and Laming followed them soon after.

'We crawled along these dark water sewers but to our horror discovered that our exit wasn't the railway lines as we thought but was actually in a street. We lifted the lid and it seemed so bright outside, even though it was around half past six on a late October night, that we thought this can't be right. Alarmed, we crawled on. Our candle burnt out and we were eventually crawling in the pitch darkness. It was difficult to move along, and we just crawled along on our hands and knees. There were remnants of barbed wire all along in which we occasionally got caught up and which slowed our progress. In the end we decided we would turn back and get out on to the street. We had already spent three hours down there when we had been assured it would only take quarter of an hour. Our mistake had been that we had heard the voices of the first group down the left-hand sewer and had followed them, when in fact we should have turned right.'

They chanced getting out on the road and, to their relief, owing to a night-time curfew in the town, nobody saw them.

'We went to the address we had been given. They were very anxious

Detail from the 1933 map of Besançon that Gordon Laming stole from behind the barrack room door, on which is marked his escape route. (1) Entry into sewer through manhole. (2) Point reached before turning back and exiting at (3) through manhole onto the street.

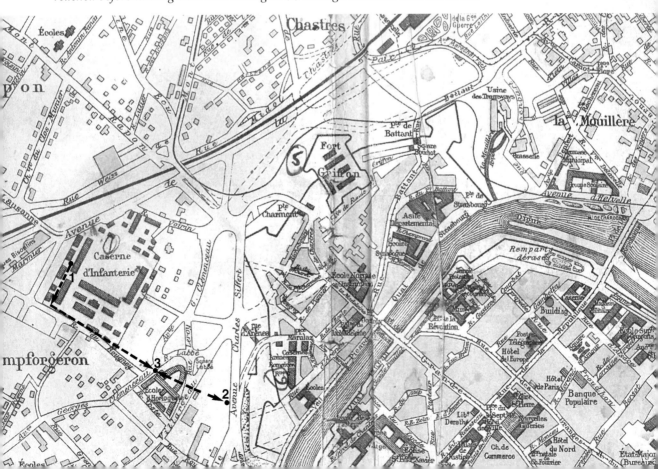

and it was, with the benefit of hindsight, very unfair of us to go there because there were notices in the town stating that anybody helping British prisoners of war to escape would suffer severe penalties.'

The next day they were taken to another house where they spent two nights in the occupants' garden shed.

'We were then taken into the country by car and put on a bus to a small town called Arbois, which was near the demarcation line. These kind people even paid our fares. On arrival at Arbois, we expected to find someone waiting for us who would lead us to a *passeur* someone who would lead us over this demarcation line. There were quite a few chaps who were making a business by conducting parties through the safe bits. However, no one turned up and in the end we were forced to gamble on confiding to a patron of a nearby restaurant. He told us to go to a place called the Café Rosa, where we would find a *passeur*. We did and this young lad saw us into unoccupied France through the forest that evening for the price of my friends' gold wedding ring and a hundred francs.'

After a series of adventures, Laming and his companions made their way to Spain and eventually to Gibraltar, where the familiar sight of a British Bobbie

The mountains that Gordon Laming crossed into Spain 21st December 1940.

Left: April 1941, Gordon Laming with Joan his girlfriend after his escape having returned to the UK. Right: 1947 Gordon and his wife, Joan, standing on the sewer exit by the School of Watchmaking in Besançon.

patrolling the streets confirmed their freedom. They had been on the run for four months.

'Our escape relied on exceptional luck coming our way. There were no established escape lines nor were there any guides. We simply strode through France and Spain, and into the Pyrenees, totally ill-clad and just hoping to cope with any of the weather hazards that late December might bring. Thankfully a measure of resolve and determination was graced by good fortune. I did not really have a sense of having done anything out of the ordinary.'

He arrived back in England on 17 March, a year and six days after leaving for

France. Following a debrief at the London District Transit Centre, he went to stay with his parents.

'Mother was working and didn't look up. She just assumed it was my father returning home from work. When she did see me there was, of course, much rejoicing. Telegrams were sent out to the rest of the family. Like most other folk, we did not have a home telephone.

'After a few days at home I, along with my fellow escapees, reported to the Corps HQ at Hillsea. To our surprise, rather than being welcomed back, the Orderly Room Sergeant just grumbled that we caused him added work. Our Commanding Officer didn't even bother to see us and, when we went to the Medical Officer to ask him for some sick leave, he told us that the CO thought we should have only two weeks "or they will only get themselves into trouble". Might it not have occurred to him that we had had our fill of trouble over the past nine months? The facts we were suffering from fatigue, stomach bugs and a poor diet were ignored completely. Perhaps it was just the army being the army. The other thing that I felt unhappy about was that I was the only one in our group who was awarded the Military Medal. This did not seem to me to be fair given that we all took our chances together so, at the beginning I did not wear the medal ribbon.'

WALTER MORISON, in Stalag Luft III, planned an escape that would involve none of the walking and weeks evading capture that so many had to go through.

'It didn't take very long before I became involved in trying to escape. One day there appeared in my room a new *Kriegie*. His name was Lorne Welch. I had a little model glider that hung over my bed, and he was a glider pilot, so we got talking. We soon discovered that we had one particular idea in common and that was to "borrow" an aircraft from the Luftwaffe and fly ourselves to freedom. A great many of our friends told us it was a barmy idea. They were all very pessimistic – "You'll never do it", "You'll get shot down", and so on.'

Morison and Welch took no notice. Their logic was even that if someone did manage to get out of the camp, he would still be a long way from home. Switzerland was some several hundred miles away and required crossing a very well-guarded border. If an escapee chose to get to the Baltic ports, he would then have to stow away or, even more dangerously, try to cadge a lift on a ship to Sweden. Alternatively, someone, who decided to escape into France or Holland, would have to endure a very long, perilous cross-country journey and then hope to get help. None of these choices were very appealing to the two men, who believed their plan would provide a far easier journey to freedom.

'Our frontier was five miles away – the nearest Luftwaffe airfield! We'd be there in less than an hour and be in Sweden in time for dinner. It had to be Sweden because that was the nearest viable neutral territory.

Navigation would be easy too. The important thing was to try and obtain a simple aeroplane. Great as it would be to go off in a Messerschmitt 110 or something, it was important to remember that these are highly complex aircraft which you couldn't just press a few knobs and fly off in.'
Their first hurdle was to try and get out of the camp.

'At about this time, Squadron Leader Roger Bushell had been re-captured and returned to camp. He was a determined escaper who hated the goons, and he firmly believed that escaping should be properly organized, so he set up an Escape Committee. This became especially important when we moved to a new big compound in the camp, as he wasn't going to let the area be spoiled by ill thought-out schemes. No one would escape without his authority. Lorne Welch was put in charge of what became known as the "Gadget factory" and we began helping with Roger's "Great Escape" plan. One day a man came into my room and said, "X would like to see you tomorrow afternoon in hut so-and-so. Three o'clock". X was Roger Bushell's code-name. Very cloak and dagger stuff, but he was a chap who the Gestapo had very reluctantly returned to the Luftwaffe, with the warning that another attempt to escape

Roger Bushell 'Big X'   IWM HU1605

would result in death. I didn't ask why X wanted to see me, because you just didn't. You never asked questions, but I couldn't think why he wanted to see me. I rather wondered if I had done anything wrong.

'When I walked into his room there were a dozen people who didn't seem to have anything in common. To my surprise, Lorne was there. We all sat around and then Roger Bushell walked in. He was a barrister by trade and had a considerable presence. "Well gentlemen," he said, "I got you together here because I am going to march you out through the gate." He then proceeded to explain briefly how he was planning to do this, and it was the most brilliantly conceived escape scheme that I had ever heard. The breakout depended on the discovery of a louse. The significance of this was that, if a louse was discovered, the goons took everybody from the infected hut to be deloused, which meant taking all the blankets and so on and putting them into a big oven. You would then be given a hot shower. The point was that the delousing plant was in another part of the camp and could only be reached by going out through the main gate, along a public road and back into the other part of the camp. It was one of the very few reasons why the goons would take prisoners outside the wire. The reason they were so anxious was that lice carried typhus, which was – in those days particularly – a very dangerous illness that could spread like wildfire through barracks. With this in mind, the Escape Committee devised an ingenious plan.'

The men were to be escorted through the gate by false guards, who needed to be impeccable German-speakers equipped with a formidable array of passes. The whole operation had to be very carefully timed, because two genuine guards would come into the camp to collect the party going to the de-louser. As this was happening, the party of escapees would be taken out of the camp by quite different guards, in short *kriegies* disguised as goons. It was also necessary that the guard on the gate should change between the time the genuine guards came in and the time when the escapees would go out with their false guards. Otherwise the guard on the gate might have recognized the different personnel. All this required minute timing. Then once they got out onto the road the party would melt away into the forest, which was on the other side of the road, and go their respective ways. Morison describes what happened next:

'Once we were given this fairly earth-shattering information about being marched out of the front gate, we went off to make our preparations. Lorne and myself had to decide which airfield we would go to and what sort of aircraft we wanted. A navigation map was also needed to show us the way to Sweden and so on. I discovered that Lorne had discussed our plan with Roger Bushell. Roger had recognized that the "*kriegie* guards"

Main Gate at Stalag Luft III drawn by Alex Cassie. Roger Bushell's plan was to march a party of prisoners out, with false guards, under the pretext of attending the delousing sheds.

would throw off their uniforms because they wanted to escape in civilian clothes, and we could then use these uniforms, as it would be desirable to be properly dressed when wandering around German airfields. Bushell had an economical mind and he thought it would be a pity to throw away two good German uniforms which had absorbed enormous resources to produce.'

Incredibly, the plan worked exactly according to plan. The party went through the gate and disappeared into the wood.

'Lorne and myself then headed for our airfield. We knew there would be a hue and cry, not least because the number of people who got out was double the original twelve. Time was of the essence because it would not be long before the sirens would sound and the border patrols would be alerted. Unfortunately though, the airfield we planned to nick our aircraft from turned out not be where we thought it was. We never found it. This was partly because it was Whitsun and, as the Luftwaffe were on holiday, there were no aircraft movements. We ended up walking around the area for eight days having a look for a suitable airfield. To begin with we never moved except at night. But eventually we decided that the German searches would have spread out and we did walk round by day. This always made us feel edgy, to put it mildly, as we only had a couple of words of German between us.'

To their disappointment, none of the places they visited were suitable. Either there was something wrong with the airfield itself or it had the wrong type of aircraft. In the end, exhausted by their efforts, they reluctantly returned to the airfield closest to camp, which they had initially turned down because nearly all the planes were bombers, which were far from suitable. It was their last resort. As they set off they passed a village where they were relieved to see that the Nazi party notice board had nothing to say about escaped prisoners of war. Little did they know that a special issue of the *German Criminal Police Gazette* had been issued with Morison's and Lorne's

Special edition of the Criminal Police Gazette *published by the Gestapo in Berlin, 16 June 1943, six days after the 'Delousing Party' escape from Stalag Luft III.*

97

photographs, along with the most lurid description of these two RAF pilots who, it stipulated, had to be recaptured 'at all costs'.

'We arrived at the airfield too late to do anything, so we waited until early the next morning. There was a gate in the fence on the far side of the airfield from the hangars. Using a skeleton key, we unlocked it and walked around the inside perimeter track, wondering whether there would be any likely aircraft. As we were doing this, a nice little aeroplane came in to land and taxied up to the control tower. A three-man crew got out and walked away. It looked an ideal aircraft – a Junkers 34. Our mistake was that we then hesitated before eventually thinking, "Well, it is now or never, and this is our aircraft". So we walked towards it and climbed on board. It had plenty of fuel, and even had some maps inside. It was perfect, except that it didn't have electric starting.

A Junkers W34 of the type Walter Morison and Lorne Welch attempted to take in their bid for freedom.

'The thought of getting out to wind up the engine was a bit daunting. I still had a very weak arm so Lorne got out with the handle and began searching for the hole to put it in. At first he couldn't find it. When he eventually did, disaster struck. "Christ, we've had it," he whispered. I looked up to see the rightful crew walking towards us. This was very embarrassing. I switched off everything that had been switched on, namely the petrol and the ignition, and then clambered out. As I was dressed as a Lance Corporal of the Luftwaffe, I decided to salute smartly. The pilot then said something which I could not understand, so I saluted him again. It seemed to be the best thing to do in the rather hopeless circumstances. Again he said something, and once again I didn't understand. He must have thought I was totally thick-witted. Then, after what seemed an eternity, he gave the classic sign for winding up an aeroplane which I understood all too readily. I now had to try and get the engine to start so that he could fly away in our aeroplane! So nothing for it – I wound, but I hadn't eaten much for a week and had a groggy arm, and the engine wouldn't start. Lorne meanwhile was fidgeting about on the ground and looking agitated, so I said, *"Mein kamerad kommt"* ("My friend's coming"). He was a bit stronger than me and thankfully managed to get it going. We both slid off the wing and stood and watched as our beautiful aeroplane flew off into the distance. It was very sad, and we retreated to recover morale. The gleam of Sweden was distinctly fading from our eyes at that particular moment.'

The two men decided to take refuge in a barn.

'It proved to be a bad choice as the goons came and spent the afternoon there doing we don't know what, while we shivered out of sight. We had a nasty experience soon after they left when, on wandering past a senior German NCO, we failed to recognize his rank and didn't salute him. *"Halt! Konnen Sie nicht gruben?"* (Can't you salute?). So I said, *"Ja"*, to which he replied, *"Gruben!"* So I nudged Lorne and we saluted and it passed off. We walked on, and decided that we would have another go the next day. Once again as we arrived an aeroplane flew in – not as ideal as the one the day before but it was fine. It was now or never. Adrenalin began to rush around as we climbed in. We got the engine turning over but it would not start. At this point an NCO walked out and shouted to us, *"Was wollen sie mit die maschine?"* ("What do you want with this aircraft?") Well, there didn't seem to be a satisfactory answer. So I summoned up all my courage and said, *"Wir sind englische offiziere"* ("We're English officers"). He remained remarkably calm and just said, *"Ach so! Komm mit!"* and led us away.

'In due course we were taken back to camp with an escort of five Tommyguns, having been ordered to take our boots and trousers off. I suppose this was to stop us escaping but it was somewhat undignified and we protested that such a garb did not become an English officer. They took no notice and we were met at the camp by the very stately old commandant. I did my best to behave properly and said, "Good afternoon, Sir!" He just snorted and walked away – rather rude, but there you are. We were then escorted to the cooler. One of the camp officers, Hauptman Peeber, later came in to see us. He was a very decent chap and said, "Herr Morison, such a pity. It was a good try." I think he actually meant it. Unfortunately, others were not so sympathetic and we were endlessly interrogated. They mumbled things about courts martial and sentences of death and so on. I didn't believe them. It was this business of wearing German uniforms that most upset them, and of course wandering on Luftwaffe airfields could, I suppose, be construed as espionage. Eventually, after six weeks in the cooler, it was decided that we should be sent to Colditz.'

Morison recalls that, with the benefit of hindsight, it was probably a good thing

'Obergefreiter' Welch and 'Gefreiter' Morison at a German photo-call following their failed
attempt.

that his attempted escape failed:

'We subsequently learned that our intended route would have taken us slap over the German V2 rocket research station at Peenemunde. This would undoubtedly have been very heavily defended and any untoward aircraft would probably have been shot out of the sky. I did ask Lorne a few years ago whether he thought we would have actually made it. He said, "Of course, we wouldn't," but he was beginning to die at that point and perhaps his morale was sinking. Even if we had made it and got flown back from Sweden to England, we would have gone on operations again and probably been killed, so perhaps we were lucky.'

As a result of this escape attempt Walter Morison was sent to Colditz.

JACK COMYN'S life as a prisoner of war in Italy was considerably better than some of his fellow officers incarcerated in Germany.

'We were actually paid whilst we were imprisoned. There was some extraordinary agreement, which must have been made before the war, between the British and Italian governments that allowed for us to get part of our normal salary. So there we were getting some income and being treated really very well. We were at this camp at Mont Albo which was situated in lovely countryside and the Commandant even allowed us to go for walks with just one or two armed guards. A verbal understanding was made that we would not try and escape during these walks and we respected it. As a result we had a delightful time walking around this beautiful place with a couple of bottles of wine. Perhaps most extraordinary of all, our senior British officer in our camp was a Catholic and he arranged with the Commandant an agreement that Catholic officers would be allowed to go to the local village church for Christmas Eve Mass. I was in the party that went. This little church was crammed full of villagers, Italian soldiers of the camp garrison and a number of us British officers. This was 1942. It was rather extraordinary, and very moving, that we were singing Christmas carols with the enemy. It made one feel that one day we'd all come to our senses.

'If Mont Albo was splendid – so too was Fontanellato where towards the end of our time in Italy we were moved. We were place in a magnificent building with marble floors and walls. Nuns lived next door and used to do our washing, and sometimes send us little notes enclosed with the clean laundry saying they were sorry for us and that everything would be all right and so on.'

Despite these relative comforts, nothing could dampen his desire to escape. One day he spotted an opportunity.

'We were sent clothes parcels from home, but the Italians, seeing that these were mostly civilian items which could be used in escape attempts, decided to confiscate them. However, although they were not given to us, all the clothes were meticulously stored in a little wooden shed just outside

February 1941, Jack Comyn, second on the right, prisoner of war at Homs, Libya. This photograph was taken by an Italian officer.

the wire. It was promised that they would be returned at the end of the war. I was selected by the commandant to help with the book-keeping of these clothes.'

Comyn went out and found himself alone on the other side of the wire with an Italian sergeant. Such an opportunity to escape was too great to miss. He persuaded the senior British officer to tell the Commandant that he found the work heavy and needed another officer to assist him. The Commandant agreed.

'I got hold of this great friend of mine and we went out together. I told him, "Hugh, your job is to keep that sergeant talking in one of the rooms, while I am busy in the other". I got together some chocolate and money, and off we went. Once in the hut, he began talking to this sergeant. Meanwhile I was next door fishing out some suitable clothing – corduroy trousers and an old shirt. To go with this I had made a little paper hat that I noticed all the Italian builders wore. I then rubbed my face in concrete dust off the floor before just dropping out of one of the windows in this little hut and walking past the camp with a hammer in my hand and looking like a builder's mate. Suddenly, from behind a tree, a military police sergeant stopped me and said, "Where do you think you are going?" in Italian. Well that was too much for me. I couldn't possibly reply. "You're a prisoner aren't you?" he said, before taking me back toward the camp.

'I was taken to see the Commandant. His name was Vichi Domini and he was a charming old Italian colonel – a retired regular army officer brought back for the war. I was still in my escaping clothes and he looked at me disbelievingly and said, "You're not Comyn, are you?" I told him that I really was. "Well look, Comyn, when you were walking past the camp my sentries might easily have shot you. Then what would your mother have said?" It was a rather amazing thing to say in wartime! However, I didn't get let off scot free and was sentenced to a month's solitary confinement, which was the proper punishment for the offence.'

A year later Jack Comyn found himself in the bizarre situation of being on the run without having actually escaped. On 8 September 1943 Italy capitulated leaving Comyn and other prisoners in Italian camps in a strange predicament.

'The Allies had conquered Sicily and landed on the mainland of Italy. Mussolini had been expelled from the government, which was now under the King and Marshal Badoglio who had surrendered to the Allies. They had promised to protect Allied prisoners of war in Italy from the Germans who of course occupied the whole country. We were getting secret messages from London telling us that we'd be alright and ordering us to stay put. The War Office must have thought that it would be easier to deal with us that way than have us roaming over the Italian countryside.

'On the day of the surrender, loudspeakers around the camp proclaimed that hostilities were going to cease and that all prisoners would be protected. Our Italian sentries told us they were going home. We hoped we might be going home too, as we were all optimistic that the Allies could occupy Italy and turn the

Lieutenant Colonel Hugh Mainwaring, General Staff Intelligence HQ Eighth Army, Alamein 1942.   IWM HU69746

Germans out. In the meantime Colonel Mainwaring, our Senior Officer, organized us in true military style into companies and battalions. He then went to see the old Italian Commandant and arranged with him that if the Germans were seen approaching the camp the wire would be cut and we would be set free. Mainwaring was absolutely right because it would have been nonsense to stay waiting for further captivity under the Germans. The next day we were told about these arrangements and were in the middle of getting down to a huge lunch of what was left of our Red Cross parcels when a bugle blew signalling that the Germans were on their way from Palma to round us up.'

The prisoners fell into companies and battalions as arranged and were marched out in fours through a big gap in the wire, and across country to a ravine about two miles away from the camp that had been reconnoitred by Mainwaring earlier. There they remained, some six hundred of them, crammed into this hideout.

'A little later an Italian interpreter arrived with some potatoes. He informed us that the Germans had arrived in camp and imprisoned all the Italian officers, including my friend, the Camp Commandant.

'We stayed that night. I found myself as Colonel Mainwaring's Staff Officer and towards the end of the next day he confided, "We're going to have to break up. From now on people will have to just do the best for themselves. I'm going to get on a train with a Belgian officer who can speak fluent Italian and get as far south as I can by train. Do you want to come with me?" It was a difficult decision for me. By now I had many friends in the camp and I was reluctant to desert them. In the end I said no. I subsequently heard that due to the mass of confusion in Italy at the time, nobody asked him and his Belgian colleague for papers at any point on their journey. All they had to do was just sit in a railway carriage!'

Instead, Comyn joined a party of sixteen fellow comrades and they sat down to decide the best course of action.

'There were a number of possible options. The first was to head for Switzerland, but that would mean being interned. Another was to try and join Tito in Yugoslavia, but none of us really knew what the outcome would be and it frankly just didn't appeal to me. A further option was to make our way through occupied France and into Spain. In the end we decided to stay put for the time being. Our decision was to a large extent the result of the BBC, who were putting out all sorts of stories that the Allies were going to land in the north of Italy, near Genoa. The group concluded that with any luck we would soon be taken over by the Allied armies. We decided to stay put in the region, but moved into the Apennine Hills, just to the west of Fontanellato, at dusk. Italian peasants came round offering civilian clothes and food which were gratefully received. I did, however, keep my battledress in a small haversack, because strictly speaking an officer in civilian clothes behind enemy lines was liable to be shot on the spot.

'Our main problem that night was crossing the Via Emilia, a main road running through Milan and Bologna. There was a lot of German military traffic, but, once we'd managed that, it was just a long walk up into the hills where there were plenty of grapes and tomatoes with which to slake our thirst. Charlie Hadley, the eldest man in the group, found it a struggle and his feet began to pack in during the night, forcing us to stop in a little wood above a farmhouse. The next morning I went down to investigate and saw the farmer milking a cow in a little shed. He looked up at me but showed no surprise. News of our break-out must have already gone round the neighbourhood. "What do you want?" he asked. I told him that there was a big party of us up in the woods and that we'd like some milk and some hot water for one of our friend's feet. He agreed and was a great help.'

Soon after, three Italian deserters joined them in the wood. One of them offered to take the men to a bigger wood and promised to put them in touch with a 'local English millionaire'.

'The prospect of meeting a local English millionaire in this area seemed rather unlikely but we followed them into another wood and, soon after, a charming Italian called Senor Palumbo arrived on the scene. It was soon clear that he was a millionaire of lire and not pounds but he'd run a restaurant in Soho for twenty years and spoke with a broad Cockney accent. That in the eyes of the locals was enough to make him an English millionaire. Anyway, he owned a number of different small farms in the area and allotted us in pairs to all his different farms.

'I spent the next six weeks in a small farm hoping the Allies were going to land near Genoa. This was freedom and, after three years of being a prisoner, it was fantastic and exciting to be able to just walk around and hear the birds singing. In the camp it was hard not to feel that life was passing one by, and so the feeling of being free was wonderful. We slept in a hay barn, which wasn't luxurious but it was certainly preferable to a horrible prisoner of war camp existence. Not only did the poor little peasant farmers feed us throughout this time but Senor Palumbo also used to bring up a horse-cart loaded with ham, eggs, bread and wine for us every few days. I remember having a lot of fun trying to learn a bit of Italian.'

After about six weeks it became obvious to Comyn that the Allied landings in the north were not going to take place.

'Four of us got together to discuss the situation. One of the men was a captain, who was senior to me, and he believed we should stay put, saying that it would be only a matter of time before we would be relieved. A young friend of mine and I disagreed with him and a regrettable row ensued. The result was that we set off with the aim of getting to the Allied lines near Cassino, some 400 miles south of us. Unaware that the Allies had settled there for the winter, we began our journey by walking through the Apennine Mountains before passing through Florence and then heading down the Tiber. Our trek was made all the more difficult as it was necessary to avoid roads at all times.

'At one stage we came to tiny hamlet, well away from any road or telephones, consisting of old people and a number of girls and young wives of soldiers. They held a dance in our honour. These lovely girls said, "Why don't you stay with us? Just settle down here. We'll look after you and feed you. The Germans won't come near here. It is much too remote." We were sorely tempted! The next morning as we walked down this tiny hamlet street, we were given a glass of wine from every house we passed.'

After a couple of months they found ourselves in the wild region of the Sabine Hills, east of Rome. It was clear that they were getting near the fighting.

'We asked our peasant host if he had a radio. He didn't, but said the *patroni* – the landowner – who lived in a big house nearby did. That night he secretly took us there and we were greeted by a rather heavy Italian man, who was obviously the *patroni*. He asked to see our hands. When we showed him, he spoke up, "Ah yes, officers, I can see." Once our soft palms had passed the officer test, nothing was too good for us. We were put up for three days and a cocktail party was arranged, where we were presented to these rather smart Italians as his sort of trophy. He wrote to my parents soon after and told them all about our visit. We could have stayed longer but really felt that we must get on, so pushed on into this very wild country called the Abruzzi Hills in the south of Italy, which was a national park. The tracks of brown bears were clearly visible in the thick snow. At one point an Italian suddenly appeared and offered us the pistol he was carrying. I told him that if we were caught in civilian clothes with a pistol we would have hell to pay, but he replied that it wasn't the Germans we should be frightened of but the wolves!

'The snow was becoming more and more difficult to cope with and, by the time we got to a place called Opi, it was getting dark. Some Italian officers, who were trying to get to the south, told us there were hiking tracks in the mountain and that the trees along those tracks were marked out with the number of the track on it. In the dark though this didn't help and we just went on the best we could in the general direction. It was so cold that we refused to sit down and on we walked, when all of a sudden we heard voices. We lay low and, realizing they were neither Germans nor Italians, crept up to them and discovered four Sikh officers huddled together. I told them to come with us, but the oldest amongst them replied, "We are cold, we are tired, we shan't live long." There was little we could do, so we left them. Then in the early hours of the morning the fog and

Monte Cassino where the Allies were held up by the German positions across Italy known as the Gustav Line. The Allies settled down for the winter and Jack Comyn's party hoped that they would cross to safety.

snow became so bad that we just could not go on. Our only hope lay in a large stone hut that shepherds used in the summer. Smoke was coming out of the chimney, and the idea of a fire was something we just couldn't resist. Our minds were made up on seeing a British soldier running out of it to get some logs.'

Not long after, the little band of Indians walked in, having decided to follow Comyn's advice. The hut now comprised Comyn and his travelling companion, four Indians and a British other rank.

'We gratefully took off our boots and stockings and sat down in front of the fire to warm up. All of a sudden the British soldier spotted some Germans approaching. There was a burst of small arms fire outside, and he and the Sikhs rushed out. Meanwhile my friend and myself hid in a dark hole behind the fireplace. It was big enough to be a storeroom. Unfortunately, though, we did not collect our boots and socks in time. Meanwhile the Germans were

Map showing Jack Comyn's escape route. So near and yet so far...

rounding up the others. I began to think we were going to get away with it, but the German officer came into the room with the fire and saw our boots lying beside it. He immediately asked the British soldier whom they belonged to. "Oh, they are mine," he replied. The German replied, "You don't have three hats and three pairs of boots do you?" And then the search began. One of them came into our dark hiding place, lit a match and informed the German officer that no one was there. This dark room had a window though, which had been covered over by a wooden cover frame and, just as we began to get optimistic about our chances again, we heard an axe coming through the window. The next we knew was that there was a horrible German face, with spectacles on, peering in on us.

'It was the most miserable point in my life. Having got hold of us, we were marched practically all day down the mountains. I just remember being exhausted and terribly hungry to the point of hallucinating. Our journey had begun near Piacenza in the north and we had got to the south of Rome after some two and a half months. It was horrifying to find oneself a prisoner of war again after such an effort.'

Comyn was transported back to Germany and sent to Moosberg concentration camp.

'Imprisonment in Germany was very hard. As the war began to near its end, conditions further deteriorated. Hunger was ever-present and, to make matters worse, we were on the direct route from England to Berlin. This meant that practically every night British bombers came over. The American Air Force also flew over in vast numbers and their bombing was a bit random at times. Our camp suffered very badly as a result. Much of it was destroyed and quite a lot of friends were killed.'

LORD HAIG, like so many other prisoners of war in Italy, greeted the news of the Italian armistice with excitement and optimism. Here he describes how his hopes for freedom proved to be short-lived and how a mass escape took place on the train journey to Germany.

'Brigadier Mountain, our senior British officer, advised us to remain in the camp even though our guards had gone. A War Office order had been received instructing POW officers to stay put for the time being. Mountain had been assured of a warning from the Italians in case of any German move to take us over. So with this advice we went to bed fully clothed and with our bags packed ready for an immediate move. In the early hours of the following morning we were woken by the sound of machine-guns. The Germans had surrounded the camp. We were caught. Desperately we tried to escape, but the Germans had planned their operation so well that we were all rounded up. Two of our officers were found wounded, one of them so severely that he later died. Apart from that, the operation had been bloodless. We were prisoners once more. Our disappointment was terrible. We felt badly let down. The prospect of moving to Germany was grim. Our only consolation was the fact that we were not alone. In front of us between the two wires stood our former Italian guards. One of them, Count Palestrelli, said to one of our officers, "Now we are both in the sack together". I doubt whether he got a civil reply.

'At Bologna the SS herded us into cattle trucks, over forty officers in each truck. We were filled with bitter disappointment. We had expected freedom after the Italian surrender only to have our expectations transformed into German captivity. We had always been thankful, when we were in Italian camps, that we had the sun. We had lots of advantages and we knew that life in Germany was going to be pretty depressing. We were going into a grey climate with not too much light at the end of the tunnel.'

Their journey north took them towards the Brenner Pass. The train's speed decreased as it began the long climb towards Trento.

'One of our officers climbed on to the shoulder of another and dived head first through the window, just wide enough for his shoulders to pass. After he dived we heard no more. Some time later the train stopped at a small station and guards ordered us out, "*Raus, Raus*" in angry tones. As we piled on to the platform we were hurriedly counted. The SS looked

Following the surrender of the Italian government, British prisoners of war in Italy were quickly rounded up by the Germans.

grim and tense. A guard told me that many officers had escaped from those trucks which had wooden floors. In fact more than a hundred officers had escaped during the journey between Verona and Trento. In one truck an officer had managed to squeeze through a hole in the floor, crawl along the rods underneath until he reached the side of the train, where he climbed up and slid back the latch of the unlocked truck. As the train climbed slowly up the mountainside most of the officers were able to jump out in turn. In other trucks some officers had boldly crawled through the holes they had made and simply fell or jumped onto the line. For them, unless the train had been going slowly enough to crawl free, there was an almost certainty of being crushed, as the last vehicle, an electric engine, had very little clearance. A few other officers had simply dived through the window. In fact a large number survived. Some escaped over the mountains to Switzerland; some were recaptured.

'The officer in charge of the SS guard now threatened to shoot those officers who had been found in trucks from which there had been a mass escape. They were prevented from doing so by a threat made by our interpreter that for every British officer shot ten SS men in Britain would be shot as a reprisal. In the face of this warning the officer did nothing, though he realized he would be punished at the end of the journey.'

MIKE DAUNCEY had abandoned any attempt to escape from the Dutch eye hospital that had been tending his wound sustained at Arnhem, as it might have endangered the lives of the local men and women who had treated him. However, he had no such reservations once he had been moved to St. Antonio's, the German military hospital at Utrecht.

'Conditions were totally different to those at the eye hospital. We were all in one long corridor with beds running all along it. Only Major Gordon Cunningham of the 5th Black Watch, as the senior prisoner, was given a room to himself. Equipment was simple and supplies were limited. The only bandages I saw were paper ones, and amputations were more widespread as often it was the only thing that could be done under such conditions.'

Dauncey resolved to escape but time was not on his side. He was well aware that the moment he looked as though he was on the road to recovery he would be moved straight to Germany. Escaping from a camp there would be a completely different matter.

'I asked if I could go for a little walk as I was feeling a little better and this gave me an opportunity to survey the wire fence surrounding the hospital. A number of us watched when the Germans went off for their supper each evening and began to develop a decent understanding of their guard rota. I had to act fast and so I decided to inform Gordon Cunningham about my plan to leave. I thought as senior officer he should know. He had been shot through both legs, but the bullets had missed his bones and gone straight out. Despite these wounds, which had only sustained ten days before, he insisted that he should come as well. I agreed and that night we agreed that we would make our break the next evening at about half past six, when the German guards were having their supper. As we were one floor up, we couldn't just jump out of the window and so we decided to use the traditional method of knotting together various sheets.'

The time came and all went very smoothly. The two men successfully made their way down the wall

Lieutenant Mike Dauncey, Adjutant G Squadron, Glider Pilot Regiment, RAF Fairford, Summer 1944.

and into the garden. Now only the high fence stood in the way of their freedom.

'The concertina wire was very prickly, but such was the urgency neither one of us even noticed. We managed it with Gordon getting on my back as his legs were still very weak. A few moments later we were over the wire and in an absolutely deserted street. There was a curfew every night and absolutely no one was around.'

The men had planned to head for the English church in town. Dauncey had been visited by a very friendly couple whilst in hospital who lived in the Parsonage beside it. He felt sure they would help, but first he had to ask for directions.

'We took a risk early and tapped on a door to ask where the church was. It was opened by a man who was absolutely terrified at the sight of us and rushed out into the night. His wife, however, was a very different calibre and agreed to take us to our intended destination as long as we promised to walk at least fifty yards behind her. Once we approached the church she left and we made our way to the Parsonage, where we were warmly greeted by my friends Paul and Constance Breuning and their three younger children. Dr Breuning brought out a half bottle of champagne that he had been keeping until the Allied victory, which I thought was a great compliment. The relief at reaching a safe haven was unbelievable. Little

The English Church, right, and Parsonage, Utrecht, where the Breuning family so bravely gave Dauncey and Cunningham shelter.

did we know then that we would spend the next two months there.

'Their hospitality knew no bounds. At Christmas time we had a great feast which I secretly learned afterwards was their pet white rabbit. They didn't tell the children about it, although they may have guessed as its disappearance coincided suspiciously with Christmas. In fact the Breunings were generally very short of food. I can even remember going up into the attic and spending quite a while brushing up dried peas which had fallen out of a bag.

'Most of the time was spent in our room and we played an enormous amount of bridge, which Gordon was incredibly good at. He could remember each hand for a long time afterwards and the morning after would tell me what I should have done. Apart from that, we just used to talk. Somehow the Breunings had acquired a copy of a menu from a well-known restaurant called Simpsons-in-the-Strand, and we spent day after day discussing what we would choose. A doctor used to come regularly to check on Gordon's progress. A rather clever ruse on the part of the Breunings was that they made out the children had measles which explained the doctor's regular visits and also had the effect of stopping people from coming around. They were incredibly brave because, if the Germans had come round to the place, there is no doubt that Paul Breuning would have been shot, and his wife would probably have been put in prison. The only thing they expected us to do was to get out through an upper window and into the garden if the enemy did come around.'

The Germans were furious about Dauncey's and Cunningham's escape. At least one of the orderlies and several sentries received fierce punishments as a result of the breakout and a massive search was conducted. Then one day, while they were playing cards, Mrs Breuning told them that the Germans had announced that they had been captured and shot.

'I was rather upset about this but the Underground thought it was absolutely terrific because it was an acknowledgement that they hadn't been able to find us, and that they intended to waste no more time looking. In fact the Breunings had to work very hard to make contact with the Underground because security was terribly tight. In the meantime Dr Breuning had managed to get us two identity cards complete with passport photos. I was called Peter Bos and was meant to be doctor who was deaf and dumb, and some eight years older than I really was. I found it an unlikely combination but I suppose it was better than nothing at all. He also arranged, or perhaps I should say stole, two bicycles which at the time were very prized bits of apparatus because petrol was virtually non-existent.'

The escape plans changed daily because they were very dependent on the situation at the front.

'It was decided that we weren't going to do a big hook through other parts of the country. Our escape route was a straight line into the Allied sector. The whole thing sounded very simple as long as we evaded the

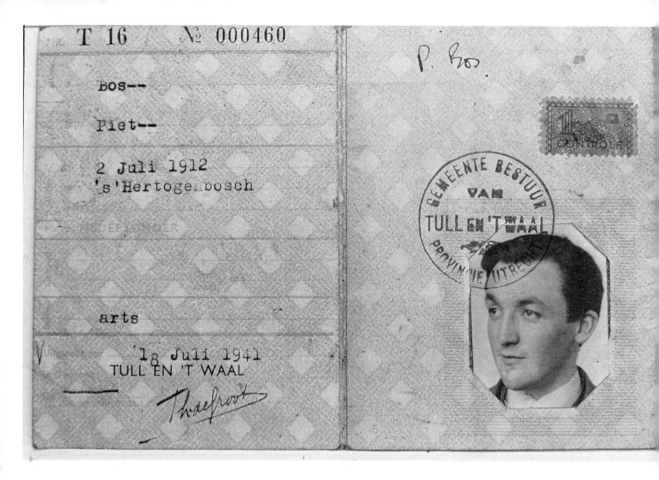

Identity Card secured for Mike Dauncey by the Dutch Underground. He passes as a Piet Bos, a deaf and dumb doctor.

Germans at awkward places. As the weeks turned into months, we got more and more buoyed up and the second month seemed to be endless.'
At last the time came when the bicycles were to put to good use. The two men bade a fond farewell to the Breunings and, led by two young Dutch women, set off towards the Allied lines.

'As we hadn't been out for some two months our cycling was somewhat shaky at the beginning, and Gordon found using his leg muscles quite an effort. The girls were very pretty and tended to attract the eye of the German soldiers so we just sailed on in their wake. I was wearing rather funny clothes – an old coat, a pink scarf which stood out a mile and black winklepicker shoes. I rather wondered if my garb didn't have the effect of drawing attention to myself rather than merging with the crowd. I decided I would wear my identity discs around my neck as it would be less easy for the Germans to prove I was a spy if I did get caught. By the end of the first day, we got to a little river called the Lek, left our bicycles there and got across on a small boat, where we were greeted by some other Dutchmen.'
Over the next few weeks they stayed with a number of Dutch people at different

places, while all the time working towards the Allied lines.

'The Underground meticulously organized our escape. It wasn't long before we were manoeuvring within six to eight miles of the front line, and of course the quantity of enemy troops in the region intensified. The key was to keep moving and we often just stopped at different little farms, houses and flats for a night before being moved on. This of course required a great deal of effort from the Underground who not only had to organize it but also had to ensure we were fed and so on. We stayed at one large farm in a village called Culemborg for some time. It employed a number of farm workers so we were able to merge in, although most days were spent hiding inside. Every evening, though, we all sat around this enormous kitchen and had the most wonderful food. German soldiers would occasionally pop in to ask for eggs, but we were told not to take any notice and just to laugh when the other labourers did. It worked marvellously and we got on very well with the labourers, not least because they loved cards and we introduced Pontoon to them which they couldn't get enough of. Indeed, some time after the war, my wife Marjorie and I came back to Culemborg to try and find the farm, which we did, and we were met by one of these labourers who roared with laughter and shouted, "Twist, Bust!"'

After ten days at the farm the two men were moved on to another small town called Buren, which was even closer to the Allied lines.

'Here we were joined by two United States pilots and two other chaps, and together we set out that night with the aim of crossing the Waal which would have got us to the other side. As we reached our crossing point, the Underground rushed us back with the news that the Germans had a troop movement in the area where they had planned. The crossing was therefore cancelled and we were taken to another farm, where we were all put up in a loft. There was further trouble the following morning when one of the US pilots came to over and informed us that he believed that one of his fellow pilots was a fraud. He smelt a rat after hearing the chap talk about England, where he had said he'd been based, because he couldn't answer some fairly elementary questions about the place. This was serious because obviously the Underground were afraid that he may have infiltrated some of their escape routes. In fact it was later discovered that he was a Dutchman who just wanted to get out of occupied Holland, but it was a rather eerie moment.'

The next day Dauncey was taken back to Buren and, while he was there, the Dutch Underground brought along a little radio transmitter, via a girl on her bicycle.

'I spoke to one of the British OP aeroplanes who wanted to know a bit more about us, and about what we were proposing to do. I think the British wished to know that the people the Dutch wanted to get over were in fact Allies and not infiltrators. In order to talk on this thing you had to wind it up, which seemed to make an enormous noise, and I felt conscious that every German could hear it all around. Anyway, as soon as we'd finished, this girl packed up the radio and disappeared. I thought it was incredibly brave of her.'

Their next hiding place was in a church in Asch, where they were placed in the upper reaches of the building.

'It wasn't long before the boredom and the constant midges got to us as we crouched in this small dusty hideout. One day, instead of staying up in the church, we went down to the main body of it when there was a sudden noise. We leapt into a broom cupboard and just hoped whoever had entered would go away. To our dismay the door opened and there in front of us stood the local priest. Unable to think about what to do, we just bowed to him and made our way back to the hideout at the top of the building. To our embarrassment, the Underground informed us the next day that he was furious and had told them that it was quite wrong for a church to be used for that purpose and that we must leave immediately.

1978 Brigadier Mike Dauncey, Colonel of the Cheshire Regiment (1978 – 1985).

'Whilst working at another farm, I and a member of the Underground went for a swim in a river. I think he must have thought I needed freshening up. At that moment a German sentry with his rifle slung over his shoulder came by and the Dutch Underground man shouted something at him, which was obviously quite witty because the German roared with laughter. I started laughing too and off he went. It once again showed me that, if you just keep calm, you could get away with the most extraordinary things.'

At last the time came for another attempted crossing into Allied lines. A party of six escapees, including Dauncey and Cunningham, were met by a guide called Jan who led them down to the river.

'Jan was a young man and I was amazed that he was prepared to take us. We reached the riverbank in darkness and there was a boat lying in the bank. This was too good to be true but Jan said no one bothered to take it because there was an enormous hole in one side of it, which would make anyone think it was useless. We all jumped in and began to row. Sure enough, water started coming in fairly quickly and before we had reached the other bank it was virtually waterlogged and well above the seats. Once we had got there, I asked Jan if there was anything we could do for him. "The only thing I would like is if you could please turn the boat over and empty all the water out," was his reply, which I thought was a rather modest request. I asked him if he wanted to come with us but he declined, saying that he wanted to go back to Holland again. It was a very moving moment. In fact there is now a memorial on the bank of the Waal to Jan and to the other men who helped ferry British and Allied soldiers and airmen across the river.

'We were now in no man's land, in a little neck of land that neither side used. Jan pointed us in the right direction, but told us to lie low and wait until it was light, when we should go forward one at a time with our hands up in order that we could be inspected by the Allies. The Allies on this stretch of the line were Belgians and I confess that I did hope that someone had told them that we were coming. As it turned out, I think they must have witnessed other prisoners coming back because they weren't wildly excited. For us, though, it was a great moment of triumph and nothing would deflate us.'

The day was 10 April 1945. It had been some four months since the two men had first escaped from the prison hospital.

'We were taken in for questioning at a reception place but my main memory is the sight of white bread again. Soon after, we were flown to Croydon. The euphoria of being home was tremendous. I was back with my fiancée Marjorie and my family, and nothing could take that away from me. On a slightly sadder note, I went back to Fairford in the summer of that year to see what was happening there and visited the Nissen hut that I had lived in with six subaltern friends for a year before I became a prisoner. I was the only one still alive. I had been very lucky.'

BOB WALKER-BROWN, 2nd Battalion The Highland Light Infantry, was wounded and captured by the Germans in the Western Desert in June 1942. He was handed over to the Italians, who treated him in a military field hospital near Danna. From there he was shipped over to Naples and then taken by train to a hospital run by nuns at Lucca, in Northern Italy. Here he received good treatment but found certain practices disconcerting.

'Although there was never any attempt at unkindness or callousness, the nuns were used to treating local Italian paupers and the way they behaved towards men who were about to die was ghastly. A number of my fellow prisoners did die there, and each time the process was the same. The local parish coffin would be brought in and placed beside the man who was about to die while he was still conscious. We thought this was terrible. As soon as the prisoner died he was put straight into this parish coffin and removed, and a few hours later back came the same coffin but empty.'

After recovering, he was moved to a prisoner of war camp, Camp 21, near

Chieti. It was a typical Italian single-storey army barracks, surrounded by a very high wall, some eighteen feet high, which had sentry boxes, searchlights and double barbed wire fencing around it.

'I was desperate to escape. Regrettably the vast majority of prisoners failed to share my sentiments. Out of 900 officers in the camp, a maximum of about forty engaged in active attempts and many of those were prepared to help, but did not want to risk escaping themselves. I was surprised by their attitude.

'The Italians were rather suspicious of tunnelling and used to have snap searches. Additional troops were brought in and on one occasion a full company of Italian soldiers doubled in through the main gates of the camp looking very impressive. On completing the search, they then doubled backwards but unfortunately several fell over on their backsides causing enormous hilarity. The Italians were not amused, rifles were cocked and shots were fired in the air.'

Walker-Brown joined a small escape party, which soon resolved to dig a tunnel out of the camp.

'We tried to sink a shaft inside the barrack blocks. These had a floor of tiles, made up of some twelve inches of concrete. The noise of the tapping could be heard quite a long way off, even though we tried to muffle it. Eventually we got through the concrete and replaced the tiles with a sort of wooden tray, but the Italians were very clever and used to come round and tap the floor. They noticed a slight change of tone and discovered our embryonic tunnel. It was time to think again.'

Bob Walker-Brown, Egypt 1942.

It was not long before Walker-Brown and his group of nine fellow escapees, undeterred by the failure of their first attempt, developed another escape plan.

'We discovered the lid of a sub-drain outside one of the barrack blocks about fifteen inches by eighteen inches. On removing it, there was a brick-made sump about forty inches deep. This was absolutely ideal, as it was out of the direct line of the wall sentries. It also had the advantage of being adjacent to open windows leading to the lavatories and ablutions. The walls of the buildings had an air space between them and ventilation plates on top and these were eventually to be used for the disposal of soil, which is the great problem when you are tunnelling. The sump was tiny, so we seized a very small officer and in spite of him saying, "What me?" we pushed him inside, sealed him down under the lid and told him to remove the bricks on the leading edge and start to dig. He could only stay down a short time because of the claustrophobic conditions and also because the perimeter was regularly patrolled by armed carabinieri.'

From that point onwards they managed to drive forwards. The first thirty feet were dug underneath a concrete pavement so there was no need to shore the top of the tunnel. All the spoil was dragged back to the tunnel mouth using Red Cross cardboard boxes on little improvised sledges, rolled into balls in the lavatories and stuffed into the double-skinned walls.

'Digging was extremely unpleasant to put it mildly. For the first thirty feet or so one was digging in dry conditions but the tunnel was tiny – it was just high enough to bring your knees under your backside, with your shoulders touching the sides. A shift went down for usually about three hours. It started immediately after muster parade and we wanted everyone out at least an hour before the next muster parade. We just kept to the same job for the whole stint so one might spend three hours digging at the face, or three hours pulling soil back or, as it later turned out, three hours in the sewer. After twenty minutes or so the little lamp one had, which was normally just a shoe lace or something in a tin of olive oil, gave out because of a lack of oxygen. From that moment onwards one had to dig in total and complete darkness. It was claustrophobic in the extreme. We had two cases of fainting at the face, which could have been lethal. Fortunately both cases recovered. Very unpleasant.

'The great fear when digging was that there would be a collapse of the tunnel behind you because you couldn't turn round. That would have been very dangerous indeed. One's chances of survival would have been minimal. There was also the ever-present worry that the Italians would, if they discovered, certainly have thrown a few grenades down it. We believed they had one or two informants in the camp, and two prisoners in particular were identified as potentially hostile. They were watched and, if they came anywhere near the tunnel, work stopped immediately. On the whole the attitude of the prisoners when we were digging was a mixture of acquiescence but non-involvement. A minority were actively hostile towards us because they reckoned it might disturb the tenor of prison life.'

Once the team had reached the end of the pavement it was then forced to construct a deep-level chamber in order to tunnel underneath the deep foundations of the high wall that surrounded the camp.

'We were working just on top of the water table so it became slippery and cold at the bottom, and shoring was necessary. This was done using wooden planks from our beds, which of course aroused great suspicion. Indeed they became so suspicious that sudden snap searches were intensified. On a snap search, a bugle would blow and the entire camp had to parade for a head count. We were very fortunate to get away with it as on one occasion we had six people working in the tunnel at the time. Dummies were arranged in beds to simulate sick people and thankfully the Italians never bothered to prod the motionless bodies, so we got away with it.'

Their biggest problem was the disposal of earth. At the half-way stage it became clear that the double-skinned walls in the ablutions wouldn't take any more. Just as they were at their wits' end as to how best to overcome this issue, the group had a further piece of good fortune.

'We came across what appeared to be a concrete obstacle in the tunnel. On closer inspection it turned out to be a sewer. We broke a section of the sewer with a digging tool. The stench was terrific but we suddenly realized that this could be the answer to our problems of where to put the earth. It couldn't just be shovelled in because the sewer would have blocked and that in turn would have led to an investigation. In the end, using more wood from the beds, we formed a sort of duck-boarding in the sewer so that the muck from three hundred Italians could run smoothly underneath it. It was the worst of all the jobs because you were literally surrounded by faeces. It was also a messy job, which added to our problems. Getting people out of the tunnel in the three minutes it took before the carabinieri patrol returned again was quite some rush, when they were naked, covered in sewage and clay, and needed to be washed up, while at the same time having to seal the entrance of the tunnel. It was very exciting and nerve-racking.'

On the other side of the perimeter wall was a big fig tree. It was decided this would be their break out point as it would provide the escapees with some essential cover. Using an army prismatic compass and an improvised theodolite, the diggers were able to ensure considerable accuracy and to work the tunnel upwards once they had gone past the perimeter foundation.

'Some Red Cross parcel string knotted together gave us our position underground. On reaching the area of the fig tree the tunnelling became extremely difficult. It was the Italian summer and the ground was rock hard, but eventually we reached the roots of our tree. A breakout chamber – using a canopy supported on four pieces of wood from the beds – was built. The aim was that it could withstand pressure from above. We also contrived a very amateur periscope, which would help us see if anyone was patrolling.'

Ingenuity, along with determination, ensured that the 150 foot tunnel took less than five months to build. By September 1943 it was ready. To their dismay, however, an order passed by the War Office declared a ban on escaping from camps in Italy.

'We were aware the Allies had landed in Sicily but we had no means of knowing what the state of the campaign was. The War Office clearly anticipated a rapid advance up the Italian peninsula and the thought of hundreds and hundreds of Allied prisoners roaming the countryside was deemed undesirable. Our Senior British Officer made it clear that anyone who tried to break out would be court-martialled at the end of war.'

It soon became obvious, however, that the War Office predictions about Allied progress in Italy were optimistic. There was no rapid advance and so Walker-Brown and his tunnelling companions went to see the Senior British Officer to ask if he would modify the instruction he had received. He refused. Undeterred and believing his decision wrong, Walker-Brown and his fellow tunnellers resolved that they would break out regardless of orders. The arrival of German troops that evening further reinforced their decision.

'German parachutists suddenly seized the camp and ordered a muster parade at first light the following morning. It was quite clear that they would be sending us all back to Germany so the nine of us went straight down the tunnel, and some of our helpers sealed the top of it. We remained there for the best part of twenty-four hours. It was like being buried alive

POWs quickly found themselves under German control after the Italian Armistice.

121

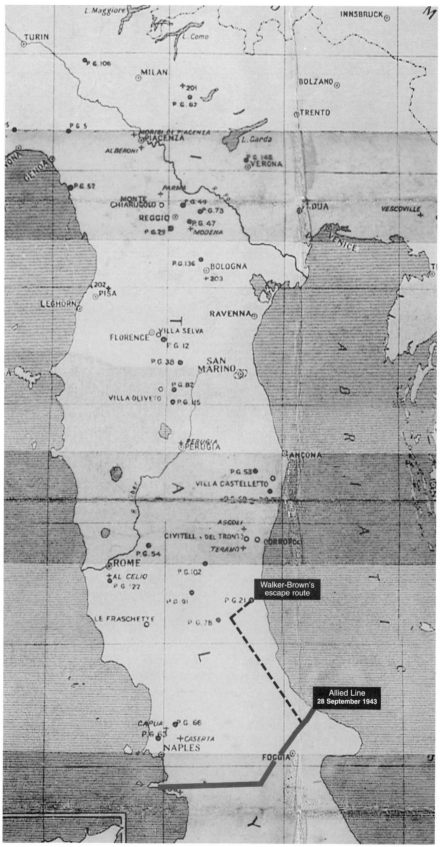

1943 British Red Cross map showing POW camps in Italy, with Walker-Brown's escape route marked from Camp PG21.

but we were buoyed up with the hope that we were about to make a successful escape. Morale was high. The time then came when we decided we would cautiously explore the situation. In fact, rather than get out of end of the tunnel, we went to the entrance. There was no sound of anyone in the camp and we correctly assumed the place was now empty. In some ways getting out by the entrance and not the exit chamber was a bit of an anti-climax after all our work, but escaping was our first priority. We emerged into a completely abandoned camp at around 2 o'clock in the morning and, thinking that it would be safer not to try our luck out by walking through the camp gate, we found a ladder and scaled the wall.'

They then split into parties of three and, in the bright moonlit night, Walker-Brown led his party towards the River Pescara.

'On our way there we passed through a small Italian village. Dogs barked but no one approached. On we walked, raiding a farmhouse along the way and stealing some clothes – some blue trousers, blue shirts and so on in order to look like Italian peasants. On reaching the river, we laid up for the rest of the night and waited until the first light to find out where we were. Having got our bearings it was decided to strike south along a spine of hills about ten miles inland from the Adriatic. Although we didn't have a map, we knew that all we really had to do was move south, with the sea on our left. We only moved when it was dark and so relied on night vision, but most of the time there was either starlight or moonlight. The great danger was that anywhere within two or three hundred yards of a farmhouse would provoke dogs barking. We didn't know the attitude of the Italians and so thought it best to avoid all contact with them. Our diet consisted purely of peaches and figs, which were very pleasant but produced some obvious side-effects.

'The journey involved crossing three major rivers. They were fast-flowing and so we linked arms to steady ourselves and went through them at about waist-height. We rightly suspected that the river banks the other side would be patrolled by the Germans, and so it was a question of waiting for the right moment before venturing across.'

On day nine they spotted some tank and vehicle movements on the crest some three or four miles to the south.

'We couldn't tell if they were friend or foe, but the sound of battle was getting louder and louder, and closer and closer. In order to get a better view, we breached our inflexible rule of never moving by day and made our way into a vineyard. As we did so, there was a shout of "Hands up" in German. I felt a cold shiver down my spine. In the bag again, I thought, after all this. We were immediately captured by a section of the German infantry. The commander was very suspicious. "*Englander?*" he asked. "*Italiano, Italiano*", I replied. He didn't seem convinced at all. He unshipped a machine gun from a mule which was covered in belted ammunition, set it up on its tripod facing us and handed us entrenching tools with orders to dig.'

Walker-Brown and his two companions assumed they were digging their own graves. Fortunately though, at that moment, the position came under very accurate and intense mortar fire from the Allies.

'The Germans decided to leave us and off they went in very good order. We waited there and just hoped the shells and mortars missed us. When, at last, the battle drew to a close, we were met by some leading companies of the 36th Infantry Brigade. They were equally suspicious of us and we were then taken back to the Brigade Headquarters where I asked to see the Brigade Intelligence officer. I told him our story and informed him that we had crossed three of the major river obstacles that stood before them, and that there was only a thin screen of Germans in between. "If you really get your act together, move now and show a bit of dash, you can probably bounce them," I told him. Our advice was ignored, however, and I went back to Divisional Headquarters where I repeated the same story. Once again my advice was not followed. Nothing, however, could blight my joy at getting behind Allied lines. It was just too marvellous to be true. I have never felt such a sense of exhilaration.'

Fifteen months after his capture he was at last a free man. Walker-Brown was told he would be sent back base immediately.

'I remember asking some officer about the air situation. "Oh, you don't have to worry about that. We've got complete air superiority." So off I went to join the back of a column of trucks going south from the forward areas. As we set off, I don't know why but I suddenly looked behind me and saw two Messerschmitts right behind the column. How I did it I do not know, but all I remember is ending up about sixty feet away in a ploughed field. As I lay there the Messerschmitts opened up with their cannon and machine guns. Seconds later there was just a column of burning vehicles. So much for total air superiority, I thought.'

Bob Walker-Brown was taken to Tunis and then on to Algiers, where he took a troopship back to the UK. After a few weeks of leave, he was posted to an infantry training battalion in Aberdeen. But he wanted to rejoin the action.

'I soon got thoroughly bored with the routine of training. One day while I was up there I met a strange character in a pub. He was covered in knives and pistols and heaven knows what. "What on earth are you?" I asked. "Oh," he replied "I'm in the SAS." "What's that?" I enquired. "It's the Special Air Service." I found out who his Commanding Officer was, picked up the phone and said I wanted to be a part of it. The end result was that I joined the 2nd SAS.'

He went on to work behind the German lines in France and Italy. His experience of the latter, acquired while travelling through as an escaping prisoner, proved invaluable.

Some time after his escape he learnt that the train carrying POWs from Camp 21 was attacked on the way to Germany by Alliedaircraft, killing many of his former comrades.

Men of the 51st Highland Division await the onslaught of Rommel's 7th Panzer Division on the River Bresle, 8th June 1940.

Chandos Blair, Lieutenant, 2nd Battalion, The Seaforth Highlanders. Captured 12 June 1940.

*Chandos Blair
1942*

*Chandos Blair
1999*

Lieutenant **CHANDOS BLAIR** was commissioned into the 2nd Seaforth Highlanders in January 1939. When war broke out eight months later his battalion was sent over to France. He was captured by the Germans at St Valery. From that moment onwards he only had one thing on his mind – escape.

'We all felt very depressed and in a state of shock. I don't think I had ever thought that I might be taken prisoner and I felt a certain amount of disgrace at having been captured. We were marched off as captives and immediately began looking for opportunities to escape. It was clear, though, that the guards escorting us wouldn't hesitate to shoot if you broke ranks and there was also the possibility that you might endanger anybody marching alongside you.'

Blair was, however, conscious that the longer he left his dash for freedom the harder it would become. On about night three, the men were all put in a field surrounded by barbed wire and a number of guards.

'We stopped there before it got dark. I met up with a naval commander called Elkins, who had got captured coming ashore to arrange the

The last organized resistance had been overwhelmed and troops of the 51st Highland Division were rounded-up in the afternoon 12th June 1940.

embarkation on the night the fiasco happened at St Valery. He was determined to get away and, along with a couple of others, we spotted that there was a patch of undergrowth – mostly nettles – quite close to the wire which it might be possible to crawl through and not be seen. The plan was considered by the four of us and it was decided that three should go and that one of us should keep sentry. Well, Elkins was obviously going to go because he was a sailor and could manage boats. There was also a French linguist so he was another obvious choice. In the end I was left as a sentry. The plan went very well and they got into this patch. They must have lain up there for about three or four hours. It grew dark and they got away. Ten days later they were back home. I never found out how they acquired a boat.'

Blair was determined to find another opportunity. After ten days of marching the captives were taken by boat from Holland down the Rhine into Germany. They were then placed on a train destined for Austria and disembarked near Salzburg, before being marched to an old chateau in Laufen – a notoriously difficult place to escape from with its high walls and watch towers.

'After we had been there for about four months, three chaps did manage to get out of a window, down the wall which must have been in shadow from the searchlights. They were all fluent German speakers and tried to make their way to Hungary, which was the only place to head to from there. After three days on the loose, they were caught. It proved that escaping from Laufen was possible, but it also showed how difficult it was to pass yourself off as a German.'

After about eight months the German Kommandant paraded the men and announced that German Luftwaffe prisoners had been mistreated by their Canadians captors in French Canada. As a tit for tat measure, he had been ordered to send three hundred prisoners to a punishment camp in Poland. Blair was among those sent there.

'We were incarcerated in an old fort underground that had been built for some previous war. It was a pretty depressing place because all the rooms were underground, but you had a window onto the moat, which by then was a dry moat. I teamed up with two or three others to try and make an escape attempt. One of them, who I didn't know well, was a linguist. He said he had got into cahoots with a German guard and told us he thought he could bribe him with the camp Deutschmarks to be on sentry at a

General Victor Fortune.

certain place on a certain night. He felt certain that the sentry would not raise the alarm on seeing us climb in and out of the moat. We took the chance and set about building a ladder that would get us into the moat and another ladder that would get us out on the other side. We managed to do this by finding a disused locked-up cellar. Somebody had a saw and we cut off the bottom eighteen inches of the door so that we could crawl in underneath and make our ladders in peace and quiet.'

On the night in question the ladders were dropped out and the escapees descended into the moat with the searchlight full in their faces. They could see the sentry standing in the distance, but he did nothing.

'As we were about to raise the ladder to get over the wire he suddenly shouted at us and started firing shots. Whether they were at us or over our heads I don't know, but we were blown. There was little for it but to hustle down the moat and get under the drawbridge, where we waited quite a long time in the shadow. We were found soon after but thankfully the immediate reaction and panic of the Germans had died down and they didn't shoot. Before long the Kommandant appeared and sent for General Victor Fortune, who was the SBO in the camp. I overheard the Kommandant say to him,

"Well, the first round is to me." The second round was certainly Fortune's, however, because the next day a chap called Peter Douglas managed to get clean away. Rubbish was taken out of the camp in a sort of large wheelbarrow, without a wheel – rather like a stretcher. It was just too small for a man to get into, so surreptitiously they enlarged it slightly. Peter got into it and had rubbish put over him. He got to Sweden eventually.'

Blair's punishment was a term in solitary confinement. Before long, though, the camp was closed, as it was to be used as an ammunition depot for the imminent German attack on Russia. The train journey to their new camp provided the prisoners with another opportunity to try and escape.

'Eight of us were crammed into a small carriage. It was pretty tight and some of us had to sleep in the roof rack. Now the vital thing for escaping is to have willing friends and somebody had managed to smuggle in a saw. We were in an old-fashioned wooden carriage and it wasn't long before we had a hole in the floor. The logic was that some of us might have a chance to escape from it when the train halted at a stop. We had already spent one night in the train and we didn't know where we were going. Our only advantage was that we had picked up a civilian map on the train wall, so we could at least follow our progress. We reckoned that we had at least another night on the go so that would give some of us the opportunity to escape at night. We drew lots and the lot fell upon a pair of Gordon Highlanders. Then the rumour started that we were going to Ulm. I don't know how we got to hear – some German guard may have dropped a hint to somebody. Ulm was bad news because we realized we would probably reach it before nightfall.

'We hurriedly agreed that the two lads should make their break the next time the train halted, which proved to be a stop in the countryside. The chaps got down onto the line and, as we moved off, we all held our breath. The train must have gone a quarter of a mile when suddenly began braking. There was a whole lot of shouting, a little shooting and a chase, which we couldn't see. Eventually the pair got recaptured. Either they had stood up off the line too soon or the German guard who was still hanging onto the handrail saw them at the back of the train. It was a good try anyway.'

Their new camp posed a very different challenge from the one in Poland.

'It was brand new with huts surrounded by a formidable double barbed wire fence and searchlights. At least anybody getting out wasn't going to be faced by six-foot-thick stone walls. Tony Rolt, Bill Chain, Maurice Martin and myself managed to all get put into the same room. We decided that our best chance of escape was to watch the gate. After about three weeks we noticed a working party of British soldiers, because the Germans never used officers to work, being brought into the camp to remove wooden beds out of one of huts. They pushed along a handcart, which could hold about three of these double wooden beds. After loading up in the camp, without a guard, they rumbled it around the gate, picked up a guard and moved off. We didn't know where to at this stage.

'When the working party returned we got hold of the soldiers, put on their gear and took their places in order to find out what the situation was. We soon discovered that, having picked up the guard, they would go round the perimeter and put these beds into a large tank hangar at the back of the camp and outside the searchlights. It was clear that we ought to be able to get somebody into the cartload and wheel him round to the tank garage. Then it was just a question as to whether your hidden man could get out of the cart and into the garage without being seen. Germans loved cigarettes and we thought that if we offered the guard a cigarette and got him out of the wind and round the corner to light it then we'd have a chance.'

The idea was cleared by the Escape Officer in the camp. They would put their plan into action in the early afternoon, as it was estimated that the working party's task would be completed within a couple of hours. It was now a question of determining who the escapee would be.

'We agreed that, if we got one person into the garage successfully, the last thing we should do was to muck it up on the second trip so only one would go. We threw dice to decide who was to go and I threw fourteen with three dice and won handsomely. So we loaded up a palliasse with an assortment of kit, food and things and put the plan into operation. I was lying under the palliasse on top of the beds. It worked without a hitch until somebody, who knew Tony Rolt was an escaper, came round on the exercise ground and jokingly said, "And who have you got in here?" as he lifted up the palliasse. He soon realized that there really was someone in the cart, but fortunately none of the guards saw the incident.

Major Chandos Blair, 1944.

'So off we went round to the garage and, when we got there, the pre-arranged thing about the cigarette was done. Somebody loudly whispered, "Now", and I leapt out and nipped into the garage. We'd seen some big bales of straw there and so I nipped in behind one of these and hid. The palliasse with the gear in it was chucked in beside me, and they went away. Another trip was made and then the garage door was closed. I now had to work out how to get out. Was the place searched with dogs every evening? I just didn't know.'

Once it grew dark Blair began to feel more confident about moving about in the garage. He piled up the straw bales towards a skylight window at the back, some ten to twelve feet high.

'To my delight it opened and I noticed that there was an old traction engine onto which I could lower myself down and avoid possibly spraining my ankle or something if I just jumped. I got out of the window and shut it again in case somebody else wanted to get out the same way on another occasion. The only thing between me and the freedom of the fields outside was a chain link fence about six feet high, which I leapt over with no bother at all. Then I was free, although still slightly apprehensive. The ambient light from the searchlights was present on the field so I crawled for about 150 yards and then got up. For the first half-mile I didn't feel my feet touch the ground.'

He had left the camp with an envisaged route made up on a copy of the map taken from the train. His plan was to follow the railways down to the Schafthausen salient of Switzerland, a distance of about seventy-five miles away as the crow flies. It was the only part of Switzerland not to be bordered by either Lake Constance or by the Rhine. A French prisoner had told him earlier that it was no good even contemplating crossing the latter as an escaper.

'I decided that I would only walk at night, which in the middle of July was a problem as the nights were so short. There was always a terrible temptation to start too soon. A quarter to eleven was about the earliest I could think about setting off, and I had to stop again at about four o'clock.

'Walking down roads was too hazardous, even at night, because somebody could come up behind you without you even hearing. My aim was to follow the railway as much as possible and go cross-country the rest of the time. I had as much food as I could carry – a loaf of bread, two pounds of chocolate, two rounds of dairylea cheese and some other bits and pieces, like raw potatoes which proved impossible to eat. I was wearing a roughly made civilian pair of trousers and a sort of black jacket that I'd got from a French medical orderly. The cap was one that I had made myself out of a blanket. I don't think my home-made compass worked. It was a darning needle and a piece of magnetized card. Thankfully, though, I was blessed with clear nights and the North Star was nearly always visible.

'My worst night was the second night, when I was trying to hit the railway that went west. The track seemed to be heading north and I decided that I must have gone wrong somewhere. I cut south again and reached a very large, swampy wood. It started to rain and, thoroughly demoralized, I just lay on a pile of wood and waited for daylight. An hour's sleep recovered my morale completely and I later found my way to the edge of the wood. On hearing a railway I climbed a tree and saw in the distance a station with its name marked with enormous letters on its roof – Woddsee. I looked for it on my map and realized that in fact I had been on the correct railway the night before.'

Progress was initially terribly slow. After three nights he had only gone some twelve miles from the camp.

'I knew I had to push on faster and the next night I took the risk of

The original map used by Chandos Blair to make his escape from Oflag VB, Biberach, to Thaingen, Switzerland in 1941.

walking straight down the railway line and not bypassing the small town. All went according to plan until I realized that there was a party going on at the station guest-house. Guests began emerging on the platform. I hid behind some sleepers and after a while they duly departed.

'Much of the time was spent hiding up in the woods, as I was on the edge of the Black Forest. It was difficult not to feel almost pleasure being out in the wild. There was a sense of being hunted and I actually began to enjoy trying to outwit the Germans. It was very uncomfortable though. The crops were up and covered in dew. By the time I went to sleep I was soaking wet and would wake up an hour later with my teeth chattering. It was then just a case of waiting until the sun came up when I could take my clothes off and hang them on a bush to dry. The other problem was the mosquitoes and flies which were horrendous. I ended up with a face like a tomato. I couldn't recognize myself in the mirror.'

After seven nights he was aware he was approaching the frontier.

'I passed a place called Singen and knew the border was only about five miles onward. I went to sleep in a patch of bushes quite close to the railway. Suddenly I woke up conscious that somebody was looking at me. And there standing within five yards of me was a small boy with a bag of fircones that he was collecting. He took one look at me and ran off down the path to fetch somebody. There was a very good bushy fir tree nearby and rather than start moving about in the wood I decided I would climb up it. Sure enough, about ten minutes later the boy returned with either an elder brother or his father but they couldn't see me.'

Blair realized the next night would either lead him to success or failure. He was very close. His problem was that the frontier in that area was complicated, with lots of little salients.

'I really didn't know what to expect. There may have been minefields for all I knew. I left the railway and made my way across country. In the distance I could see a moderate-sized town. I needed to find a signpost which could tell me where I was heading, so I made for the road.

'As I reached it, a man suddenly leapt from behind a tree with a pistol. "*Halt*", he shouted in German. I instantly thought "Good God, I've come all this way and I've blown it". I was fluent at French and replied, "I'm sorry but I don't speak any German. Would you please speak in French." To my relief he replied in French with the words, "What are you doing here?" I told him that I was American and that I was staying in Singen. It was such a marvellous night, I said, that I thought I would come for a walk. He asked me for my passport and I told him that I had left it in my hotel room. "In this part of Switzerland anybody I find has got to be taken to the police station," he replied. On saying these words, I fell on his neck and kissed him. I forgot about the pistol! I realized that I must have crossed the frontier without even knowing it. He then carted me off to the police station in very amicable form, where I was then incarcerated for the night.

'My big worry in the cell was whether I would be handed back, as I

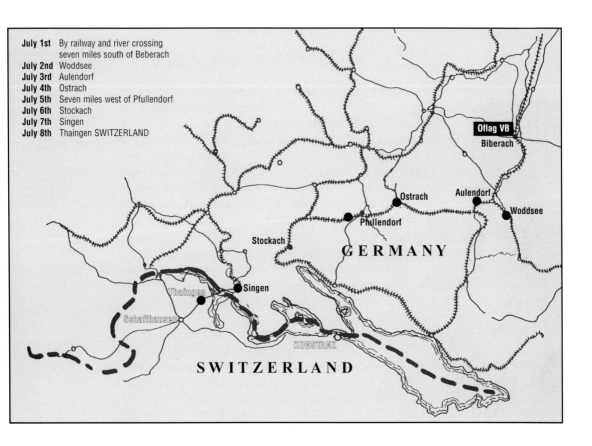

July 1st	By railway and river crossing seven miles south of Beberach
July 2nd	Woddsee
July 3rd	Aulendorf
July 4th	Ostrach
July 5th	Seven miles west of Pfullendorf
July 6th	Stockach
July 7th	Singen
July 8th	Thaingen SWITZERLAND

didn't know how far over the frontier I was nor did I know what the liaison between the Swiss and the Germans was on this subject.'

The next day Blair was taken to a larger police station at Schafthausen, a few miles away. He prevailed upon the police there to allow him to ring the military attaché, Colonel Henry Cartwright, in Berne. They agreed.

'Colonel Cartwright was most assuring and told me that he felt certain he would be able to fetch me. After a number of interviews, I was taken to Berne where I met Cartwright and was placed in British hands.'

Blair spent a month with Colonel Cartwright, but was anxious to return to England, put his uniform back on again and rejoin his regiment. The problem was that Switzerland was surrounded by France, Italy and Germany, all of were hostile. A way had to be devised to get him back home. In the course of investigating possible means of getting out, he discovered that there was a passport control officer called Farrell who lived in Geneva. Colonel Cartwright agreed that he could stay with him. Farrell's first plan was to send Blair off with a number of Swiss Jews who the Germans were allowing to go to Palestine and he began growing a beard for the disguise. The plan never came into fruition.

While he was staying with the Farrells, Wing Commander Peter Gilchrist, a fellow escapee, smuggled himself into Switzerland. He had done thirty-three operational raids so was badly needed in England and there was considerably more money available to use to get him back. Blair teamed up with him and together they discovered that the Bolivian Consul was selling false passports.

May 1942, Chandos Blair, three months after his return to the UK.

'A plot was soon hatched whereby we would have two false passports, which declared us to be Bolivian watchmakers who had been studying our trade in Switzerland and were now returning home. The snag was that neither of us spoke Spanish and neither had dark hair. Despite this, it was decided that the plan should go operational. The War Office approved and the passports costing £400 each were paid for. The Bolivian Consul also agreed he would escort us as far as Barcelona and from there would arrange a guide to take on the rest of their journey to Lisbon. By this stage I'd been in Switzerland for six months.'

Most of the journey could be done by train, but the most tricky part was the beginning in which the men would need to go by taxi into Vichy France. After numerous nerve-racking moments at various frontier posts along the way, the two successfully got to Barcelona. Here they were met by the Bolivian Chargé Affaires, who agreed to escort them to Madrid, despite losing his nerve on the train and refusing to speak up for the two men when detectives and ticket collectors came round. But Blair and Gilchrist bluffed their way through and successfully reached Madrid, where they made for the British passport control office.

'We rang the bell and were let in by a doorman. The first thing we saw lying in the hall were copies of *The Field*, *Country Life* and *Tatler*. I just thought – My God, we've made it.'

They, and a further twenty other escapees, mostly airmen, who were hiding there, were taken to Gibraltar and then back to England.

'I was terribly lucky and my escape was in large part thanks to marvellous friends. There were many others who made much more daring attempts, suffered much worse hardships and were just less fortunate. I was the lucky number.'

CHAPTER FOUR

The Great Escape

In April 1942 the Luftwaffe's most famous camp, Stalag Luft III, was opened up at Sagan in Lower Silesia, about 100 miles south-east of Berlin. It was set in the northern edge of a dense forest, which runs unbroken for some twenty to thirty miles towards the Czechoslovakian border. Originally built with just two compounds, it was intended to be the chief camp for British and American air force officers. When the numbers of air force men shot down exceeded German expectations, Stalag Luft III was expanded and by the end of the war over 10,000 officers were housed in six compounds in the camp. The prisoners were accommodated in single-storey wooden barrack huts raised on piles above the ground, measuring about 160 feet by 40 feet, which were divided into rooms. Each hut contained a small kitchen where prisoners could heat food and boil water, as well as a primitive urinal. Drainage and running water did not exist.

Escaping over ground was virtually impossible. The camp was surrounded by strong and heavily interlaced wire, a twelve-foot double fence of bristling spikes. Arc lamps hung above the wire and at intervals along the fence stood the goon boxes – small sentry tower boxes on stilts above the wire, each of which

One of the watch towers at Stalag Luft III, Sagan in eastern Germany.   IWM HU21018

was manned by two guards armed with machine guns and connected by telephone to the main guardroom at the prison gates. Each goon box had a searchlight that continually swept the camp at night. Meanwhile, on the ground, well-armed guards patrolled the wire between these sentry boxes.

Tunnelling provided the main hope for escape and in the summer of 1942 alone some thirty to forty attempts were made. All but one were unsuccessful. There were a number of reasons for this. Firstly, the sandy soil made digging difficult and it was necessary to shore up the tunnels with wood in order to prevent falls. Secondly, the distance from the barracks, which were the most feasible places to start a tunnel, to the wire was never less than sixty yards. Thirdly, by 1942 German anti-escape measures included the use of buried microphones which could detect digging noises to a depth of approximately twelve to fifteen feet.

The failure of tunnel after tunnel forced the escape experts to try and form a better-planned system. It was imperative that no tunnel encroached on another and escape committees were set up in the different compounds to approve, oversee and advise on all attempts. In the North Compound the committee code-named 'X' was led by South African-born Squadron Leader Roger Bushell, who had been shot down over the beaches of Dunkirk. Tony Bethell remembers:

'Roger, known as 'Big X', was the senior officer of the escape committee. He had already made one or two brilliant escapes but had been caught after several months in Czechoslovakia. They brought him back to camp and had told him he would probably be shot if he escaped again. He was a London barrister, a French and German speaker, and a brilliant brain.'

Under Bushell it was decided that all efforts should be put into three elaborate, substantial and properly planned tunnels, which would be built at the same time. The logic of building three was that there was a greater chance that the Germans would not discover all of them. If at any time the Germans showed signs of suspicion then the digging would be suspended for an indefinite period. The three tunnels were called *Tom, Dick* and *Harry.* Ken Rees recalls that, 'As a security measure, we were not allowed to use the word tunnel at all and it was made clear that no one was to

Antagonists in the ongoing battle of wits between prisoners and guards: Roger Bushell (Big X), Leutnant Eberhardt (German Security), Paddy Byrne (who later successfully feigned insanity and was repatriated).

136

show any interest in the huts where the tunnels were to start from.' After careful planning the location of the tunnels was decided on. *Tom* would run some 280 feet west from Hut 123 towards the forest. *Dick* ran in the same direction but from Hut 122, while *Harry* started in Hut 104, ran in a northerly direction and went the furthest distance.

On 11 April 1943 work began. The first phase of tunnelling was critical as trap doors had to be constructed. This was an extremely delicate and dangerous phase in the operation, as Rees explains:

'The problem was that the huts were raised some two feet off the ground. Only the concrete from the stoves and the washroom touched the earth. So one had to go through the concrete, otherwise the tunnels would have been found. The Poles were brilliant at making traps, by going through this concrete. The trap for *Tom* was in the concrete just outside the cookhouse. Some fifty yards further into the camp was the hut for *Dick*, where a trap was made in the centre of the washroom. The trap for *Harry* started from a stove. The stove stood on a tiled concrete base. They loosened all the tiles, reset them on a wooden tray and put it back into place. So all that was needed when we needed to put the trap back on was to put the tray on the area and put the stove above it. *Harry* was the furthest from the wire – some 300 yards and I don't think the Germans would have even considered the possibility of building a tunnel from there.'

The second phase involved the construction of vertical shafts, which needed to be dropped down about thirty feet and then shored up with wood from bedboards and floorboards. The latter was possible because the

This stove, in Hut 104, hides the entrance to the tunnel code-named **Harry**.   IWM HU2122

prisoners just removed the lower half of the double-skinned floors in the barracks. Three chambers were built at the bottom of these shafts so that there was a room for an air pump, a room for storing sand and another which was used as a workshop. Digging then began in earnest. Ken Rees was one of the

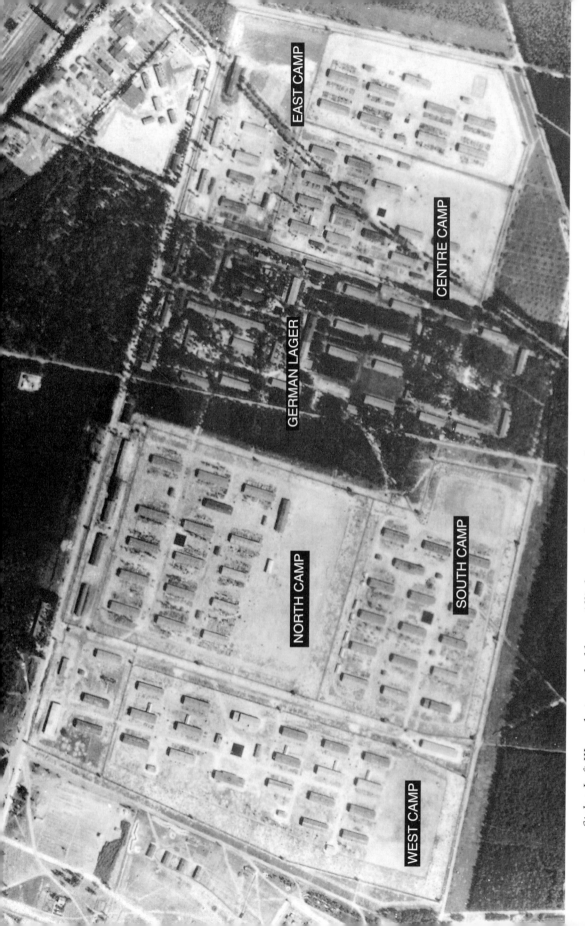

EAST CAMP

CENTRE CAMP

GERMAN LAGER

NORTH CAMP

SOUTH CAMP

WEST CAMP

Stalug Luft III as photographed by an Allied reconnaissance aircraft.

The stove is lifted out of the way and the tiled trapdoor removed to reveal the entrance to **Harry.**

IWM HU21246

team of tunnellers who worked down *Harry.* He describes the working in the tunnels:

'There weren't many of us diggers. Each tunnel had a couple of teams of about half a dozen people. I worked on *Harry* mostly. When I first went down *Harry* the trap had obviously just been built by the Poles and only two of the chambers at the bottom had been completed – one was for the air pump and the other was a bit of a workshop. That was all. So, although I worried about whether I was going to get claustrophobic, I never actually did because you just grew up with it. We used to strip off and then descend into the tunnel. Most of us preferred to dig in the nude, which meant that when you came out again all you had to do was get some cold water thrown over you and then get dressed.

'The way we did it was that the front digger went forward and his number two went backwards. This was a bit of a nuisance to start with and it wasn't long before they decided that we must have a

Entrance to escape tunnel **Harry.**

IWM HU21235

At the bottom of the shaft and looking along the tunnel; a wooden trolley on wooden rails built by the prisoners for removing spoil from the tunnel head. IWM HU21243

little railway to transport the sand. So the engineers and carpenters set to work and made rails from beading and battens off the walls in our rooms, wheels with hard wood, axles from the stove in the kitchens, and so on. They developed a perfectly good railway and trolley. The trolley had two boxes on it. One would dig using a small shovel and push the sand behind you. Then your number two would scoop up the sand and put it on the trolley. We would work feet to feet. When the boxes were full, the number two would pull the cord and the trolley was pulled back. It worked very successfully. The danger was that if you dug more than six inches forward before shoring you could get a fall. As you were right forward, the chances were that it would come down on you. If this happened, the number two would have to quickly heave at your feet and pull you out of it. The scary thing was that a fall would generally put the oil lamp out and so you would be surrounded by darkness. We shored the tunnel with bedboards. By the time the tunnel was complete, people were almost falling through their beds, In fact quite a few people decided to make string beds.

'Once we had dug about a hundred yard it was getting more and more difficult to pull the trolleys, so it was decided to build a halfway house, which we called *Piccadilly* for security reasons. This was the widest section of the tunnel and could take two people. You could almost sit with your head up. Two people generally manned it. The forward person would lift the box off and pass it back to the other one who would put it onto another trolley. This was very successful and after a further hundred feet we built

Dried milk tins soldered together privided ducting for air circulation within the tunnel.

Drawing of the ingenious, hand-operated, bellows contraption used for pumping fresh air through the workings.

another halfway house which we called *Leicester Square*.

'As the tunnel got bigger, we needed more and more air moving up it so an air pipe made of *klim* tins was laid along it. This was connected to a pump, which was comprised of two kit bags with wire inside. When you pulled one way, you deflated one bag and sent air up the tunnel while filling the other with air. It was a kind of rowing movement. You deflated one, inflated the other and air shot down the tunnel. This was necessary because if air didn't get through our lamps would go out. It was hard work doing the pumping and generally three people took it in turns.

'On one shift alone, by the time the tunnel was nearing completion, there would be three chaps on the pump, two in *Piccadilly*, two in *Leicester Square* and two doing the digging. I preferred digging to any of the other jobs. This was because if you were in the halfway houses you tended to have much more time to think about where you were. It was hard not to think that if this caves in it could be nasty. When you were going up the tunnel one

141

noticed some of the boards did have a slight bow in them which was a little worrying, but they seemed static and didn't appear to alter. You just hoped these bedboards would take the weight. The depth of the tunnel was about thirty feet. This was partly due to the soil type but also because the Germans had sound detectors under the wire. I remember sitting in *Leicester Square* with Joe Noble when suddenly there was a rumble and we thought Christ the whole thing's coming down. For a few moments it was a nasty shock, but it turned out to be a horse and cart. On the whole, though, we were reasonably confident.

'Each job had its problems. The main drawback to front digging was that it was awkward and you got stiff as you couldn't change your position much. Pump duty was the most tiring. One would row for about fifty minutes and then somebody else would take over.'

When Tony Bethell was taken down *Dick* he was astounded at the sight:

'It was an extraordinary thing and incredibly designed. I was just amazed at the ingenuity of so many of my fellow prisoners. Inevitably, the first time I crawled along the tunnel I had a slight sense of claustrophobia, but I was in the company of others and I actually for the most part enjoyed the experience. This was partly because I was amongst people who had been working down it for a long time and knew what they were doing. It felt wonderful to be part of the team involved in such an impressive construction achievement.'

There were falls nearly every day but amazingly no one was killed. As the summer months passed by all three tunnels were making good progress. The most time-consuming part of the digging was the dispersal of the earth. The bright whitish-yellow sand brought up from the tunnel starkly contrasted with the darker top soil and could provide the Germans with a giveaway sign that tunnelling was in progress. Carrying the soil away from the hut and finding places to conceal it proved an extremely tricky operation. Jimmy James:

'Dispersal was run by Lieutenant Commander Fanshaw, who had the brilliant idea of hanging a trouser bag, about two foot long, inside each trouser leg. The two bags had a brace suspended round your neck and were operated by a string from your pocket, which would let the sand out. In this way people walked around the compound sprinkling this sand. This then needed to be concealed by somebody shuffling along behind them. Sometimes one would go up to people sitting gardening or just idly lounging around, and these people would have a hole ready, so all the person would do was just pull the cord and the sand would go in. They would then casually sweep the dark earth over it. In all, there were around two hundred penguins, as we called them, tramping around the compound that summer and they managed to disperse about one hundred and thirty tons.'

A German guard demonstrates the mean used to distribute tunn soil around the camp compound.

Incredibly, there were few signs that the German guards were suspicious of any tunnelling activity. To a large extent this was due to the tight

142

German guards talking to Allied officers at Stalag Luft III caught on camera by 'goon-watchers'.

security established by the Escape Committee. James was part of a large team that watched the German guards night and day.

'I was in the security organization, which was run by a Canadian Air Force chap called George Marsh who was a great organizer. Our purpose was to know exactly where all the German guards were in the camp. This would enable the tunnellers, and also the various back-up departments within the Escape Organization, like the forgery department, the mapping department, the compass department, the clothing department and so on, to work in safety. I was one of these watchers and was also sometimes the duty pilot at the gate, which involved keeping a record of when the Germans walked in and out of the camp.

'I remember one amusing story of how Glimnetz, the German officer in charge of the compound, went up to the duty pilot and said, "Mark me out will you". Not surprisingly our man was rather surprised and reported this to the Committee. However, it was decided that we should keep a person in the same place as we had to have a person near the gate and Glimnetz would probably find where the new position was if we moved him. About three weeks later Glimnetz went up to the duty pilot again and said, "Has Heinz been in today?" The chap looked at his list and told him he hadn't. "Oh well, Heinz is for the cooler." Heinz was one of the ferrets and, as a result of our records, got seven days in solitary confinement.'

Tony Bethell was also a member of the security organization:

'When I arrived in the north camp there were a lot of people who were involved in the project. I indicated that I wished to be part of it. I soon became a "stooge" and found myself standing on the corners of buildings keeping my eye out for "ferrets" and other Germans. As soon as you saw a German you reported it with a sign. It was a very, very efficiently run system. For the first time since I had become a prisoner I felt happy that I was putting a lot of energy into a good end. Security was vital because the success of being able to dig tunnels was dependent on one's ability to open and close them very quickly.'

Despite these precautions the first crisis came in June 1943. The Germans began building a new West Compound to house American prisoners in the area *Dick* and *Tom* had aimed to break from. It was clear that digging two tunnels in that direction was futile. Time was not on the Escape Committee's side and they decided to abandon *Dick* which was only eighty feet long at that stage and concentrate on *Tom* in an effort to finish one of the tunnels before the West Compound was completed. *Harry* was temporarily shut down as all efforts were put into *Tom*.

All was going according to plan and the tunnel shot forward. By September it was some 280 feet long and well outside the wire. Then disaster struck. Ken Rees takes up the story:

'After Big X had made the decision to blitz *Tom*, we began to take more chances. Good progress was made and the tunnel soon reached the wire. Before long, we were just about in a position to start on the exit when the ferrets had another search of the block. They noticed a bit of sand there and I think they had an idea that a tunnel was going on but they just didn't know where. They began scouring all around the camp and in the block, in particular, but found no evidence of anything. At the end of this search, they were just standing around the hut idly waiting to be moved off when one of them began prodding the concrete with a kind of metal spear – a thing he pushed into the sand to see if there were tunnels. Suddenly this spear went through the edge of the tunnel. The German immediately realized it was the trap and that was the end of *Tom*. Everyone was thrown out of the hut and during the next few days they flooded it and also put some dynamite down the shaft.'

Jimmy James recalls the feelings in the camp:

'The Germans were absolutely delighted at finding it, not least because it was within a week of completion. For everyone connected with the tunnel, though, the discovery was a huge disappointment. The only light moment was when the Germans overdid it with the dynamite and very nearly blew up the nearby guard tower. It sank down into the hole made by the blast at a crazy angle. So *Tom* had done his bit for the war effort.'

A grin of success from a German ferret, nicknamed 'Rubberneck', after Tom *had been discovered.*

144

Tunnelling resumed two days after the discovery of *Tom,* but the Germans remained suspicious. The camp swarmed with 'ferrets' and, after more thorough searches, Big X decided it was necessary to lie low for a while. All tunnelling operations were ceased for an indefinite period. This would give the Germans a false sense of security. All hopes now rested on *Harry.*

The tunnel reopened on 10 January 1944. The advantage of working during the winter was that the Germans didn't expect tunnelling to take place. There was a disadvantage, however. The snow on the ground meant that dispersing sand became almost impossible. It was firstly decided to refill *Dick,* the tunnel they had been forced to abandon a few months before. No sooner had this begun to get full when the Escape Committee came up with another brilliant idea for disposal. Jimmy James was in the room:

> 'We had to find a different means of disposal. One day one of the Escape Committee said, "What about the theatre?" Roger Bushell thought about it for a second and then replied, "That's a damn good idea, James. Go and have a look at it". So I went along with Peter Fanshaw and "Scharnhorst" Cross (so named because he had been awarded the DFC for bombing the battlecruiser *Scharnhorst*). A trap was made underneath one of the seats and we realized that it was a perfect place for disposal – absolutely first class. There was a sloping auditorium so you could almost stand inside it. I was put in charge of a disposal team and we managed to get rid of the soil that way.
>
> 'The tunnelling was done in the daytime between morning *appel* and evening *appel*. All the earth would be stored in the dispersal chamber. Then in the evening it was taken by penguins via a secure route after dark to the theatre, where it was poured down the trap. This was possible because the doors to the huts were open until ten o'clock. About ninety tons was dispersed this way.'

While the digging of *Harry* progressed, preparations were made for the intended mass breakout. Over 600 prisoners were members of the escape organization and nearly all had a part to play. The vast majority were involved as members of the dispersal and security teams. Some, however, had particular skills and worked in the more specialist departments set up by Bushell. A tailoring department, for example, made civilian suits from blankets and dyed and altered uniforms and clothes of all sorts. It even managed to make two German uniforms. There was also a food factory, where dietary experts produced compact and nutritious rations for each escapee – a concentrated fudge made up of raisins, condensed milk, oats and chocolate, which was intended to last ten days. Individuals were also given the task, by hook or by crook, of accumulating enough German money to make it possible for the escapers to buy train tickets and so on. One Lithuanian pilot was an expert on transport in Germany and, using German newspapers, compiled a travel guide which included railway timings. People were also busy making travel maps, while the forgery department, known as 'Dean and Dawson', after the pre-war travel firm, made fake documents.

Alex Cassie

'I sometimes dreamed of escaping but, at the same time, I realized that these dreams would never be put into operation because I didn't have enough confidence in myself to battle with the difficulties of being in a foreign country without adequate knowledge of the language. However, one had to do something and the obvious thing for me to do, once I'd found my feet, was to work in a forging capacity. I'd always liked maps and so I joined up with Desmond Plunkett who was in charge of making maps. Soon after, I discovered there was also a section making and forging passes and documents, which was run by Tim Whelan. That appealed to me rather more, particularly because I'd always been rather fond of lettering. Whelan's department was called "Dean and Dawson" and specialized in passports, German Guard passes and escape and travel documents of all kinds.

'Many of the papers were typewritten temporary documents, Urlaubscheins. These were intended to give some semblance of security to a person who had no other qualifications for travelling in a foreign country in strange clothes. They would explain the absence of an official document; eg a chap purporting to be a Polish worker in Germany might have a document saying that he was being allowed some leave and that his normal official pass was in for renewal or re-stamping and so on. We did these laboriously by drawing them out at near-life size in pencil to imitate ordinary typescript from a commercial typewriter. It would then be given to a sympathetic German guard. I know of one case where he would take it to his wife in the Ruhr Valley when on leave, who would then type it out on a wax flimsy. The German would return, rolling it up in his jackboot and then pass it to our organization, 'Dean and Dawson', where we had a home-made printing press. We could then roll off a number of copies. I never knew who the German guard, or guards, were who did this but they were obviously taking a tremendous risk and the reward was pretty poor – a packet or two of English cigarettes, which were deemed a great luxury, or a cake of soap, or coffee or tea. But that was all.

'The most difficult but satisfying forgery jobs were the ones in which you made an actual document like a German guard's pass or the standard pass that the border guards had. The first thing we required was a copy of a pass. Well, among this pile of RAF officers you're bound to find a few pickpockets and they were used to good effect. The Germans had a habit of shoving their passes in the great big cuffs they had on their heavy coats. It was quite possible for someone to chat with a guard after appel while somebody else would go up on the other side and carefully take the pass out of his pocket. Another way was to lure a German into a room to have a cup of tea and a cigarette. That was a great treat for them. In the meantime the pass has been taken to Tim Whelan at 'Dean and Dawson', who'd taken a strip off, made a quick tracing of the size, the lettering and so on, and then handed it back. Very often it was back in the German cuff without the guard ever knowing it had gone.

'Most of the forging took place in the afternoon during what we called the "ferret-free period". Of course, many of these documents required photographs and there was a little branch in X Organization that provided these. I don't know how but I presume they had an illicit camera of some kind. Really one only concerned oneself with the area you worked in. The fewer people who knew the details, the greater the security. One of the most difficult jobs was forging a stamp with a relief on it. We were never very good at that and were always conscious that it didn't look very good. Anyway, you were at least always guaranteed a pretty stamp and there was an Australian wing commander who was very good at carving out things from rubber boot heels. Another member of 'Dean and Dawson' was Gordon Bretell who was an absolute genius at doing the Gill Sans type lettering, which I believe Hitler had wanted as he felt the old German script lettering was too old, fashioned. It was a very crisp clean lettering and was particularly difficult to do. Gordon managed it by filing down the pen nib until it was very sharp. My speciality was lettering, especially gothic script ones. It's very easy to do because there are so many wiggles on it that you don't have to be so precisely accurate as you had to be with the Gill Sans type lettering. Most of our work was just done laboriously by hand and was so trying on the eyes that some had to give it up.'

Samples of the art of the forger: passes, permits and identity cards; necessary documents for the escapee in Nazi-occupied Europe.   IWM HU21214

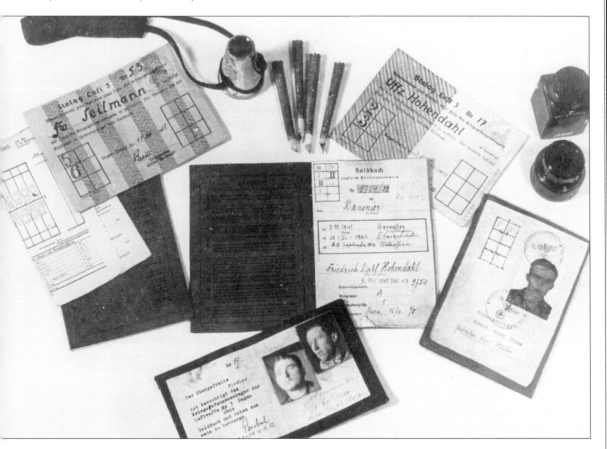

Harry was completed on 14 March 1944. The tunnellers believed they had at least reached the wood and an exit shaft was built and shored up to two feet of the surface. They had then put boards on it to ensure it was secure if anyone walked over it. Now it was up to Roger Bushell to make the critical decision as to when the breakout should happen. The Committee received advice about what would be the best night to break out. Moonless nights, for example, were essential, but they also had to bear in mind train times and so on, which might be affected on certain days like Sundays. Ideally there would be some wind to cover up the noise and it was also hoped that there would not be too much snow on the ground, but neither could be planned. The date was set for 24 March and was final. It was not subject to change as the forgery department had to date the 400 forged documents they had made and a delay would effectively destroy their whole painstaking production.

Clothes now needed to be decided on, equipment collected and escape routes planned and finalized. Meanwhile Bushell had to work out the quickest means of getting the most possible inmates down and through the tunnel, as well as to work out the best means of regulating the arrival of the escapees into Hut 104. It would get dark by about nine o'clock and begin to get light again at around five thirty. This gave him eight and a half hours to work with. Then, of course, there was the issue of who of the six hundred members of the escape organization should actually go. Jimmy James recalls the process:

'The task of choosing the people to escape was a rather delicate one, because everybody wanted a crack at going out. Roger Bushell decided that the first thirty would be chosen according to the likelihood of getting out – either on the basis of language, nationality and so on. A lot of them had been out before and had also done an enormous amount of work on the tunnel. This first group of thirty were chosen and all had suits, papers and money, so that they would be fully equipped to travel hundreds of miles across Germany into neutral territory.

'The next seventy were also chosen on their chances of getting home and on how much work they had done for the escape organization. The last five hundred were chosen out of a hat. I had learnt German on the camp and was chosen as Number 39 with papers claiming that I worked on the local wood-mill and stating that we were on leave. I was, according to the papers, a Yugoslav and was fitted out with a pair of middle-eastern trousers, which I dirtied to make them look like workman's clothes. I also put some civilian buttons on my tunic. My partner was a Greek fighter pilot. I had been asked if I would like to go with him and I thought it might be a good idea because we could go down to the Danube, into Greece and then he'd help get us over to Turkey which was neutral.'

Ken Rees found to his disappointment that his name had not been drawn out of the hat.

'Neither Joe nor I were on it and we thought that was the end of it all. But then Johnny Ball told us not to worry as we had been picked as despatchers. "We need experienced tunnellers down there," he said. Most

1943 Stalag Luft III, North Camp, Ken Rees (second from left) and his navigator Gwyn Martin (on his left), with fellow POWs.

of the escapers had never been in the tunnel, so it was bound to be quite daunting for them. I was to go down Number 50 and, after helping some people through, would come out at about seventy-five.

'Joe and myself were escaping together. We altered our uniforms and changed their colour slightly by taking some black binding off some books and boiling them. This didn't work very well, and we finished up looking like tramps. At least it didn't resemble anything like a military uniform by the time we had finished. Other people had suits – the so-called expert escapers who could speak the language and had a good chance of escape. These people were treated a little better. We were just normal escapees, known in the camp as "hard-arses" – people who were going out as foreign workers and whose plan was just to get to one of the borders. We had settled for a walk through Czechoslovakia and Yugoslavia as Norwegian workers – a bit silly on reflection as we were heading the opposite way to home. We made some fudge under the direction of a nutrition expert and before long we were ready to go. I was full of enthusiasm and I really thought we could make it.'

Not everyone in the escape organization seized the chance to break out. Alex Cassie was one of the men who decided against escaping, despite all his work in the forgery department:

'I was put somewhere in the first fifty to escape, but I decided to turn down my chance to go for two reasons. Firstly, I had already gone down the shaft of *Harry* and I was really thoroughly thankful to come up at the

Prisoners wore widely differing forms of clothing, some items of which would be utilized to represent civilian garb. Alex Cassie (seated) second from right.

end of it. I knew there was goodness knows how many yards to go before you got to the mouth of the tunnel and so my decision was partially guided by the fact that I really didn't enjoy the sensation. I also knew that they were going out in the very cold winter weather. I just didn't feel like submitting myself to those rigours. I knew it could be a case of sleeping rough and that weather just didn't appeal to me. These may have been my rationalizations for just being frightened. But, whatever it was, that's what I told myself were the reasons for not going in the tunnel.'

Jimmy James remembers the atmosphere in the camp as the hour for the breakout approached:

'There was tremendous excitement in the air. You could feel it. Before I left my hut the cook in the room gave us a particularly good feed. I was the only one going from my room and happened to have stored 4,000 cigarettes. I told my companions that they were welcome to them, but one of them rather rudely replied, "You keep them. You'll need them when you come out of the cooler." No words could, however, dampen my excitement. So off I went, with my pack and rations, and routed by secure means to Hut 104.'

Emotions ran high as the 200 men chosen to break out began to assemble in Hut 104. Alex Cassie:

'The night of the escape was probably the most unique and memorable night I can ever remember. The whole atmosphere in the camp was quite electric and there was a tremendous amount of activity going on. Two hundred people had to be got into Block 104 after dark with their travel equipment and so on. It was chaos with the people leaving making arrangements and leaving messages with mates such as, "If I don't come back, will you get in touch with my family?" and so on. I found it pretty stressful. I had lived in close contact with my room mates and all five were now leaving. We had got on very well together and had all devoted ourselves to doing our bit for the tunnel, so it was a difficult parting. One thing was certain – whatever happened, it was going to be a complete change of life for me. I tried not to resent the arrival of five new people who came in to take their places that night, but it was of course tricky. Furthermore, I knew I couldn't discuss the thing with them. They were complete strangers to me.'

As zero hour approached, Block 104 began to fill up with escapees in their breakout disguises. Ken Rees was amazed at the scene that greeted him as he arrived in the hut.

'Block 104 had been emptied of all occupants that night, who were then spread out in different parts of the camp and 200 of us escapees then assembled in the block after dark. It was an incredible sight. There were people walking around looking like city gents. I had a brief moment of panic, though, when I saw two German soldiers in among the crowd until I recognized one of them as a fellow prisoner. They looked absolutely marvellous, with belts made of paper and painted, and guns that were simply carved wood.'

Things from that point on, however, went far from smoothly, as Jimmy James remembers:

Prisoners in their home-made civilian clothing and briefcases as they were dressed when they left Stalag Luft III via **Harry.** Museum of Martyrology For Allied POWs, Zagan, Poland

Routes taken by the three tunnels,
Tom, Dick *and* Harry.
In the event only Harry *was used.*

'Our first difficulty was that the trap-door had iced up. The two chaps who were expected to get through it at around 8 or 9 o'clock took an hour and a half to prise it open. The next problem was that on getting the exit trap opened, they discovered the tunnel was some twenty-five feet short of the wood. This was serious because the exit hole was within view of the wire when the searchlights were on and there was a guard patrolling this area. Roger Bushell immediately ordered that a man should go and hide behind what we called a ferret fence, which was in fact a bush at the edge of the wood that the ferrets used to hide behind to watch us. The man was sent out with a rope, part of which was left hanging down from the top of the exit hole. The system was simple. One tug meant that it was okay to leave the exit hole, two tugs indicated danger. Once this had been established, it was left to the person exiting the tunnel to take over at the ferret fence.'

There was no question of turning back. The unforeseen trouble with the exit hole and the conference on how best to work out an effective and safe method of getting from the tunnel to the wood had, however, taken up valuable time. Use of the rope was a remedy, but it meant the breakout would take considerably longer than envisaged. Tension in the hut was electric as men waited in turn to make their way down the shaft. Eventually it got to Jimmy James' turn:

'I presented myself to the trap controller at the top. His job was to see you didn't carry too much luggage or weren't too bulky. He passed me and so I went ahead heartened, and climbed down the thirty-foot shaft. It was like going down a ship's hold. At the bottom there was a chap working the air pump. I lay flat on the trolley, yanked the rope, thus signifying I was ready to be taken down the tunnel and off I went, pulled by a chap at the first halfway house, *Piccadilly*. There I changed trolleys and got pulled to *Leicester Square*, where I got on another trolley and was pulled the last hundred feet up to the exit by the haulers at the end of the tunnel. On reaching the exit hole, I stood up and saw the stars above me. It was a very euphoric moment. I didn't think about what might happen, the fact was that I had got out of the camp. I was free at last. I thought of the old RAF motto "through difficulty to the stars". I climbed to the top and received the signal from the man behind the ferret fence. With that, I crawled out onto the snow and joined my group.'

Soon after James had reached the wood there were further problems in the tunnel which once again lost the escapees valuable time. Ken Rees:

'Somebody went down the tunnel with far too much stuff. I think he was trying to take a suitcase or something. The result was that he knocked one of the shorings and there was a fall. Two diggers had to go down, clear and then re-shore it. This caused another hold up. Then the RAF decided to raid Berlin. All the lights in the camp went out and so too did the lights in the tunnel. Joe Noble had stolen some wire and bulbs had been put throughout the whole length of the tunnel. Now, as a result of the raid, we were plunged into darkness with people who hadn't been in the tunnel before. Oil lamps had to be passed down but once again this slowed the process up.'

Tony Bethell was in the tunnel when the fall took place. His job was to haul twenty people through *Leicester Square*, the second of the halfway houses, before he himself would make his way toward the exit hole as number sixty-five. At the time he had no idea why no one was coming through.

'Twelve came through without any problems at all. It was all smooth going. You lay on your front and just pulled people up on a trolley. He then crawled round you, got onto another trolley and went up to the other end to the exit shaft being pulled by whoever was up there. Your only form of communication was the rope that pulled the trolley and you knew when to start heaving because there was a tug on the rope. It must have taken about half an hour to get twelve people through and then suddenly there was no tugging. It dawned on one that nothing was happening. I shouted but then two thoughts occurred. One was that noise does not travel very far in a constricted area and two that if I shouted I might bring the tunnel down. So I thought I'd better shut up and hope that something happened. It was hard not think that I was some thirty feet below ground and in what you

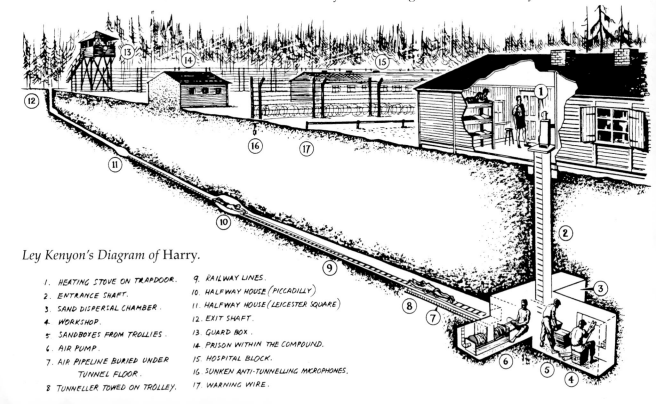

Ley Kenyon's Diagram of Harry.

1. HEATING STOVE ON TRAPDOOR.
2. ENTRANCE SHAFT.
3. SAND DISPERSAL CHAMBER.
4. WORKSHOP.
5. SANDBOXES FROM TROLLIES.
6. AIR PUMP.
7. AIR PIPELINE BURIED UNDER TUNNEL FLOOR.
8. TUNNELLER TOWED ON TROLLEY.
9. RAILWAY LINES.
10. HALFWAY HOUSE (PICCADILLY).
11. HALFWAY HOUSE (LEICESTER SQUARE).
12. EXIT SHAFT.
13. GUARD BOX.
14. PRISON WITHIN THE COMPOUND.
15. HOSPITAL BLOCK.
16. SUNKEN ANTI-TUNNELLING MICROPHONES.
17. WARNING WIRE.

Ladder up the shaft of **Harry.** IWM HU 21245

Ley Kenyon's sketch showing the rope-signalling system used on the night of 24th March 1944.

might call a rather large coffin. The more I thought about this the more frightened I got. I think for probably the only time in my life I sweated with a cold sweat of sheer fright. I don't know how long this period of inactivity in the tunnel took, but it seemed to go on for ever. Then at last a tug came on the rope and the panic subsided. Life was still going on in the tunnel. Eventually the twentieth man came through and it was my turn to make my way down the final part of the run. The reason for the delay was that there had been a fall in the tunnel.'

Bethell successfully made his way along the tunnel and out into the wood. A few others followed him but it was nearly becoming light and, at around 4 o'clock, the decision was made to close the tunnel down, even though nowhere near the planned two hundred escapees had got out. Number 87 on the list would be the last man. Ken Rees was at the bottom of the shaft when he was given the news:

'Two people were sent down to pass the word to myself, Clyde Saxobe and Joe that we were to press on to the tunnel exit. We were to be the last to get out. I started to make my way down and had reached *Leicester Square* when suddenly a shot ran out from the exit end. "Oh God, it's been found," I thought. I hurriedly began pushing my way back to *Piccadilly*. A few moments later Joe came screaming past me. Then Clyde Saxobe came clambering past me. Saxobe was six foot four and not used to the tunnel, and once he had passed me he began holding me back. He was going down the run in small kangaroo leaps and I seriously thought he was going to pull the whole thing down at any moment. All went well though, and, as I made my way along, I kicked out the lights. My main aim was to get round the slight bend in the tunnel as I was afraid they were going to shoot up the tunnel and make an extra hole where I didn't want one. Nothing of that sort happened and we got back to the block and shut the tunnel down.

'All mayhem was going on in the hut. People were burning their forged documents, maps and money, but no one could get out of the hut, although I believe one or two people did leap out of the window and rush back to their own rooms. Most of us, however, were left in the room with burning paper all around us. Everyone was eating as much of our escape rations as we could, as we knew it would all get confiscated. It wasn't long before the first of the German ferrets and a dog handler came in. He was grabbing stuff but was having trouble controlling his dog as we were all feeding it food, which it was loving.

'After about half an hour things got really bad. The Commandant came in fuming, along with all the other officers and ferrets all armed with rifles and machine-guns. We were marched outside the hut. One of the guards who I had a few differences with during my time on camp saw Joe and myself and ordered us to strip. By this stage we were feeling very despondent. We had missed our chance to escape and we started slowly taking our clothes off. The guard got annoyed and stepped forward and started pulling my coat off me. This annoyed me and I pushed him away.

He raised his revolver and it looked as if he was going to bring it down on me when the Commandant stepped out of the hut and called something to him. Anyway he lowered his gun and I quickly took the rest of my clothes off down to my long johns and vest. Joe did the same and we were then marched off in a rather undignified way, with a Tommy gun in out backs, for fourteen days in the cooler.'

It transpires that, as Number 87 was making his way down the shaft, a German sentry had been walking along the perimeter disconcertingly close to the wood. He was still a good distance away, but the man holding the rope behind the ferret fence could see that if he continued along on the same line there was a serious danger that he would walk right on top of the exit hole. Meanwhile the escapee, Number 80 on the list, lay motionless in the snow beside the tunnel mouth as he waited for the all clear signal. The sentry got closer and closer. To the rope controller's horror he stepped about a foot away from the hole and was even nearer to the man on the ground. At that point the sentry spotted a slushy track leading from the exit hole to the woods, and then spotted a prisoner some thirty yards away. As he raised his rifle to shoot, the man behind the ferret fence decided the game was up and waved his hand with the shout, "Don't shoot". The German not surprisingly panicked at the sight of yet another prisoner on the loose and shot. He missed and regained enough nerve not to fire again. Instead he blew his whistle. *Harry* had been discovered.

If the discovery of the tunnel had come too early for Ken Rees, it had come too late for the Commandant of Stalag Luft III, Oberst Lindeiner-Wildau. Alex Cassie witnessed the scene.

'Daylight came and the Commandant was absolutely speechless with rage. Everything had gone wrong for him. He was a real gentleman and some of us actually felt very sorry for him. It was awful to land this thing on his shoulders.'

A few days later, he and some of his officers were relieved and put under immediate arrest. He suffered a heart attack while under arrest but was later tried by courts martial and sentenced to a year's imprisonment. While his appeal was being heard, he had a nervous breakdown. His other officers were also imprisoned, but their terms were shortened by the end of the war.

While there was pandemonium in the camp Tony Bethell was attempting to make good his escape. He recalls his time on the run from the moment he made his way out of the exit shaft:

'As one climbed up the ladder one could see the sky and feel the temperature. I waited for the nine other people in the group, then took them round past a station at the north end of the woods, steering clear of a transformer box which was said to have police dogs in it. Once past it, our aim was to head west to get into open country and from here the ten of us dispersed. We were only a hundred yards from this place when the first shot was fired and the tunnel was discovered. So we all ran like scalded cats and found ourselves kicking tins in front of another camp. What had happened was that I had gone completely round this

*A German guard emerges from the exit shaft of **Harry** shortly after seventy-six prisoners had used it to escape into the German countryside. The repercussions from this Great Escape would be tragic for both RAF escapees and Luftwaffe captors alike.*

transformer thing and had got to a Russian and French camp to the left of us. So there we were kicking these things and making a noise from hell. Anyway we managed to scamper back into the woods and then all split up as arranged. I went off with Cookie Long in our planned direction and the others went off in pairs on their respective routes.'

Jimmy James had got away in the group before Bethell:

'After joining my group in the woods, we were led off round the camp by a Squadron Leader Williams. It was a freezing cold night and we must have walked about ten miles before we reached our objective, which was a country station called Tshiebsdorf where we knew we could take a train south. I was feeling terribly excited. The plan was that we would get down to Czechoslavakia. After a short wait we got on board a train and travelled south to another country station – just north of the Czech border. We expected a check at the station but it was nine o'clock in the morning and obviously the alarm had not reached the station yet. At this point the group split up and I went off with my partner Skantzikes , a Greek fighter pilot.

'We proceeded to climb over the Reisengebirge – or giant mountains – with snow up to our necks. Not only was it tough but we knew that if we had another night in those conditions we would probably freeze to death. Rather than proceeding on we walked into Hirschberg West Station secure in the knowledge that we had good passes and some money. At the ticket office we were intercepted by a civilian policeman who asked us for our papers. We presented them airily and he looked at them and put them in his pocket. "Hey, what's going on? I'm German and I'm just off to see my old mother in Belgrade," I told him. "We'll talk about it in the station,"came his reply. We were taken down to the police station, where there were already four other members of our party locked up. Two more came in later. By the end eight of us had been caught in the local area and all eight of us were interrogated and then taken to the civilian jail in Hirschberg, where we were each thrown into a cell. It was only some twelve hours since our escape. We were prisoners again and it was shattering. We didn't have any idea what was going to happen. After a couple of days four of our names were called out – Skantzikes , a Canadian and Pawluk and Kiewnarski, two Poles. They were told to pack up their things and go. Our natural reaction was that we thought they were going to be taken back to the camp. In fact they were taken off to be shot.

'By now a national alert had been raised and Hitler had had a meeting with Himmler and other top Nazis. They'd flown into a rage and said all seventy-six people who got out should be shot. However, someone had reminded them that, if you shoot the whole lot, it will look much like murder and they will shoot our prisoners. As a compromise, Hitler decided that fifty were to be executed and left it to Himmler to chose the names. He then passed the job over to a Gestapo general called Nebe. It seems Nebe just looked through the names on a card index which stated age and marital status. All the Poles and eastern Europeans were shot along with other escapees who were selected on a seemingly random basis. They were taken from their various jails, taken to an autobahn two or three at a time, invited to perform natural functions and just shot in the back of the head.

'The three others were also taken away and I was left on my own with a rather queasy feeling. At one point during that week the Gestapo came in and I thought they were going to interrogate me, but in fact they wanted me to get out of the cell so that they could interrogate some other unfortunate. Anyway, after about seven days, the Meister, a rather unpleasant little man, looked round the door at about 5 o'clock in the morning and said, "Raus, Schnell". I dressed, picked up whatever small things I had and went down the stairs where I was greeted by the Gestapo. One of them pulled out a revolver and told me not to do anything stupid. They marched me off to Hirschberg station and took me by train to Gestapo Headquarters, which I was glad to see had been bombed and was in a rather rickety condition. I sat there for about three hours and was then driven out of Berlin, escorted by an SS man beside me and two in the front, with no idea of where I was going. The car stopped beside a dark wood and as we went through it a big wall became visible, with electric wire on top of it. It was all a bit sinister. I had arrived at Sachsenhausen concentration camp.'

Tony Bethell was also later captured.

'The first time I actually felt freedom was once Cookie Long and myself had actually got into open country. It was getting to be broad daylight and we found ourselves some cover in a small pine forest, with trees going down to the ground. It was ideal. That was the moment when you could literally sit down relatively safe and realize that you were free. I hadn't felt any such emotion when I had got out of the tunnel because there was too much to focus – such as the simple things like counting in all the men I was waiting for before leaving and so on.

'Our prime law not to break was that we must only walk at night. We were "hard-arses" which meant that we had no ability to protect ourselves with the German language. We had passes but we didn't have any papers that would stand close examination so our best protection was the dark. We therefore waited until dark and spent that night walking up a railway line that we had found. Then it was a question of finding somewhere to lay up. A barn came to our rescue and we dried up there. Someone did actually come into it that day but wasn't remotely interested in us and just disappeared. It was a great place to be and we managed to dry our socks out and generally make ourselves comfortable.

'Then that night we went out and continued up the railway line until we got to a small junction. Our attempts to walk round it were, however, unsuccessful and we got thoroughly stuck in ploughed fields. It was awful so we decided the only thing we could do was to go back, find our barn, de-mud ourselves and then try again. Exactly the same thing happened the next night and we thought we can't spend our lives just trying to get round one silly railway station, so we broke our rule and waited until midday when we thought everybody would be at lunch. We struck out to walk round this place and we were halfway from our cover to the railway line when from behind us came two *Feldpolizei* with the words that had become so familiar, "For you the war is over". They didn't know we were Brits. In fact they thought we were Russians who had escaped from a work camp

SS Feldgendarmes checking the documentation of Russian prisoners.

just down the road. It was just bad luck, but we had broken our rule and that is why the thing went sour. We might never have reached home but I'm sure we would have gone a lot further had we stuck to the night. Luck is obviously needed as any escapee would acknowledge, but we had not helped ourselves.

'They put us in this little village jail. Our room was whitewashed and had straw on the floor. The Germans themselves were perfectly civil once they discovered we were British and not Russian, but that was little consolation at the time. We just felt very deflated. Some time later we were taken to the Gurditz – a fortress-like building which was the Gestapo jail. There were anywhere from four to six in each cell and already they had about thirty-five of us. I suppose there was a somewhat comforting element to finding myself surrounded by fellow escapees. Whether it is just that misery loves company or something I don't know, but I did feel better.

'People were interviewed and shifted around. I talked to the chaps in my cell. They had been interrogated before me and their stories varied as to the severity of the treatment. Certainly the threats by the Gestapo included things like we would lose our heads, you would never see home again, you would be shot and those sorts of things. My interview was conducted by two men. There was a woman present who appeared to be a secretary. They began by being very hostile – shouting and making a hell of a lot of noise. It was a very threatening environment indeed. I tried to deal with them by appealing to them as gentlemen and officers. I also suggested that they stopped shouting because there was a lady in the room. And they did. In fact, after about fifteen minutes they really just lost interest in me. They didn't pursue me in the way they had obviously pursued some of my fellow officers.'

He recalls seeing people taken away from the Gestapo prison and mistakenly assuming that they were the lucky ones being taken back to camp.

'I heard some transportation drawing up in the courtyard so I hauled myself up by the beams and from there I saw some lorries and a couple of cars, as well as people dressed in uniforms. I couldn't identify the uniform but they came with rifles. The next I heard was the sound of cell doors opening and shutting, and a load of shouting. Soon after I saw some of the lads being shepherded into one of the trucks. One's reaction was that they were jolly lucky and that they were going back to Sagan. You knew they'd get at least three weeks' solitary, but at least they'd be back there.'

* * * *

Unaware of the fate of their comrades, the prisoners in Stalag Luft III began to try to settle back down to something resembling their old routine. Then one morning the Senior British Officer, Group Captain Martin Massey, was summoned over to the office of the new Commandant, Oberst Braune. Braune informed him via Massey's interpreter, 'Wank' Murray, that some forty officers

Oberst Braune took over as Commandant after the Great Escape and had the unpleasant duty of informing the Senior British Officer of the executions of escapees.

had been shot resisting arrest. When Massey asked how many had been wounded the German officer said he could not say. Massey persisted with the question again and again, until the Commandant replied that as far as he was aware none had been wounded. Later the number of those shot rose to fifty. Alex Cassie remembers the moment the news was broken to the prisoners on the camp:

'Bill Jennings, the camp adjutant, came through all the rooms in the camp saying all senior members of every room must attend an important meeting in the theatre at 2 o'clock. Well, I decided that I was the senior member and went to the meeting which was led by the Commandant and Group Captain Massey, who was known for using pomposity as a weapon against the German. But on this occasion he was clearly very moved and broke the tragic news that over forty officers who had escaped had been shot. You could almost feel the shock in the packed theatre. I asked the Commandant how many were wounded but he said that he had no further information. The Commandant was obviously upset. This was the sort of thing that a regular German officer, with a high code of conduct himself, would have regarded as quite unforgivable. I think he felt a deep sense of shame himself. But of course we hadn't many thoughts for the Commandant. It was for the ones who had gone out and for the ones they'd left at home.'

Ken Rees also remembers the reaction of the Germans on the camp to the news of the shooting of the escapers:

'The Germans on the camp were very quiet. They wanted to make it very clear that the shootings had not been anything to do with them, but had been by the Gestapo. They were really shaken and really tried to distance themselves as far as possible from the murders.'

At the time when the camp was informed, Ken Rees was in the cooler contemplating his misfortune at being caught when he was so near to breaking out. News of the fate of his fellow comrades gradually began to reach him though.

'The cooler was a place with single whitewashed rooms with walls about ten foot long and four foot wide, possessing a bed, a chair and a table. There I spent the next fourteen days. I could have cried after all the work. I thought it had been my only hope of gaining freedom and getting home. Even if I had been caught along the way, it would have been wonderful to have just been free and out of the camp for a while, but it was not to be. After a while people began to shout across to us what had happened to some of the escapers. I then began to think that perhaps it had been a good thing that I hadn't got out. All of us in the cooler began wondering whether they might be looking for more people to shoot at.

1. Birkland, H. 2. Brettell, E.G. 3. Bull, D. 4. Bushell, R.J. (Big X) 5. Casey, M.J.

6. Catanach, J. 7. Christiansen, A.G. 8. Cochran, D.H. 9. Cross, K.J. 10. Espelid, H.

11. Evans, B.H. 12. Fuglesang, N. 13. Gouws, J.S. 14. Grisman, W.J. 15. Gunn, A.

16. Hake, A.H. 17. Hall, C.P. 18. Hayter, A.R.H. 19. Humphreys, E. 20. Kidder, G.A.

21. Kierath, R.V. 22. Kiewnarski, A. 23. Kirby-Green 24. Kolanowski, A.W. 25. Krol, S.

Roll call of the fifty Great Escapers murdered

162

26. Langford, P.W. 27. Leigh, T.B. 28. Long, J.L. 29. McGarr, C.A. 30. McGill, G.E.

31. Marcinkus, R. 32. Milford, H.J. 33. Mondschein, J.T. 34. Pawluk, K. 35. Picard, H.A.

36. Pohé, P.P. 37. Scheidhauer, B.W. 38. Skantzikes, S. 39. Swain, C.D. 40. Stevens, R.

41. Stewart, R.C. 42. Stower, J.G. 43. Street, D.O. 44. Tobolski, P. 45. Valenta, E.

46. Walenn, G.W. 47. Wernham, J.C. 48. Wiley, G.W. 49. Williams, J.E. 50. Williams, J.F.

after capture on the direct orders of Adolf Hitler

(Adapted from a photograph) courtesy of the Special Collections Branch of the USAF Academy Library

THE FOLLOWING OFFICERS WERE SHOT BY THE GERMANS
"WHILE ATTEMPTING TO RE-ESCAPE."

F/Lt	H. BIRKLAND.	R.C.A.F.	F/Lt	J. LONG	R.A.F.
"	G. BRETTELL.	R.A.F.	"	S. KROL	POLAND
"	L. BULL.	R.A.F.	"	P. LANGFORD	R.C.A.F.
S/Ldr.	R. BOSHELL.	R.A.F.	"	T. LEIGH	R.A.F.
F/Lt	M. CASEY.	R.A.F.	Lt	N. McGARR	S.A.A.F.
S/Ldr.	T. CATENACH. D.F.C.	R.A.A.F.	F/Lt	G. McGILL	R.C.A.F.
F/O	A. G. CHRISTENSEN.	R.N.Z.A.F.	"	R. MARCINKUS	LITHUANIA.
F/O	D. COCHRAN.	R.A.F.	"	H. MILFORD	R.A.F.
S/Ldr.	I. CROSS. D.F.C.	R.A.F.	"	T. MONDSCHEIN	POLAND.
F/O.	H. ESPELID.	NORWAY	"	K. PAWLUK	POLAND.
F/Lt	B. EVANS.	R.A.F.	"	H. PICARD	BELGIUM.
F/O	N. FUGELSANG.	NORWAY.	F/O	P. POHE	R.N.Z.A.F.
Lt.	T. GOUWS.	S.A.A.F.	Lt	B. SCHEIDHOUER	FRANCE.
F/Lt	A. GUNN.	R.A.F.	F/O	S. STANZIKLASS	GREECE.
"	W. GRISMAN.	R.A.F.	F/Lt	C. SWAIN	R.A.F.
"	C. HALL.	R.A.F.	Lt.	R. STEVENS	S.A.A.F.
"	W. HAKE.	R.A.F.	F/O	R. STEWART	R.A.F.
"	E. HUMPHREYS.	R.A.F.	"	D. STREET	R.A.F.
"	A. HAYTER.	R.A.F.	"	J. STOWER	R.A.F.
"	G. KIDDER.	R.A.F.	F/Lt	P. TOBOLSKI	POLAND.
"	R. KIERATH.	R.A.A.F.	"	E. VALENTA	CZECH.
"	A. KIEWNARSKI.	POLAND.	"	G. WALENN.	R.A.F.
S/Ldr.	T. KIRBY-GREEN.	R.A.F.	"	G. WILEY.	R.C.A.F.
F/Lt.	W. KOLANOWSKI.	POLAND	S/Ldr	J. WILLIAMS D.F.C.	R.A.F.
F/Lt.	J. WILLIAMS	R.A.F.	F/Lt	J. WERNHAM.	R.C.A.F.

A list of the murdered Great Escapers on a page from Tony Bethell's Wartime Log.

Such things go through your mind when you are stuck in a little cell with absolutely nothing to do but just sit and think.

'After fourteen days, I was released on to the camp. By that stage the number of people murdered had risen to fifty and their names were up. I was absolutely shattered then because Johnny Bull, my room-mate and one of my best friends, who had picked me when I had first arrived and had got me in the digging team, was on the list. His bunk was right opposite mine near the side of the room and it was now empty. I knew him so well. He had a child that was born after he was a prisoner. He used to show my the photographs, and say how much he was looking forward to getting home and seeing the child for the first time. It was quite heartbreaking and the whole period after the shootings was a really low time as far as I was concerned.'

Tony Bethell also heard the news of the shootings whilst in the cooler. He was one of the few captured escapers who had been returned to Stalag Luft III from Gurditz, the Gestapo prison.

'Word came through via a guard that the prisoners had been shot. I greeted the news with complete disbelief. Shock, horror and disbelief. It was only when we all got out of solitary that we learnt it was true and also found out the full measure because I think the first report was that forty had been shot. Then it finally became clear that the number was over fifty.'

He could not help but question why he had not been chosen to be shot:

'Those men who had been murdered, as became clear at Nuremberg after the war, were shot on the direct orders of Hitler. He apparently wanted all of us escapees to be killed, but Goering and some of his general staff warned him that the allies might take reprisals and a compromise number was agreed on. It seems General Nebe, who selected who was to be shot, just went through the cards with pictures and chose according to various random points such as age, status and so on. At the time I thought it must have been because I was what you might call a pretty good Aryan specimen. I was blue-eyed, young, reasonably fit and that sort of thing. Cookie had a heavy jowlish face and looked quite Jewish. I believe that I wasn't shot because I was the youngest escapee but Arnie Christensen, a New Zealander, who was a day older than me, was. I once used to speculate endlessly as to why Cookie Long, who I had gone out with, had been shot and not me. He was one of the last to be shot and he must have had a very frightening, sad and lonely death.'

A list of the officers who had been shot was put up a few weeks after the announcement to inmates that fifty had been murdered. For Alex Cassie seeing the names of so many of his close friends was particularly painful. He had lost five room-mates and had the job of dealing with their personal belongings.

'Word passed around that a notice had been pinned up on the camp notice board at the end of the administrative block. There was a constant stream round there. Anybody who went there came away shocked. Everybody knew somebody or a number of people listed.

'We were told that we were not to mention anything about it and the Germans would censor our mail and rule out anything about the escape. I remember when I got back home the first thing I had to do was to write to Gordon Brettell's parents, to Tim's parents and so on, to let them know and explain why I hadn't been able to write to them beforehand. Some weeks after the news the administration set about dealing with the property of those people who had escaped. He sent for me. "Cassie, most people have of course lost only one room-mate in this. You've lost five. We wondered if you would feel able to cope with dealing with five sets of property or would you rather have somebody else helping you?" I had a think about this. Not a very long think though and decided that I probably knew them better than anybody else in the camp and so should deal with it myself. Wing Commander Howell said, "Is there anything in particular that you would like to keep as a personal memento?" Tim Walenn had a rather nice green, paisley-patterned silk scarf, which was almost a trademark, and I said that I'd like to take that. He also had an engraved gold watch which he had been given on his twenty-first birthday by his parents. I took it and, at the end of the war, gave it back to them.'

Life in the camp changed following the escape, as Tony Bethell recalls:

'After the shootings the camp was not the same. I suppose we felt a bit of a sort of blank inside. You'd lost your sense of security. We were more vulnerable – collectively and individually. The whole X organization had been destroyed. Roger Bushell, who had led it, had been one of the men shot and most of the people who weren't shot of the X organization had been moved to other camps. So it was all rather like the chicken without the head, compared to what it had been like.'

Nevertheless, the inmates were determined that the memory of the men who had been captured and shot should not be forgotten. That summer permission was granted by the camp authorities for the prisoners to build a stone memorial in the forest outside the camp. A vaulted altar, designed by a prisoner who had been an architect before the war, was erected and three scrolls were inscribed with the names of the fifty men who had been executed. Prisoners were given permission to tend it while they remained at Sagan.

Of the seventy-six men who got clean away on the night of 24/25 March 1944 three reached England. Fifty were shot. Of the others, fifteen were returned to Stalag Luft III, two were sent to Colditz, one to a camp in Berlin and another to a camp at Barth on the Baltic Coast. A further four were taken to a special compound attached to the notorious concentration camp at Sachsenhausen. Jimmy James was one of them.

'I had no idea where I had been taken. On arriving in the camp, I was greeted by "Wings" Day. "Oh, hello Sir," I said, "is this Colditz?" "No, I wish it was," he replied, "This is Sachsenhausen Concentration camp. The only way out of here is up the chimney". We were under no illusions of the fate that awaited us should we attempt to break out.

'In fact conditions for us were not too bad at the beginning. We were

Prisoners at Sachsenhausen hauling a wagon. Some escapees from Stalag Luft III ended up in this camp and became aware of the appalling treatment meted out to victims of the Nazi regime.

given adequate rations and the guards treated us fine. In effect we were political prisoners. Our first introduction to the main compound, however, gave us quite a shock. We would be taken over there for showers. In this compound, there was a semi-circular area which was used for roll calls but was also used as a boot-testing place, and had different surfaces along it – grass, asphalt, stones and so on. On this track miserable, thin, stripped figures were made to test boots for the Russian Front. They'd be driven round all day – walking some twenty-five kilometres carrying a thirty-pound pack on their backs whilst living on starvation rations. If they dropped, they were kicked and dogs were set on them. At the head of the *appel platz* was a gallows on which inmates were hanged publicly for the

Crowded living conditions at Sachsenhausen.

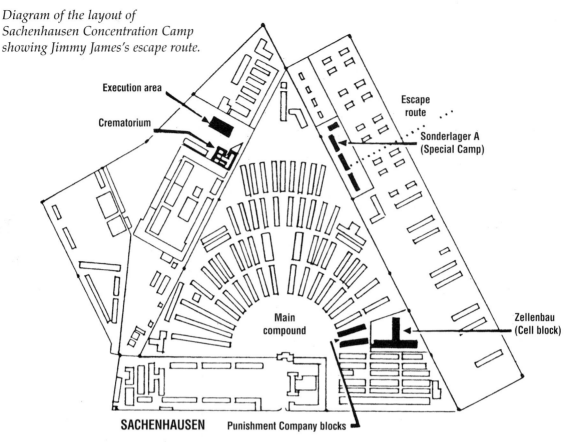

Diagram of the layout of Sachenhausen Concentration Camp showing Jimmy James's escape route.

Execution area

Crematorium

Escape route

Sonderlager A (Special Camp)

Main compound

Zellenbau (Cell block)

SACHENHAUSEN Punishment Company blocks

smallest peccadillo. If anyone escaped the whole compound was lined up until they were caught and were then made to watch a public hanging.'

Remarkably, Jimmy James successfully tunnelled out of Sachsenhausen – an unprecedented feat made all the more extraordinary in that it was James' eleventh escape attempt since his initial capture in 1940. He was caught, along with Jack Churchill, by elements of the *Volkssturm* (Home Guard) near the Baltic. They were taken back to the camp and placed inside the main compound in the *Zellenbau* – a building containing eighty cells used for solitary confinement. James was now no longer a witness to the brutality but a victim of it.

'It contained prisoners they didn't like and the expectation of life there was not very long. We knew that we were in a bit of trouble after fifty had been shot in the Great Escape, and didn't think a further escape attempt would be viewed very benevolently. In fact Hitler ordered our execution but later commuted it to imprisonment in the cells. The camp commandant was treated less leniently. He was shot for not thwarting our escape.

'Even after our sentence had been commuted, it was really more a case of having a delayed death sentence because anyone who went into the cell block was very likely to be taken to one of the places of execution later. There was a place called "Station Z" where people were shot, and another place for hanging. There was also a gas chamber. One further method of execution on the camp was the *genickschuss* installation – which in German literally means "neck shot". The way they did this was that you were shown in to a room where you would be greeted by a man in a white coat, who you naturally presumed was a doctor. He beckoned you to stand on some scales and would measure your weight and then height. Unbeknown to the victim was that there was a hole in the wall behind you through which an SS man would shoot you in the back of the neck while loud music played in the background. The blood would be wiped away and then "Next please". They shot something like 18,000 Soviet Army personnel using that method in October 1941 alone. The SS guards who did it were given a holiday in Capri as a reward.

'We knew the dangers of being in the cell block. You could smell the smoke from the crematorium. The SS sergeant who was in charge of it was a man who went round and murdered people in their cells with his own hands. His normal method was strangulation. We didn't know the details but we knew some nasty things went on. Whenever the door opened you didn't know where you were being taken or what would happen. It wasn't a very nice feeling at all.'

James found that only way to overcome one's fear and boredom was to establish a routine.

'I'd be screamed at in the early morning at around 5 o'clock. I'd then have to empty my bucket and be screamed at again on the way back by the SS guard, who would then give me a broom to sweep my cell out. I got a bit tired of this screaming after a while and rather unwisely I screamed back. It was a bit of a gamble and I think I was only saved by the fact that I was a British officer. Anyway he calmed down after that. Much of the time was spent meditating and things that you thought you'd forgotten came back to you. In that respect, it was a rather interesting period. The other thing one could do was watch the prisoners exercising outside through the bars at the top. You had to get up on your bed to do it and be very careful. The SS guards outside wouldn't hesitate to shoot if they saw you. Then you would walk yourself round your cell which was some three foot by seven foot. By then it might be lunchtime, which consisted of some sauerkraut soup. In the afternoon you would try and rest but, if the guard looked through the peephole and saw you, he would open the door and shout, "*Raus* – rest forbidden". For an hour every day we went on a walk in what they called *Hitler Strasse* – an exercise area around the other side of the wing from where the cells were; once again there were plenty of sights of torture, including an underground bunker where they put people to starve. In the evening I played chess with myself using pieces of wrapping paper. I always won which was at least a morale raiser! Then it was bedtime, feeling that you'd had quite a full day. That was how I coped.'

He was held in solitary confinement in the cellblock for five months.

'They had a tannoy in the camp and I remember that on Christmas Eve they played *Silent Night*. It was the most incongruous thing hearing this beautiful hymn in such a satanic place. Quite a lot of commandos came in and were executed the next morning on account of Hitler's Commando Order. Among them were Commander Cumberledge and three sergeants who were in a commando group that had been captured blowing up the Corinth Canal during the Greek campaign. They arrived in Sachsenhausen after terrible tortures and Jack Churchill managed to communicate through tapping on the wall. They were taken off and shot soon after their arrival. During that month, out of a population of eighty, only thirteen were left by the time we were moved on.'

Soon after leaving Sachsenhausen, Jimmy James was forced to endure yet more horrors at Flossenburg concentration camp.

'The SS greeted us with loud shouts and screams of *"Schnell! Schnell!"* We were then taken to the Kommandant who decided that he wanted us executed at once. "There's no room for these people here" he said. Fortunately an SS guard who had escorted us to the camp spoke up and said, "If these prisoners are shot there may be some awkward questions asked. Anyway they may be useful for bargaining with the Allies." So we were spared.

'It was a terrible place. We were put into the hospital block to start with because there was no room in the cells. We were fairly high up and had a good view of the camp. From our windows we could see inmates being worked to death in a quarry every day. They died at a rate of fifty a day. The crematorium couldn't take all the bodies so they burnt them in bonfires at the side of the camp. I remember one day we saw three stretchers going past. The ones on them were covered in blood. We learnt later that they were Pastor Bonhoeffer, the famous theologian, Admiral Canaris who had been head of German Intelligence, and General Hans Oster, his adjutant. At around the same time thirteen British agents were executed in a cell in order that there was room for us.'

Jimmy James was later taken to Dachau, before being taken by bus into the Austrian Tyrol where he was liberated by the Americans. So ended an ordeal that had begun with his recapture following the Great Escape, a break-out which in terms of scale, daring and ingenuity was unprecedented.

Colonel Jack Churchill, ex-Commando, and Jimmy James standing near the once entrance to a cell block, and now memorial, at Sachenhausen in 1975.

170

CHAPTER FIVE

Colditz – Two Perspectives

Colditz is perhaps the best known of all the Nazi prisoner of war camps. More likely to be the setting of a Bram Stoker novel, the very word brings up images of the fortress castle. It was an unusual prison, far removed from the purpose-built, hastily erected barbed wire camps housing the majority of those Allied servicemen captured between 1939-45. Yet it was no stranger to wars. Since 1014 it had been subject to sieges and sackings, captures and recaptures. Originally built for Saxon Kings, it had been put to many uses before the Wehrmacht took it over at the beginning of the Second World War. Indeed, from the early 19th century Colditz had been a prison and in 1828 its bare and comfortless rooms were used to house the mentally insane. When the Nazis had come to power, they firstly used it as an offshoot of the Buchenwald concentration camp complex, before employing it as a Hitler Youth training centre. Yet, with its high, grey granite walls and steep terraces all round, the Nazi authorities soon realized it was their answer to the maximum high-security prison they required for habitual escapers. As a result, the Wehrmacht decided that it should be used

Colditz Castle 1999, little changed in 55 years.

as a *Sonderlager* – a special camp. Before the decision was ratified, Hermann Goering visited the austere, unyielding castle and confidently proclaimed that it was indeed escape-proof.

Yet the Nazis miscalculated the determination of these inveterate escapers and underestimated their ingenuity and daring. Furthermore, by bringing together the men who had proved themselves most adept and willing to break out, they succeeded in concentrating an international array of talent, from forgers to locksmiths, under one roof. Over three hundred escape attempts were made from the castle. Most failed in their initial stages, but some hundred and thirty prisoners did get out of the castle before being caught. Thirty men made successful home runs.

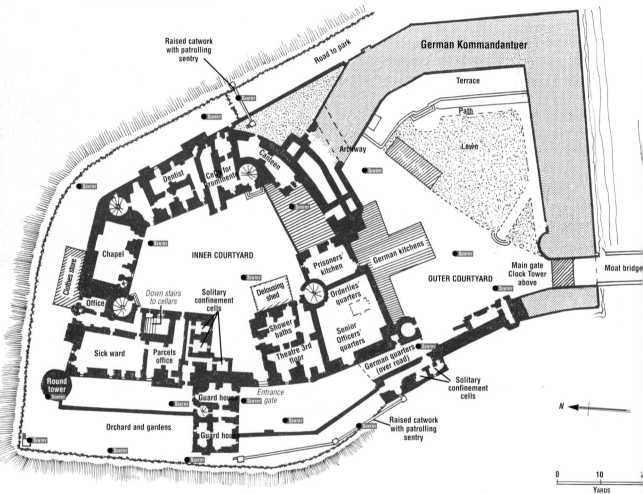

Plan of Colditz Castle

WALTER MORISON was sent to Colditz after his daring escape from Stalag Luft III when he attempted to 'borrow' an aeroplane from the Luftwaffe with his friend Lorne Welch. Escaping was petering out by the time Walter arrived at the Castle.

'Enthusiasm for escaping was beginning to go out of fashion by the time I got to Colditz in August 1943. This was partly because the large number of loopholes in the castle had been more or less exploited. Also we were becoming increasingly aware that the allies were going to win the war. A further reason was that the Germans got fed up with us playing this escaping game. They issued a notice to all prisoners of war which stated that breaking out was no longer a sport. When fifty people were shot trying to escape from Stalag Luft III, their point was further reinforced.'

Walter Morison in home-made German uniform.
IWM HU21188

Nevertheless, some people continued to devise means of breaking out. Perhaps the most famous example of these in the latter stages of the war was the building of a glider within the castle confines. Morison takes up the story:

'This glider was built in the castle without the knowledge of the goons. The plan was to launch it off the roof. Of course, the main purpose was to get a couple of guys out, but it was also probably a lot of fun building the thing. The war was coming to an end but the project was kept going, and it was virtually totally completed when the Americans entered the castle. In fact a simple aircraft is relatively easy to build. It only needs some wood, which could be acquired from things like the floorboards and the backs of cupboards, and a bed-sheet or two to cover the wings. Although the materials were relatively simple, the task of designing such a craft should not be underestimated.

'The main difficulty was how to conceal the thing. The top floor provided the solution as it possessed an unoccupied room some seventy feet long. This was secured with a very sophisticated lock but they managed to somehow measure its dimension and make the necessary keys. They then built a false wall across the end of the room, leaving about fifteen feet or so for a workshop. The goons never noticed and just used to open the door, glance around to check that nothing was going on, and then leave. Parts were in fact built all around the place. I made some wing rims in my room. If there was a cry of "goons" you would just slip the objects under your blankets or something.

'Sadly, the glider had to be left there when we were rescued. They later tried to get permission bring it home, but by then it was in the Russian zone and had disappeared. Very sad, because it was a fantastic achievement to make a properly designed aircraft in such circumstances.'

To all Prisoners of War!

The escape from prison camps is no longer a sport!

Germany has always kept to the Hague Convention and only punished recaptured prisoners of war with minor disciplinary punishment.

Germany will still maintain these principles of international law.

But England has besides fighting at the front in an honest manner instituted an illegal warfare in non combat zones in the form of gangster commandos, terror bandits and sabotage troops even up to the frontiers of Germany.

They say in a captured secret and confidential English military pamphlet,

THE HANDBOOK OF MODERN IRREGULAR WARFARE:

". . . the days when we could practise the rules of sportsmanship are over. For the time being, every soldier must be a potential gangster and must be prepared to adopt their methods whenever necessary."

"The sphere of operations should always include the enemy's own country, any occupied territory, and in certain circumstances, such neutral countries as he is using as a source of supply."

England has with these instructions opened up a non military form of gangster war!

Germany is determined to safeguard her homeland, and especially her war industry and provisional centres for the fighting fronts. Therefore it has become necessary to create strictly forbidden zones, called death zones, in which all unauthorised trespassers will be immediately shot on sight.

Escaping prisoners of war, entering such death zones, will certainly lose their lives. They are therefore in constant danger of being mistaken for enemy agents or sabotage groups.

Urgent warning is given against making future escapes!

In plain English: Stay in the camp where you will be safe! Breaking out of it is now a damned dangerous act.

The chances of preserving your life are almost nil!

All police and military guards have been given the most strict orders to shoot on sight all suspected persons.

Escaping from prison camps has ceased to be a sport!

174

Perspective One:
A Colditz Guard

ALFRED HEINRICH

Officers, senior NCOs and civilian staff at the Castle.

Inner courtyard of Colditz looking towards the solitary confinement cells on the west side (see diagram on page 172).

Alfred Heinrich
1999

ALFRED HEINRICH was wounded in Russia, some fifty kilometres from Smolensk. A Russian armour-piercing grenade exploded beside him. Two pieces of shrapnel hit him in the legs and one in the eye. The eye could not be saved and had to be surgically removed in Dresden. As a result he was deemed no longer fit for action at the front and was assigned to the *Landesschutzen* (Riflemen) – soldiers who carried out guard duties in the Reich. His first posting was to a large Russian prison in Muhlberg.

Alfred Heinrich
1939

'It was a nasty place and very exposed to the elements in winter. Four weeks later I was informed that my guard squadron was being moved to a place called Colditz. I had never heard of it, but my roommates told me I was fortunate. "Wow, lucky you, if Colditz is where you really are being sent to. It's a little town with a castle. You will have a good time." So I arrived in Colditz in March 1942 and was to stay there for two years, an unusually long time, as guard squadrons were normally moved every six months to prevent them becoming too friendly with the prisoners.

'We arrived there in winter and there was a lot of snow on the ground. The population was friendly and there were plenty of pubs in the town (about seventeen, although a lot have subsequently closed down) so that improved our morale! High on the hill stood the castle. We had a wander around the grounds and the park, and thought to ourselves, "The prisoners are not doing too badly here".

'Many of the inmates had escaped from other camps on one, two or even more occasions. We were to pay special attention to these "seasoned tourists", as they were called, who seemed rather partial to go a-wandering.'

There had already been quite a few escape attempts in 1940 and 1941, and Heinrich and the other new guards were shown the various attempt routes that the prisoners had tried to use.

'Some of the attempts had been ingenious. For example, in the afternoons those who wanted to were allowed into a fenced-in park just outside the castle, having been counted, where they could walk, lie down, play volley ball and so on. It was an area surrounded by guards and there was also a dog handler with an Alsatian who would patrol the area. During the autumn a couple of prisoners had made a large blanket with leaves from the trees sewn to it. They relied on the fact that their fellow prisoners would, by pushing forwards and backwards, and generally being obstructive, make counting the numbers so difficult that the NCO in charge would get fed up and just say that it must be the correct number. He didn't, however, and the two of them were discovered.

'The officers at the headquarters ultimately carried the can if someone did escape. Most were comfortable at Colditz and did not want to be replaced so any attempted escape was generally kept very quiet. It was more like a game between the prisoners and us. It suited both not to have

The guardroom on the ground floor. Attempts to escape by walking through the main gate in disguised as a workman or German soldier were often thwarted from this room.

the feared Gestapo or Waffen SS involved. That would have been very dangerous.'

The guard squadron consisted of three sections of guards. One section on duty, another on standby, ready to be deployed if any prisoners escaped. They would then get on their bicycles and occupy certain points round Colditz, such as stations and bridges within a radius of fifteen to twenty kilometres. The third section had their time off and were free to got to town, visit the cinema and pubs until 2200 hours, when they had to return to base.

'Often when I checked the beds at lights out, I would find an empty bed here and there. The next morning I would say to the guard, "Where the hell were you? You were not in your bed." And they would admit they were in such and such pub. Some pubs were given some kind of codename; for example one was run by two hefty ladies and was known as the "Four Buttocks".'

Each guard had a post where they had a bell button. If they noticed anything, such as a noise on the roof, they would push the button and the number of their post would drop into the guardroom.

'If Post 6 had rung the bell, then the duty NCO would go and find out what was the matter. On his return he would decide whether to ring headquarters or inform the senior duty officer. The guard was, however, entitled to act if he had seen a prisoner on the loose in his area. We were under strict instructions that we had to shout "stop" three times. If he did

178

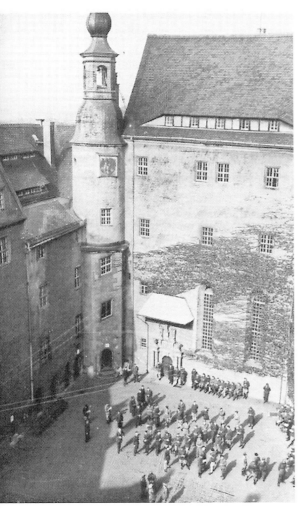

Appel *took place in the small prisoners' courtyard.*

not stop we were entitled to shoot.' Heinrich recalls only one incident when a prisoner was actually fired at.

'One of the guards, who was marching up and down the yard, was being "shot" at by a prisoner using pebbles and a catapult. He rang the bell and I went and investigated. He told me the situation. "You are joking!" I said. "No," he replied, "I really am being aimed at." At that moment there was a "Thwack" and a pebble hit the gate beside us. "If they don't stop, just fire a warning shot." The guard told me he knew where they were and agreed that he would fire a warning shot. I went back in and heard a shot. Unfortunately he had aimed a little too close to them and the bullet had hit the bars and ricocheted from the bars into the room and gone straight into the French Lieutenant's shoulder. He was taken to a military hospital and later returned to Colditz. My colleague was less lucky. He was taken away and dragged from one court to another. The fact is that imprisoned officers had quite a few rights, and if some incident like that occurred, the Red Cross were on to the scene immediately.

'We were therefore extremely reluctant to shoot. I recall on one occasion one of the guards rang me up (I was the guard on duty) and told me that there were some noises on the roof, near the chimney. I went up to investigate and, using the searchlight, instantly spotted them. "Right," I said, "You shoot to the left of the chimney, and I will shoot to the right. We are not going to shoot him down." We shouted, "Stop" three times and then shot. Some tiles came off followed by a shout of "Don't shoot". I told the guard on patrol to go up there and he discovered five men – one of them had trapped his leg. It was really lucky that we hadn't fired at it as we probably would have shot one or two of them dead which would have been a whole lot more serious for everyone.'

Apart from guard duty, Heinrich and his colleagues were also required to carry out roll calls or *appels*.

'The rows were counted – the English, for example, stood five rows deep, so five heads were counted and multiplied by the number of lines. This would then be reported to the Captain, who would confirm the correctness of the count. Then we would move on to the French who stood four rows deep and the Dutch who, being the smallest group, would stand three deep. We had to look out for cheating as such a process meant that a prisoner could squat down and crawl back to another position to be counted again. They also made skin-colour plaster dummies, which had a hat and jacket on the wooden frame. Those who stood to the left and right of the dummy held it upright. This was tried several times until one day, while the counting was going on, someone let go too soon and a guard spotted the dummy falling sideways. We had largely caught hold of this ploy by 1942, but before then a few successful escape attempts had taken place as a result of using this trick. What it did, of course, was provide the escapees with some valuable time to get away without the guards getting on their bikes to go looking for them.'

Despite their relative proximity to the prisoners, the guards did their best to avoid contact with them.

'If we had developed any sort of relationship with them we would have been removed from Colditz, and Colditz was a good posting for us guards. I remember one occasion when a young Englishman approached me and offered me a glass. "Would you like some wine," he asked. "I'm not allowed to," I told him. The truth was that I wondered where the wine came from. I think they made it from dried raisins that they received from their Red Cross parcels. One guard, Warrant Officer Kipper, was not as restrained as I was and drank several glasses. He had to be carried out of the camp as a result.

'There was a case of one soldier who got friendly with the prisoners. He had a stationers' shop in Leipzig and he brought in different things from there – type character sets, rubber stamp pads and so on. When this was discovered he was taken away and got fourteen days' arrest in a barracks in the neighbouring town of Grimma. I picked him up myself on a Sunday. He was later taken away by the Gestapo and a few weeks after we were told at the duty roster that he had been shot dead for military subversion. Such incidents only confirmed one's view that it was very dangerous to talk to prisoners, although sometimes it was difficult not to as among the English there were some who spoke German. Another incident involved a laundry woman. She got friendly with an English officer who carried the washing out. He brought it to the gate, the car would be driven up – the clean washing was then handed over which he then counted and she would then take the dirty washing from it. She would, however, smuggle things like dyes and Indian ink to write with in amongst the clean clothes. In return she got a nice piece of soap or some chocolate. The Gestapo found out though and took the woman away. We never heard what happened to her.'

Ironically Heinrich believes that the prisoners were in some ways better off than

Alfred Heinrich (centre) with some of his fellow guards enjoying a beer and a smoke. In some respects the prisoners were better off when it came to luxuries, especially cigarettes. British and American brands were keenly sought after and were sometimes stolen from prisoners' quarters during searches. However, these then had to be smoked away from the camp as the aroma was a sure give-away.

the people guarding them.

'German soldiers used to get so-called Smokers' Coupons, but they provided you with only a very small quantity of tobacco products. They were meant to last you all month but, in reality, the allocated cigarette rations were smoked within a week. A guard – being permanently bored – would smoke a lot. When we went through the prisoners' day rooms, however, we were all shocked. Whole cartons full of loose cigarettes stood on the table. The waste paper baskets were full of French and Belgian cigarettes which apparently they did not smoke at all. Well, we soldiers had no choice. When all the prisoners were asleep and nobody was about in the day rooms, one would just grab a carton or two. The only problem was that we couldn't smoke the English cigarettes in our rooms because of their sweet and perfumed smell. If one of our officers had come near he would have noticed it immediately. So we could only smoke them outside the Castle on our days off. These cigarette thefts in the end got out of hand. Our sergeant had to tell us that the English officers had complained about this spate of cigarette thefts and that they had decided to poison their cigarettes to find out the culprits. I do not know if that was true but the prisoners began to hide them in their rooms out of our reach.'

The guards were also victim to baiting from their captives.

'We certainly received a fair amount of teasing. I recall that a young

English lieutenant addressed me and said that one day I would be here on the inside and he would be on the outside. I told him I thought that was unlikely. That was in 1942 and we did not believe we could lose the war. The propaganda was still strong and there were victories all around. It was only after the fall of Stalingrad that we began to realize that things weren't going well. A loud-speaker used to relay the progress of the German army. The announcement would begin with a great trumpet noise and then it was announced that so and so many transport ships had been sunk by the Germans, that certain towns had been captured and so on. Then suddenly one noticed that the announcements got less and less. The prisoners made little charts for themselves with flags showing the progress of the allies. They obviously had radios and often heard the news before we did. They used to laugh when we heard about a great victory, because it wasn't really true and they already knew that we had retreated from such and such a

Colditz guards on parade. Surprise inspections by the Gestapo, usually mounted at dawn, were as much dreaded by the guards as by the prisoners. The whole complement of guards was turned out whilst the leather-coated security police searched the prisoners' quarters.

position. The propaganda we received was so strong and we were confident that the V-bomb would finish the war. Any German who contradicted this was instantly handed over to the Gestapo and sent to concentration camps where they scarcely ever came back.'

One thing that both the prisoners and the guards had in common was fear of he Gestapo.

'When they arrived we were all dragged out of bed. We weren't allowed to put the light on. They always wore these leather overcoats. We got dressed amidst much cursing and went into the prisoners' courtyard. The prisoners' rooms were then occupied in a flash and they were all hauled out of bed and forced into their recreation rooms. Their beds were then taken apart and searched for tools and other items. Sometimes things were found but more often than not it was useless and a waste of time. We couldn't complain though. You really had to be careful when they were around.'

The searches for the most part were futile, but occasionally the guards would find something.

'If anything was discovered it would tend to be something hidden under a floorboard or bed. Maybe money, or stolen tools from the workmen who came into the castle. When a bricklayer came in, for example, they might steal a chisel or a hammer from him. On one occasion an apprentice came in and they stole his cap. He came out in tears, but they needed such items if they were going to dress in civilian clothes. We would always send a guard in with the workman to keep watch. But the guard was often distracted in one way or another by the prisoners and they would take their chance with great speed. Even if the guard did see something, they would just throw the object from one to the other and then it would just disappear into a room. The guard couldn't just fire his gun as he wasn't allowed to, so in some ways he was rather helpless.

'The prisoners were a resourceful lot when it came to trying to escape. The Dutch had a grey-green uniform which looked just like our uniform if you dyed it a bit. They managed to copy quite a lot of German uniforms. I once discovered a sack full. Either the French or the Dutch had a sewing machine, which they used to good effect. One chap impersonated Stabsfeldwebel (Sergeant Major) Rothenberger. He had exactly the same uniform – the medals, the Iron Cross first class, the coquettes on the cap, the moustache, everything. You had to be constantly on the look out. While Captain Eckert was in a meeting with the English officers they stole his cap and it was copied

Stabsfeldwebel Rothenberger runs over procedures with Colditz sentries. His distinctive moustache begged imitation and a British officer saw an opportunity to make a break...

perfectly. Sergeant Schadlich, the kitchen sergeant, had real problems when his identity pass went missing. Once again they made a copy of it and then it suddenly appeared again. A rifle was also stolen from one guard. The prisoners were all made to line-up and told to give it back. They all jokingly turned out their pockets saying they hadn't got it. And nothing was found upstairs. The gun had disappeared. At first the Commandant wanted to leave the prisoners standing in the courtyard until someone produced it. But that took too long and he angrily agreed that they should be allowed back into their own rooms. The next day the rifle was on the courtyard wrapped in rags. The prisoners knew the score, that if they

Lieutenant Michael Sinclair (known as the Red Fox because of his persistent escape attempts) impersonated Stabsfeldwebel Rothenberger (right) and almost got away with it, but was wounded in the attempt.

184

A wooden rifle carved from a drawing of one 'borrowed' from the guards.

stole weapons it would get really dangerous for them. And that is why they handed it back, but not before they had made a detailed drawing of it, which they could make a copy from.'

Whilst he was based at Colditz he witnessed numerous attempts to gain freedom.

'On one occasion I thwarted an escape attempt myself. One of the prisoners had impersonated Boehnert Willi, the electrician, and very nearly got away with it. In front of the gate there was a spring lock and when there was a knock the guard would look through the peephole and open it if he recognized the person. So the guard, thinking it was Willi, opened the gate and it was only when the rearmost guard drew him into conversation that it was discovered that he was an impostor. As a result, we decided to put a sergeant in the area to stand guard at all times. It was my turn to go on the two-hour shift. I had pretty good hearing and felt sure that I could hear a noise. It seemed to be coming from the manhole cover. I called over the officer on duty and we listened. "There is something," he agreed. We brought over a couple more men and lifted the cover. And there, to our amazement, were

two Englishmen looking up at us. They had discovered that they couldn't go any further as there was a metal grille that closed the drain off and had caused the noise by trying to remove it. Their comrades had obviously managed to distract the guard in the courtyard – playing football with him or starting a fight amongst themselves or whatever – to such an extent that the escapers had managed to lift up the manhole cover in the middle of the yard and got down into the drain without being spotted.

'Any chance of escaping was seized upon by the prisoners. A tunnel had been discovered under the stage in the hall and a

Willi the electrician and his imposter, the real Boehnert Willi is on the right.

Alfred Heinrich on duty in the Colditz guardroom. Behind him is the board with brass, numbered discs which were issued to every sentry or civilian workman entering the prisoners' courtyard. The number was recorded in a book and a check was made as the individual left. Failure to produce a disc resulted in an immediate arrest.

horse and cart was brought in to remove the debris. The litter men shovelled the debris onto the cart baskets or buckets. When it was pretty well full the guard was distracted and one of the prisoners in a flash got onto it and was covered from his legs up to his neck. They covered his head with a beer crate, which had gaps in it, so that he could get air and he lay there like that. The cart was then driven out through the entrance gate past the guard. A woman looking out of her house spotted the prisoner trying to get himself free and attracted the driver's attention. "Hey you," she shouted. He instantly turned round and called up to the guard post. If the woman had not seen him, he would have got away.

'There was a similar incident involving waste baskets which was more successful. Big woven baskets were carried off by two litter men on their backs. These would be full of paper and cardboard, much of which was the result of the Red Cross parcels. A guard went out with the litter men, and the waste would then be tipped out, and later burned. Two men managed to crawl into one of these baskets and then covered themselves with paper. That evening we discovered that two prisoners were missing and, on reflection, we realized that they must have got out via the baskets. At the next roll call the prisoners were informed that from now on every time the baskets were taken out they would be bayoneted. And that was the end of that.'

Some escape attempts were fuelled by sheer desperation.

Escape tools discovered during a search at Colditz.

Collection of food hoarded by the prisoners to be used as escape rations.

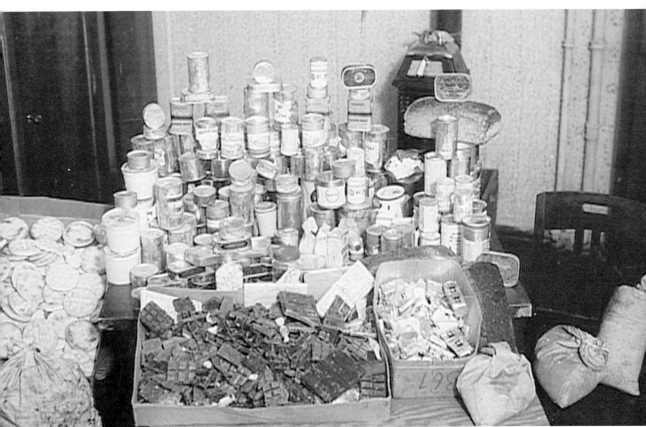

'I was taking a couple of prisoners down to a prison hospital when one of them just tried to jump into some water from a parapet. I was actually going to reach for my pistol, but the English officer with him told me not to and together we stopped the man. He later informed me that this prisoner had been guarded by his comrades for the last few days. Apparently he had cracked up after hearing that his brother had been killed in Africa and that his parents had been killed in a bombing raid in London. He wanted to take his own life. On the train he actually scared me. He sat opposite with this fixed stare and was shaking. In many ways it is not surprising. If you are imprisoned for years and then hear news like that you might just go crazy.

'For most of the men escaping was more of a game. Almost like hide and seek. The English, Dutch and French were protected by the Geneva Convention. The Poles were not, as Poland had been totally destroyed, and they had to be more careful. We were not bitter about the escape attempts and in many ways it made our life more interesting, especially when, instead of being on stand-by duty in our rooms, we were out in the countryside looking for them. Some escapes were of course successful, particularly in the early years. One Englishman who escaped in 1940 sent a postcard to the commandant from England.'

In March 1944 Alfred Heinrich was moved from Colditz to Luckenwalde, where he was given the task of training the so-called Blasov Troops (Russians who were fighting on the side of the Germany). He was later captured by the Americans and imprisoned in a vast prisoner of war camp at Hersfeld. On his release he returned to Colditz to be reunited with his wife, whom he had married during his time as a guard there.

Colditz guards during a period of relaxation.

Colditz guards on parade before dispersing to their assigned sentry posts around the prison. They had to be especially watchful of the VIP prisoners lodged at the Castle – the **Prominente** *as they were known.*

The *Prominente* were men who, due to their family connections, were treated

Perspective Two:
The *Prominente*

as maximum security inmates by their German captives. They were imprisoned in Colditz Castle. Among them were Giles Romilly (nephew of Clementine Churchill), Dawyck Haig (son of the Commander of the British Forces in the First World War), Charlie Hopetoun (later the Marquess of Linlithgow and son of the Viceroy of India), John Winant (son of the wartime U.S. Ambassador to Britain), Max de Hamel (thought by the Germans to be a distant relative of Churchill), George Lascelles (then a Viscount, and a nephew of George VI, later Earl of Harewood), and John Elphinstone (nephew of Queen Elizabeth The Queen Mother). They were held under close supervision and, as such, had a very different experience of life behind the wire.

Giles Romilly was the longest serving member of the *Prominente* to be held in the castle. Guards, like Alfred Heinrich, arriving at Colditz for the first time, were immediately informed of his importance.

'On entering the guardroom, we were all instantly shown a photograph of Romilly, Churchill's nephew, and had to commit his face to memory. He was the best known prisoner in the camp and it was imperative that he should not be able to get past the guards. Our instructions were simple – to be alert at all times.'

Heinrich and the other guards were well aware that they would be in terrible trouble should Romilly, and later the other members of the *Prominente*, manage to escape.

'We could not afford to lose these men. At a place called Konigstein, the eminent French General Giraud managed to escape and the entire German guard squadron was replaced. All of them were sent to the Punishment Company, where you could be fairly certain of either being sent to a very dangerous place, with minefields for instance, or you might just simply be killed. There is no doubt the same would have happened to us. We therefore always had a guard outside Romilly's room, who had to record his observations in a logbook at certain intervals by looking through a spyhole in the door. So he would see him lying in his bed and record: "Romilly asleep". Romilly would sometimes hang a jacket on the door to obstruct the view. On one occasion a guard noticed that he hadn't moved at all in bed, so he went in and discovered that he had put a self-made dummy in his bed to fool us. The alarm was raised and a huge search began before it was discovered that he was in a room with some fellow comrades! There was a certain amount of cat and mouse.

'Romilly, in particular, gave us a hard time. We had to be very careful because he would complain about anything. We all used to wear hobnailed boots and he once made a big scene that the guard patrolling outside his room was making too much noise thus preventing him from sleeping. The result was that the Red Cross arrived from Geneva and soon after a red carpet was laid on the concrete floor outside his room to dampen the sound!'

Romilly had arrived at the castle in the

Winston Churchill's nephew, Giles Romilly – kept as a possible bargaining chip on Hitler's orders.

summer of 1941 and was joined by Michael Alexander fifteen months later:

'It was snowing and rather dark as I went through the gloomy portals of this medieval castle on the hill and entered the cobbled courtyard, which was to become so familiar after a time. I was shoved into a small room with Giles Romilly. After a long time of no conversations, it was really nice to find myself with somebody, and we had lots to talk about. It was all a bit cramped and dingy, but, having spent many months in a very small cell with a death sentence hanging over me, it was bliss – freedom practically. Our rooms were nicer than most rooms that inmates had to live in. We were locked in every night and always had a private guard patrolling outside our door which had been fitted with a spyhole. We were very much separated from the other prisoners at Colditz and were only allowed to exercise in the narrow interior yard. None of us were in any doubt that we were being used as "special" hostages. Inevitably this played on the mind of our group. They were quite alarmed at what might happen at the end of the war. We all tried not to make a thing of it, but the situation was somewhat ominous.'

Michael Alexander, wrongly thought by the Germans to be a close relative of General Alexander. This undoubtedly saved his life as he was a Commando and subject to Hitler's notorious execution order.

As the war went on, the numbers of the *Prominente* swelled with the arrival of men like Dawyck Haig, son of the late Field Marshal. He recalls the moment he became a political hostage at Colditz.

'At the beginning of November 1944 I was sent to see the Senior British Officer at Hadamar camp, General Fortune, who told me, "The Germans say because you are your father's son you are going to be taken to a more comfortable place". With little warning I had to pack and be ready to leave that evening. An order had come through from the High Command of the Wehrmacht instructing the Commandant to dispatch me with two guards to a camp near Leipzig. The camp was Colditz Castle and I arrived there on 11 November, exactly twenty-six years since the signing of the Armistice.

'The castle was like a beehive full of cells humming with bees of many kinds. The bees had all been selected by the Germans for special guarding because of their escape records. The majority were British army officers, but amongst them were sailors and merchant navy men as well as Poles, Dutch, Belgians, French and Americans. Our little party had a curious appearance when seen as a whole, and had little of the glamour that one might expect from people with such distinguished backgrounds.'

George Lascelles, previously imprisoned at Spangenberg, arrived at the same time as Haig as a result of his German captors discovering that he was related to the Royal Family.

'When I was taken prisoner, there were at least two guardsmen who were also captured from my battalion. Unfortunately I was taken off one way and they were taken off another. They must have let slip that I was a nephew of the King. As a result in the winter of 1944 I was taken to Colditz to be one of the Germans' *Prominente* hostages. Prisoners used to refer to Colditz as a *Straflager*, a punishment camp, and everyone there either had a record of escape or some punishable offence. Mine was to have prominent relations.

'The journey by train was uncomfortable and I arrived in the evening to be shoved into a cell with a double bunk, the bottom one of which was already occupied. A cavalry-moustached head poked out which turned out to be Dawyck Haig. The last time I had seen him had been as a fellow-page at the Coronation in 1937.

'The next day I thought I should go and report myself to the Senior British Officer. I was instructed to go to a particular building and up some stairs. I arrived at the bottom of the stairs to meet tumbling down them a figure in air force uniform which I duly caught, to be met with a volley of oaths from the tumbler who was evidently less steady on his pins. It was the famous Douglas Bader, with two false legs and a propensity not only to fall downstairs but to berate whoever caught him, insisting that he had to make his own way.'

Dawyck Haig, son of the late F Marshal, commander of the Bri Army on the Western Front during 1914-1918 war.

Despite their confined surroundings, Alexander remembers that the prisoners at Colditz did their best to keep themselves occupied:

'The main rendezvous was the courtyard and you'd walk round and round it in a rather hopeless way. We played games there too and did a lot of talking. There were lots of foreigners of course who I got on very well with – Dutch, Poles, French and Belgians. I never went to university and I suppose Colditz was my university. We even had plays in an old theatre and set up an orchestra.'

The *Prominente* did enjoy some advantages over the other prisoners in the castle. Alexander:

'As a sort of *quid pro quo* for the stringent surveillance and lack of freedom afforded to our group, we were not required to come out for *appels* – roll calls in the early morning. We used to hear all the other inmates coughing and spitting in the cold while we lay in bed. The guards just used to count us through the window, which was a great asset. A *Gefreiter* would just look in to our rooms, find us present and shout for the reassurance of the German officer taking the parade.'

As the men were forbidden to exercise in the park below the castle with the

Kr.-Gef. Offizierlager IX A   Ausgestellt Spangenberg
Hauptlager
Zweiglager   am 1. 8. 194 4

Kennkarte für Kriegsgefangene

Nur gültig für den Lagerbetrieb und in Verbindung mit der
Erk.-Marke Nr. 133760

Dienstgrad : Oberleutnant

Name : Viscount Lascelles

Vorname : George Henry ~~Umbert~~ Hubert

Lichtbild

Zur Beachtung !

Die Kennkarte dient als Aus-
weis der Krf. gegenüber den
Organen der deutschen Lager-
kommandantur. Sie ist wie
die Erk.-Marke stets mitzu-
führen u. mit dieser auf
Verlangen bei namentlichen
Appells und beim Verlassen
des Lagers vorzuweisen.
Verlust ist sofort zu melden.

Der Kommandant

George Lascelles POW card. He was held at Colditz because of his royal connections, he was nephew to King George VI.

other prisoners, a further concession was made in 1944. Alexander recalls:

'The security officer, Captain Eggers, came in and told us that we were to have privileged *Prominente* walks, twice a week, over a choice of five routes. "You will like the countryside round here. It is just like your English Cotswolds," he told us. We replied, "Captain Eggers, it isn't in the least bit like our English Cotswolds. Our English Cotswolds go up and down a bit. This is Saxony. It's as flat as a pancake." "Well, you will like the walks anyway," he said. So off we went under the escort of guards with machine guns and rifles. It was rather like a school walk. I think the guards were more worried we might be rescued by somebody than that we might run away. It was as though they thought some plane might come and pick us up!'

Alfred Heinrich was one of those guards who escorted the group:

'I happened to be the duty NCO on the first of their accompanied walks. Five of them went on it with three guards with rifles and an extra NCO carrying a machine gun. The prisoners at first refused to go, saying that they had given their word of honour and that they did not need armed guards. It was then explained to them that we were there more for their own protection than for anything else. This actually proved to be correct because during the night there had been air raids on Leipzig. The bombed-out refugees were arriving at Colditz station when they spotted my prisoners in their recognizable English brown uniforms. The refugees started picking up stones and I had to do my best to restrain them. Thankfully the prisoners

Guards like Alfred Heinrich feared the consequences should they lose a Prominente prisoner.

Dawyck Haig (circled white) and George Lascelles (circled black) at the Coronation of HM King George VI, 1937. They were next to meet in Colditz seven years later.

were unharmed, but it was a difficult situation for me having to turn against my own people and, if need be, order my men to use our weapons. They were good lads and we believed in their word of honour that they wouldn't try to escape, but those walks put us in a difficult position. We couldn't take any chances.'

As the war went on life in Colditz became more and more uncomfortable. Lascelles recalls:

'Winter was particularly disagreeable because the Castle was such a cold place. Furthermore, by late 1944, Red Cross parcels began to dry up and by the end we were sharing one parcel a week between six or eight of us. It was very, very weakening. I lived on the bottom floor but ate meals at the top of the building, some three floors above. To go upstairs meant either a pause every dozen steps or a temporary black-out. An English doctor told us we were just below the starvation level of a bed-ridden patient. A typical day was one spoonful of soup with some meat and a potato in it and a hunk of bread. My diary records that I weighed 83 kgs on 9 October at Spangenberg, and 73 kgs at Colditz on 20 December.

'We spent a lot of each day in bed, fully dressed, in order to warm the bed and keep the damp out of the sheets, which we sewed into sleeping bags. Reading in winter by day was also done in bed, because it was too cold outside and the little fuel we had was kept for the evening.'

By the early months of 1945 it was clear that the Allies were going to win the war. The guards, often disgruntled and bored, proved easy sources of information and this, combined with a secret camp radio, helped clarify the situation. Whilst news of the advancing Russian forces in the East and the Americans in the West was welcome to the majority of prisoners at Colditz, it was greeted with apprehension by the *Prominente*. Their war was far from over and much speculation began as to what would be their eventual fate. They knew their situation was perilous.

It seemed increasingly likely that they would be moved out and most believed that their eventual destination would be Hitler's Final Redoubt up in the Bavarian mountains. By early April tension reached fever pitch. Haig remembers:

'Every now and then I would have a sort of visual picture of a nasty noose, but then I would put it out of my mind. We knew that we weren't there for nothing and our continued residence on this planet was not necessarily guaranteed. A senior diplomat from Berlin arrived on the camp, and I decided to take the opportunity to meet this visitor, Baron von Beninghausen. During the talk, though I was aware that the Baron was not a staunch Nazi, I also realized he was unreliable and that his assurances meant nothing. He promised to do all in his power to see that the *Prominente* were not moved. Because of my anxiety, I went to see the Commandant. The Commandant, whose name was Prawitt, was equally evasive; he told me that he had been trying to get the Wehrmacht High Command to promise not to hand us over to the SS, but he was not helpful abut the chances of getting such an undertaking.'

For some members of the group the suspense had become too much, as Lascelles recalls:

'More than one of us succumbed to some kind of nervous breakdown at this last stage of the war; others tried to immerse themselves in writing – novels, theses, solutions to the problems of the world or, in my case, just notes on what I had read.'

The *Prominentes*' suspense did not last long. On 12 April they heard the sound of distant American gunfire. On the same day the Commandant warned them that they were to be moved out that night. Haig:

'Our fears now became very great. We knew that we were going back to join the last remnants of Nazi forces. What had simmered for months in the back of our minds now became a reality.

'On the orders of Hitler and Himmler we were to be taken away from Colditz. We had little alternative but to comply with the German order. The Senior British Officer, Colonel Willie Tod, had done his best to help us by threatening the Commandant with dire punishment after the war if he handed us over. It would, he argued, be a violation of the Geneva Convention which stipulated that we be given twenty-four hours', notice and be told our destination.'

Tod's efforts were in vain. The Germans were adamant. As they hastily packed the few possessions they had, every man knew that the group could well be victims of Hitler's last act of vengeance.

Hitler and Himmler gave specific orders concerning the Prominente. *As the situation in Nazi Germany deteriorated, the likelihood of their being assassinated in a fit of revenge increased.*

CHAPTER SIX

Liberation

Few of the POWs captured in 1940 could have envisaged that it would take nearly half a decade before their moment of freedom. As the Third Reich collapsed around them, all they could do was hope that their day of liberation would come sooner rather than later. In the months of April and May 1945 their wishes finally became a reality. Yet for many of the prisoners it was not merely a case of sitting and waiting for the Allied armies. A number found the days and weeks leading up to freedom were as much of an ordeal as the years of captivity preceding them. Food shortages affected all, but there were further dangers. Some, like the *Prominente*, were only too aware that their lives hung in the balance. They were not alone. The inmates of Stalag Luft III, for instance, were

In the Winter and Spring of 1945 Allied forces relentlessly squeezed the Third Reich from the East and West. Left: An elderly German citizen appears bewildered at the presence of these American GIs on the streets of her town. Right: Russian T34/85s with supporting infantry on board.

197

Germans flee during the closing stages of the Allied onslaught on the Third Reich.

forced to endure a gruelling and hazardous march away from the encroaching Allied armies. For these prisoners the war had entered its most dangerous stage yet.

THE FATE OF THE *PROMINENTE*

On the night of Friday 13 April, amidst cheers of encouragement and support from their fellow inmates, the *Prominente*, along with General Bor Komorowski and some Poles, passed through the prison gates. They were greeted by a double line of SS soldiers, armed with sub-machine guns, forming a passage leading to two buses.

LORD HAIG recalls:

'As we drove through the town, the clock struck midnight. It was now Friday, 13 April. We went through Dresden and witnessed endless wastes of empty ruins looking eerie in the moonlight. Some thirty miles on we began climbing upwards and then, when the bus could go no further, we got out and saw towering above us the fortress of Konigstein. Charlie Hopetoun, who was in no fit state to climb, was helped along the tortuous climb.

'On passing through the great archway at the top, we entered a new world of German fantasy. The reality of the night before became obliterated by a new unreality. We were welcomed by a group of Wehrmacht officers who, with great courtesy and much saluting, showed us into our rooms where for a while we rested, before being offered coffee and rolls. The Germans did their best to thaw the atmosphere. Not long after the Commandant, Colonel Hesselmann, came in and announced in solemn tones the news he had just received. President Roosevelt had died.

We all stood up, Germans and British together, in a moment of sad silence.'
On the second day John Ephinstone, the leader of the group, was told that orders had come through from German Army High Command for their immediate transfer south. Aware of the dangers that lay ahead, Elphinstone resolved to persuade the Commandant that Charlie Hopetoun should remain in Konigstein in view of his trauma. Initially, Dawyck Haig also decided to ask for permission to stay with Charlie as his friend and companion.

'Now when the situation was definite John made his demands, but, finding that I had become ill with dysentery during the night, put forward my name to take his place as Charlie's companion. This was an act of supreme selflessness since at that time salvation seemed to lie at Konigstein rather than in the journey south, a journey which might well bring about the end of us all. The German Commandant needed no prompting and on his own initiative agreed to keep Charlie and myself

Viscount Lascelles and the Master of Elphinstone in Spring 1944.

without communicating with higher authority.

'With a feeling of intense personal relief, and with great concern for the safety of the others, we waved them goodbye. The Commandant, anxious to speed our recovery, moved us to a more comfortable room in the basement of his own quarters where we had paintings to look at and furniture to enjoy. Outside in the garden, his two boys played and laughed and reminded us of a life without war, without any of the cruelties and hardships that we had endured. We were given food from the Commandant's own kitchen. With these benefits we both felt better. Charlie's tension disappeared and he regained his poise and sense of fun. The problem now was that his recovery was so great that we would lose our excuse for staying and the German Commandant would lose his excuse for keeping us.'

Three days later, Himmler sent a telegram ordering the Commandant to send Haig and Hopetoun south to immediately join the others. Hesselmann was now in a tricky predicament.

'It was an order that Colonel Hesselmann found difficult to disobey, realizing that if he did so he was putting his own life at risk. However, he was prepared to do so providing he could do it with a clear conscience on the grounds of our sickness. He knew Charlie was better. The question now was whether my illness might be used as a justifiable reason for keeping us at Konigstein. It was agreed that the camp doctor would be asked to examine me and report on my condition. Charlie and I decided to take no chances and, as an added incentive to my innards, we got down to cooking up some prunes and figs which were in our Red Cross parcel. When these were ready, I proceeded to swallow as many as I could stomach in the hope that they would stimulate the irrigation in my plumbing system. When the doctor arrived and began to prod my intestines, he might have been squashing a hot water bottle. Amazed by the liquid state of my insides, he went off to compile a report which would corroborate my evidence and which would justify the Commandant in disobeying the order to move us south. Charlie and I relaxed once more.'

About a week later Haig heard the news that Admiral Doenitz had taken over what was left of the Third Reich and was ready to ask for an armistice. They also heard rumours that Hitler was dead.

'Some days after that the Russians arrived. The evening before had been spent with the Hesselmanns in the cosy atmosphere of their candlelit sitting room. At one point we heard Colonel Hesselmann issuing orders to a local garrison which was under his command to surrender to the Russians. Some time during the evening he discussed the disposal of the Saxon Crown Jewels, which were stored in twelve suitcases and were worth some £3,000,000. In his anxiety to prevent them falling into the hands of the Russians, he asked whether we could take them home with us as a present to the British Royal Family. We agreed to do so, subject to finding transport.

'Towards the end of the evening a haggard and distraught-looking German officer arrived and confirmed that the Russians were within five miles and would arrive next morning. He told us they were burning and raiding and were out of hand. Having delivered his report, our visitor put his field glasses and map on one side and sank exhausted into a chair. Charlie and myself then went to our room to collect a small present of coffee for Frau Hesselmann as a token of our appreciation of her care and kindness to us. Colonel Hesselmann in turn took off his small ceremonial sword and gave it to me as a token of his respect and, perhaps, of his surrender, since he preferred to acknowledge the British rather than the Russians as masters of the field. I still have it. His only wish was that we should do the utmost to help the German women, of whom a hundred or more had gathered together for shelter in the fortress and for protection from the Russian assault.'

The next morning the Russians could be seen crossing the Elbe in small boats. Yet, though their moment of freedom was imminent, Haig and Hopetoun were disturbed by the behaviour of their liberators. The two men watched as these

Russians land on the west bank of the Elbe. Their conduct terrorised the German population and shocked the liberated **Prominente***.*

troops slowly moved toward the castle, looting, burning and causing havoc as they went.

'Soon, without any military formation and without haste, motley groups began to make their way up the hill to take over the castle which now had a white flag flying over the tower. The castle became a turmoil. Russian soldiers, many of them drunk, were charging around without purpose other than to assuage their thirst for food, drink, property and possibly women. The condition and behaviour of their officers was no better.

'During this senseless orgy the German soldiers, with Hesselmann at their head, were formed up and marched off, according to rumour to Siberia, while we were left surrounded by hysterical women clamouring to us for protection. Charlie and I, anxious to protect the dependants of our enemies in the face of the ferocity of our allies, helped some girls to hide and then went off like policemen on separate beats to protect other women from the Russians. I tried to enlist the French Generals, who had also been imprisoned in the castle, for their aid but they did nothing, preferring to merely watch the misfortunes of these unhappy women. During this turmoil a German officer, who had hidden from the Russians, shot himself dead.'

Once the Russians had left the castle, Charlie Hopetoun and Haig were free to walk around at will while they waited for some transport to take them westwards. Two weeks later the Americans arrived. They did not have enough room to take the twelve suitcases of Saxon Crown Jewels. However, the jewels survived and are now safely on view in the Dresden Museum. Haig and Hopetoun were taken to the American Divisional Headquarters at Chemnitz and the following morning onto Brussels, where they were flown back to England. Several years later Colonel Hesselmann was handed over to the French authorities. Haig spoke up for him in the House of Lords in an effort to have his name removed from the list of War Criminals. John Hope, brother of Charlie Hopetoun, also brought up the issue in the House of Commons. Hesselmann died that same year from a duodenal ulcer, but his name was later cleared.

* * * *

While Dawyck Haig and Charlie Hopetoun had remained at Konigstein, the rest of the *Prominente* were driven southwards, crossing the Elbe and entering Czechoslovakia. The gap between the Americans advancing from the West and the Russians coming in from the East was closing fast, but their fate was still very uncertain. After a long journey, they were placed in a large concrete barracks at Klattau. The next day the convoy of buses continued on and crossed the wide Danube at Passau. Late that evening they reached a large block-like building. A couple of the party recognized it immediately, having spent time there during their early imprisonment – it was Laufen. Things had changed since then and it was now being used for civilian internees.

Michael Alexander remembers:

'John Elphinstone grasped that the moment was critical. If we entered this place we should no longer be under the reasonably correct control of the Wehrmacht but at the mercy of less responsible groups. Other Germans had now arrived and were repeating the order for us to get off the bus. Then John went white with rage and began to lash them in their own language and style. On no account would his party stay in a civilian camp. Anyone who tried to make them would suffer for it after the war. "We are English officers and we must be treated as English officers," he argued. The Germans went away. Telephone calls were made and then, scowling, the escorting officer climbed back into the bus and slammed the door.'

They were driven away and after some time began an ascent towards the castle of Tittmoning, near the Austro-Bavarian border, inhabited by Dutch officer prisoners.

'These Dutchmen were very kind but most of the time we stood about in depressed consultations on the nagging theme – our further move south. Anxiety fed anxiety until one Dutch officer broke through our stagnant depression and helped to resolve our crisis. Captain van den Heuvel was famed as an organizer of escapes and had in fact been banished from Colditz for that very reason.'

Van den Heuvel had reconnoitred an escape route and had also constructed a hide, both of which were intended for use in an extreme emergency. The predicament of the *Prominente* was such a case. It was agreed that Romilly would, along with two Dutch officers, use his escape plan which involved a descent down the castle wall by rope. The rest would go to ground in the hide that same evening. With any luck the Germans would think that they had all escaped.

Oflag VIIID at Tittmoning, where the majority of the **Prominente** *were held as the war drew to a close.* IWM HU65294

Giles Romilly, escaped from Tittmoning with Captain van den Heuvel's help.

'Giles went on his way. Meanwhile we all went to bed fully clothed ready to go ours. At 11 o'clock a Dutch officer broke into our room using a master key, and told us that all was ready. We each took a blanket and a small supply of food and followed him up the stone stairways and along endlessly creaking wooden corridors. Our single file finally came to a halt in the deep recess of a window in the castle wall, which at that place was at least eight feet deep. He got on his knees and, by the light of a small torch, began to ease a knife blade between the great stone blocks that formed the wall. A stone slid out and revealed the entrance to the hide, a hole just large enough for us to wriggle through one by one.

'From the tiny entrance chamber a tunnel about six feet long and three feet high led to a vertical shaft three feet square and twelve feet high. To accommodate us all, the only possible arrangement was for one person to sit on a stool provided at the bottom of the shaft, while another sat above him on a wooden plank; two people could lie in the tunnel side by side, while the remaining person sat with head bowed on the lavatory pail that had been installed near our point of entry. Each place had its attendant disadvantages. To give variety to our lives and relieve to our anatomies we arranged to change places at regular intervals. The lavatory seat was perhaps the all-time favourite, especially if a turn there could be put to useful purpose.'

When dawn broke it became clear from the great commotion outside that the men's disappearance had been discovered. From the hide they could hear excited shouting and the clatter of boots. They were in little doubt that an extensive search for them would be held both inside and outside the castle, and a little while later they heard the German guards sounding out the walls. Thankfully, van den Heuvel with characteristic expertise had made the hide echo-proof. His only mistake had been the amount of chloride of lime that had been placed in the lavatory pail. He had not realized that this was dangerous in such an enclosed space and had it not been for Max de Hamel, who was something of a chemist, the men would have the run the serious risk of being gassed.

On the second day the architect of the hide himself checked to see if all was well and passed in a bucket of hot potatoes. He also brought the news that Romilly had so far managed to evade all attempts to find him, despite the fact that the Germans had launched a search involving three thousand men. Van den Heuvel's information about Allied progress in the area was less encouraging. The advance was apparently slow.

The next day passed uneventfully, but, from the sporadic sounds of tapping, it was clear that the Germans had not given up the hope that their prisoners were still in the castle. On the fourth day the hide was discovered.

'The knocks started early and seemed to be getting stronger and increasing with intensity. There was a determined regularity between each blow as though somebody was wielding a pickaxe. Our hearts began to beat in painful expectancy. The crashes came louder and louder and soon the hole was reverberating with the ring of metal on stone. Suddenly the wall burst open, followed by an outburst of shouting. A bloodhound leapt forward barking and pistols and machine guns poked into the hole. We emerged looking extremely stupid to find ourselves surrounded by practically a whole company of SS men. The very agitated Camp Commandant, white-faced and shaking, gestured that he would have had his throat cut had we really escaped. He had apparently just been condemned to death over the telephone owing to our disappearance. It was rather an extraordinary scene.'

That day the men left Tittmoning and found themselves back at Laufen. The Germans, keen that no protest could be made that they were in a civilian internment camp, isolated them in a room which they surrounded with barbed wire.

'Supervision was strict; all communication with the civilian prisoners was forbidden. From our wired-up window we could see them circulating in the courtyard far below. A simple plan was worked out. We put a message inside a matchbox and dropped the box out of the window, hoping it would fall into helpful hands. In this message we wrote about who we were and asked that a matchbox containing a reply should be left under the single tree in the exercise ground. We were lucky. At our first outing an answer lay ready. It was signed by "Felix Palmer" and gave sufficient information to reassure us that our contact was reliable.'

The system worked well, but one day the message in the matchbox contained some unwelcome news.

'It stated, "Bus new at Laufen parked behind the walls. They seem to be trying to keep it hidden. Rumour you are to be moved." Our newly acquired sense of security was immediately shattered. We wrote back, "Do everything you can to sabotage transport or otherwise delay departure." Transport was at a premium; if the bus was damaged it would take time to repair it or find another. That evening a late extra flash was delivered in a loaf of bread, reading, "Sabotage attempt unsuccessful. Double guards on gate. Understand bus now filled with petrol. Trying to contact the Swiss. Good luck".'

SS General Gottlob Berger, in whose hands the fate of the **Prominente** *rested.*

Early next morning the men were herded onto the waiting bus. Disconcertingly, there was a strong SS presence, who followed them on their journey southwards. They soon reached the mountains. Here they saw the signpost they had been dreading – Berchtesgaden. The convoy drove on and slowly climbed up the mountain. It stopped at a huge encampment of huts surrounded by barbed wire, where the

205

Ernst Kaltenbrunner was to be the executioner of the **Prominente**.

party was ordered to disembark. After a couple of days the group had a visitor – Obergruppenführer Gottlob Berger, General of S.S. They were aware that their fate was in his hands.

'After talking to us for a while, he then produced his bombshell. He announced that he had received a direct order from the Führer that we were to be shot. It was now known in Berlin, he told us, that he had not carried out this instruction and as a result he himself had been proscribed. Following his defection, he went on, our execution was to be carried out by S.S. Führer Ernst Kaltenbrunner, who we already knew was a notoriously ruthless personality. He would now be looking for the opportunity to carry out his orders, and was known to be somewhere in the mountains.' Berger provided the group with an escort which had special orders to defend them against all-comers. He then told them that they would be driven out of the camp, accompanied by a representative of the Swiss government, through to American lines. The next morning, as Berger had promised, a big American car with a Swiss registration number arrived at the camp and, after considerable trouble finding transport as the bus had gone, the *Prominente* were moved off in two lorries. That evening the convoy halted in a farmhouse and Berger later arrived to entertain them. After considerable amounts of drink and food had been consumed, he left them and the group returned to their lorries and set off towards the American lines. They passed the last-ditch German positions and noted the youth of the men whose job it was to stall the inevitable collapse of the Third Reich. The convoy drove on. Alexander recalls the moment they knew that they were safe:

The Prominente *outside the entrance of the Hungerberg Hotel 5th May 1945 on their release. Left to right: The Master of Elphinstone, Max de Hamel, Michael Alexander, unknown, Viscount Lascelles and Lieutenant Winant.*

'We drove across the bridge and towards the widening of the Inn Valley. In a meadow to the left was an old wooden barn. Creeping towards the barn were two figures carrying rifles or machine-guns. They were Americans. We cheered. Round the next corner was a troop of three American tanks. A dusty, steel-helmeted figure was peering out of the turret of the leading one. A raised hand and a slowly swivelling gun signalled us to stop. Our credentials were checked by an American who then impatiently waved us on.'

THE MARCH FROM SAGAN

KEN REES, at Stalag Luft III, recalls the months leading up to his liberation:
'Towards the end of October 1944 it was suddenly decided to dig another tunnel. Most of us had lost our enthusiasm for digging but, as there weren't many experienced diggers left on camp, Joe Noble and myself were asked by the camp authorities to join the team. The tunnel, called *George*, was built from the theatre, which was a great place to start from as it wasn't too far from the wire – only about 150 feet. There were no worries about dispersing the sand either because one could just spread it around under the auditorium. By Christmas we were under the wire and close to where we planned the exit. I was of a mixed mind as to whether I wanted to get out after the murders of my friends.'
As it happened, the Russians were getting close. The prisoners could hear their

A remarkable photograph, prisoners from Stalag Luft III on the long and arduous march from the Soviet Army. THE SPECIAL COLLECTIONS BRANCH OF THE USAF ACADEMY LIBRARY

guns in the distance and on about 14 January they received an order from the Germans that the camp was to be evacuated in a couple of hours. Rees:

'We all immediately started tearing things off the walls to make sledges as there was a considerable amount of snow on the ground. Joe Noble, who was always doing these things, had got two ice-hockey sticks, which were used as runners and had built a box to put on them. This sledge was great because, when we did eventually move off in the early hours, we were able to pile as many Red Cross parcels as we wanted on to it. Most people took two, whereas we were able to take at least three or four, and a lot of cigarettes and other such items.

'It was snowing hard and bitterly cold. We were more or less at the back of the column, which looked more like a load of refugees that a bunch of prisoners. Conditions really were desperate and people were struggling to cope. Some were just throwing things away, which Joe insisted on picking up and putting on the sledge. We walked all day and all night. People were cold, frozen and wet.

'At one place we were sheltered in a glass factory and Joe and myself quickly found the manager's office, which had a fireplace. There was nothing much to burn but we soon settled that by breaking up a few chairs and things. We stayed there for two days and then set off on our march again. By this stage the snow had melted and so our sledges were not any good. Despite this, Joe who was a 200 lbs and six foot two Canadian, was determined to take as much goods as he could. I think he must have thought I was of a similar stature because he hung Red Cross parcels, cigarettes and all kinds of things all over me and off we set. We hadn't got very far when luckily we managed to commandeer a little dogcart. This was great because we put all our stuff in it and just pulled it along. We didn't eat a lot and tried to conserve as much as possible, because we all had a feeling that the food we carried would be all the food we would have

Allied prisoners during a pause on the long march in atrocious conditions.

Elderly German soldiers assigned to guard Allied prisoners during the long marches west through Germany and then south.

A column of British prisoners on the march during April 1945.

Allied prisoners of war march through a devastated German town and away from the rapid advance of Russian, American, British and French forces.

for some time. The local villagers were actually very friendly and it was sometimes possible to trade a bit of soap or coffee for hot water. The weather continued to be foul. Some people were suffering from frostbite, whilst others had dysentery.'

A number of the weaker prisoners began dropping out. The majority of those who fell by the sides of the roads were picked up by carts at the back of the column. By the time the men had reached Spremberg they were in a dreadful state.

'Rather than resting, we were put into cattle trucks. Some of these hadn't been cleaned and all were overcrowded – in some cases forty-six were put into each truck. This was the worst period. People were being sick, dysentery was rife and many were suffering the effects of the cold. We were locked up in the train for three days and were desperately short of water and food. We managed to make a hole in the floor of the truck and this was used for everything. They only stopped on a couple of occasions and to let us get out and try and find some water.'

On reaching a place called Tarmstadt, the weary prisoners were marched through the pouring rain to a naval camp south of Hamburg. Ken Rees remembers the conditions:

'The ground was just a mass of mud. I don't think I've ever been so low. The camp had no beds but had some straw. We just pushed the straw to one side of the hut and flung ourselves onto it, and put a few wet blankets over us. Nobody took any notice of the rats going over us. Over the next week about sixty or seventy per cent of the camp were suffering from dysentery, flu and various other ailments. Many got frostbite.'

By April the men received some news on the radio that the Allied army was making good progress.

'The Germans obviously considered us as hostages and decided to march us in the opposite direction again. We knew this was likely to happen and so had made precautions. One of our fellow prisoners, a Canadian chap, had shown us how to make backpacks and so we were able to put a lot of stuff into these. The German Kommandant had also been warned by our senior officer that we only wanted humane guards to accompany us and that he would be held responsible if anything happened. Everybody knew that the end was nigh and we purposefully set off very slowly, managing only a few kilometres a day. After a few days of marching south from Hamburg we were victims of friendly fire, as they call it now. Some fighter flew along and machine-gunned our column killing four naval officers at the rear. We couldn't have looked anything but refugees and I believe they had been warned that there were prisoners of war on the march, but we were still fired at.'

Towards the end of April they had almost reached Lübeck.

'We were put in a barn. A South African chap and myself decided to venture to a nearby house, which was owned by two females. We gave them some coffee, soap and cigarettes and asked to listen to their wireless. They agreed – by that time I don't think anybody cared too much. In fact,

Allied POWs halt for a rest at a German farm.

the guards were watching us work the radio. The news was good. The allies had crossed the Rhine. The ladies asked us back that evening and I had a sit-down meal washed down by schnapps. It was an odd feeling because the German guards were sitting on the floor in the same room eating their bread and sausage, whilst we had a reasonable meal.

'The next day we were moved into an estate and took over some stables. A few of us built a little shelter outside with straw and branches and we were resting in that when, on about 2 May, a jeep rolled up with an American lieutenant and his driver. This signalled our release. The jeep was soon followed by the arrival of more Allied soldiers. We knew for us the war was now over.'

BILL ARMITAGE was also on the march out of Sagan in January 1945. Here he recounts the days leading up to his liberation:

'We marched from dusk until dawn. We were getting very, very tired. At one point, it was very stupid I know, I just lay down in the snow and nearly went to sleep. Fortunately I woke up in time and staggered back to the column. I was nearly at the back of it when I saw another chap do the same. I went along to stir him but he really was fast asleep, so I kicked him. He didn't move. I kicked him again and his eyes fluttered and he said, "Bugger off". I managed to get him up and we shuffled on. We were behind the column but the goons weren't worrying about us. Snow was falling and you really couldn't see in front but the tracks made by this column of two thousand shuffling feet were still visible. At last we caught up with them and rested among some cattle trucks. I never saw the chap again. Then forty years later, there was a reception in the Guildhall commemorating the Battle of Britain and a chap came up to me and said, "Oh, Tage". They used to call me Tage. "Oh, Tage. I'm so glad to see you. I've never thanked you for saving my life." So we had a drink on it.

'On the day of our liberation an American sergeant approached us and asked if there were any Germans still with us. We replied there were. He then asked which ones had been particular bastards. There had been one and we pointed him out. I shouldn't think it was more than ten minutes later when the story went round that there had been a terrible accident involving one of the Germans. They'd run over this fellow with a tank.

'We were later taken to Luneburg where we were deloused and about two hundred of us were sent off to a deserted aerodrome. Expectations ran high and there were rumours that we'd be flown home that day. By the time we reached there, however, it was too late to leave and so we found this dormitory block with plenty of palliasses around and made ourselves comfortable. We slept like logs and at dawn were awoken to be told the planes had arrived. I left the dormitory where we had been sleeping and, as I slammed the door behind me, I looked round and saw on it red paint "Keep Out – Typhoid". That was the last I saw of Germany.'

TONY BETHELL still vividly remembers the moment he was liberated.
'This little armoured car appeared and we realized we were free. One

As the war in Europe neared its end millions of people were on the move, German refugees fleeing from before the Soviet Army, foreign workers and prisoners of war being marched from camps in the east. Here Allied prisoners pause during the march.

It's all over! Prisoners greet their American liberators.

minute you were a prisoner and then the next minute this armoured car arrives. A loaf of bread was produced out of it and it tasted delicious. Anyone living in England would have probably thought it was bloody awful because it was just wartime English bread, but the comparison between that and the German black bread was startling.'

LIBERATION FROM COLDITZ

WALTER MORISON spent the months leading up to the end of the war in Colditz. Unlike the *Prominente*, he remained there until his liberation.

'As the end of the war approached, morale actually began to sink. One just sat, waited and wondered what would happen. There were some very unfortunate alternatives. One was that the Russians would arrive and we didn't know how that would work. Another was that the goons would take us out and march us about in the ever-narrowing space between the British and American forces and the Russians. That was not a pleasant prospect and proved pretty dreadful for people in other camps. There was also the thought that the Germans might turn nasty. We were, after all, special prisoners and some of us had been in the habit of dropping bombs over Germany, which didn't exactly endear us to them. So there could have been all sorts of unpleasant outcomes and we didn't have much to do but just sit and think about them.

'When the arrival of the Americans was imminent, our Senior British Officer asked the Commandant what his intentions were. He replied that he was awaiting instructions from Himmler. We all knew Himmler was head of the SS and a very unpleasant customer, so it wasn't a particularly nice thought that he was deciding our fate. In the meantime the *Prominente* were ordered to be moved to Hitler's redoubt and the guards were informed that anyone who let them escape would be shot. The rest of us just waited and listened to the radio. We also had German newspapers and usually if you added to the two together and divided by two you got somewhere near the truth.

'We knew that the Americans were only about 150 miles away. They slowly moved closer and closer until we could hear gunfire in the distance. Unfortunately there was an SS contingent who were determined to defend the line of the river on which Colditz stood. Eventually an American contingent was detached from the main force that was approaching Leipzig and made their way towards us. They had been told that there was a prison camp in this place called Colditz, where there were VIPs, and that they were to get there and quick. This they did, but on approaching the castle they came under attack from the SS who were on the hill behind the castle. Shells were flying to and fro over us, which was very unpleasant. A number of army officers were taking a very professional interest in the battle, standing in the windows and commenting on how interesting it all was. I didn't take that view and went and hid under the stairs in what I thought was the most shell-proof part of the building. I felt a bit ashamed of this but I had good company. Douglas Bader and a man called Tommy Kettler, who was a submarine commander, were also cowering in the same hole. I've always believed that submariners were amongst the bravest of the brave and Bader certainly was, so I felt a bit better about my actions.

'Before long the shooting had stopped. The doors of the gate then swung open and American tanks entered the courtyard. We all felt enormous relief but such was the chaos of the day that I don't think we even thought about our emotions at that point. The next day we were all loaded into lorries and taken to a Luftwaffe airfield. We were going home.'

'THE AMERICANS ARE COMING'

JACK COMYN and his fellow captives were increasingly suffering from the effects of hunger and cold in their prisoner of war camp near Brunswick in Germany. However, they knew that liberation was not far off.

'Every night you got news of how the fighting was going. We learnt a certain amount from German papers but for the most part it was from hearing the BBC news each evening on little radios which had been made. We had men keeping guard to warn us if the Germans were approaching. So in many ways it was no mystery to us as to where the Americans and British had reached.

'Nevertheless, the moment of our liberation was an epoch-making day in the lives of all of us. During the night we heard tanks and quite early in the morning a little jeep drove up to the camp gate and out jumped an American sergeant of the 9th Army. He just went round the wire ordering each German sentry to fall in at the guard gate. And they all did. It was extraordinary. A couple more jeeps then arrived and our captors were marched off just like that. Soon after, American lorries with the famous K rations, which were a sort of hard food, arrived. They started throwing these out. Despite this, there was one officer who couldn't wait to get the American K rations and whilst everyone was outside went around people's rooms taking a slice off each loaf of bread that had not been consumed. This was instantly noticed when we returned to our rooms and I think he almost got tarred and feathered. But anyway it was a great day when the Americans arrived. Wonderful.'

CHAPTER SEVEN

Back to Blighty

POWs faced a new challenge on arriving back in Britain. The years of captivity inevitably took a heavy toll on these men and they now had to set about adjusting to life in the outside world. Some found life without the wire easier to cope with than others. Many missed the camaraderie. Understandably, people found it hard to relate to the experiences these men had been through. They were seen as victims not heroes, and their part in the war was all too often neglected. Promotions and medals had passed them by, whilst many of their colleagues had risen in the ranks.

The *appels*, the dormitories, the Red Cross parcels, the goon baiting – all these things, which had become such an integral part of their world, needed to be cast aside. The men now had to put the past behind them. The world had changed and so had they. Many of those who had entered the war as adolescents fresh from school returned as men who had aged beyond their years. Fathers arrived back unable to recognize their own children. POWs now had to rebuild relationships. Some had not seen their loved ones for five years.

On their way home at last! A C-47 transport being boarded by British ex-POWs.

BILL ARMITAGE, the Spitfire pilot shot down over France in 1941, arrived back from Germany after three and a half years in captivity and having just endured the long march from Stalag Luft III to Lübeck.

'We landed in an aerodrome somewhere in Warwickshire and were given some breakfast. We then had to go through a system of being checked off, names, numbers, who we were, were we had been, etc. This was followed by a medical inspection, which I had a bit of trouble with. I was deaf in one ear and they asked, "Do you want to claim for this?" "Yes, I certainly do," I replied. "Well, a doctors' team won't be here for around four days so I'm afraid you'll have to wait," they told me. I asked them if I could go home for a couple of days and then come back. This was apparently impossible so I told them to stuff it and that I wouldn't make a claim.

'Once I'd got through all that nonsense, I went to telephone my mother. The girl on the switchboard said, "Have you got a priority?" So I said, "Yes, I've got every priority in the world after three and a half years in Germany!" But she wouldn't have it and put me through to someone higher, who then put through to my mother instantly and I was home that night.'

After leaving the RAF, Bill Armitage returned to his family's textile firm in Bolton, Lancashire. He later sold the business and set up a carpet manufacturing firm of which he was Managing Director until retirement, aged 71. Throughout this time, he maintained an active interest in flying and was the Chairman and President of the Lancashire Aero Club, the first aero club in the U.K. Other interests include family life and gardening.

JIMMY JAMES, after numerous escape attempts including taking part in the Great Escape which had led to his imprisonment at the brutal Sachsenhausen concentration camp, recalls his emotions on arriving back in England:

'It's difficult to describe one's feelings after five years behind barbed wire. I was flown back in the civil version of the Wellington that I'd been shot down in five years previously. The feeling of arriving back at Blackbushe in Hampshire was unbelievable. You were on English soil again. I went up to London and it was a bit of an anti-climax actually. Soon after, I was inspected by a doctor who tapped me all over and sent me on leave on double rations, which I couldn't eat anyway. I was told to report back for another medical in six weeks time which I did and was passed fit for flying. Physically I was all right, but mentally my experiences in captivity affected me for many years.'

On his return, James was awarded the Military Cross and mentioned in despatches for his escaping activities. He returned to Germany after the war, where he met his wife Madge, who was a Nursing Sister in the Red Cross. He later joined the Foreign Office and served in a number of posts around the world, including Prague, West Berlin, Paris and Durban. Retirement in 1975 gave James the opportunity to pursue his love of golf, skiing and sailing.

JACK COMYN, captured in North Africa in the winter of 1940, had spent two years imprisoned in a number of Italian POW camps before taking advantage of the Italian Armistice and escaping. After two and a half months on the run, he had been re-captured

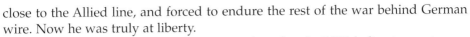

close to the Allied line, and forced to endure the rest of the war behind German wire. Now he was truly at liberty.

'When we got off the plane there were these lovely WVS ladies to greet us with tables of tea, buns and biscuits. The colonel who was commanding there then arrived and said, "How wonderful it is to see you. I'll only keep you a couple of days, but you see you've got to have a medical, and you must get your medals and uniforms and so on." He soon realized that holding us up was going to be easier said than done. And this poor colonel continued, "These are my orders – oh but damn. I've spent the whole of my career in the army mucking up the War Office and I don't see why I shouldn't do it now." We were on a train heading to family or friends within a few hours!

'I made my way down to Bournemouth, where my mother, father and old nanny were all standing on the platform to greet me. I could see them but they didn't seem to be able to recognize me though. I had to go up and introduce myself. Well, I had been away for six years at that stage and I had a small very untidy moustache. I'd lost three or four front teeth and weighed only eight stone, so it is not surprising perhaps. It was a wonderful moment though.

'The next day was the 2nd of May and news was pouring in about the German navy surrendering and Hitler shooting himself and so on. I just wasn't interested. All I wanted to do was get on a bicycle and go biking along the country lanes around my home near Wimborne in Dorset. The countryside looked so lovely. I relished the peace and quiet. It was fantastic to be able to go into a pub and have a pint of beer.'

Jack Comyn remained in the Army; he was recommended for Staff College and passed out in the top four in May 1946. He retired from the Army in 1950 to farm in County Cork, Eire. A decade later, he moved back to England and joined a large farming company in Essex, where he became financial director. He retired in 1980 but continued to pursue his two great passions, writing and fishing.

ALEX CASSIE had spent the last three years in Stalag Luft III since his Whitley bomber had been shot down in 1942. During this time he had become an accomplished forger whose documents had been used by many would-be escapers, including those taking part in the Great Escape. He found that freedom needed adjusting to.

'After a couple of nights in ambulance barracks I went up to Edinburgh where my cousin, aunt and uncle were living. They had been almost parents to me when I was a student at Aberdeen before the war. My uncle decided to put me in a private room in the main building. My first thoughts were that it would be wonderful as I hadn't had a room to myself for two years and eight months. But in fact I felt distinctly uncomfortable. There was no one to talk to. I felt lonely. I remember hearing an aeroplane go over and I suddenly became worried that it could be an enemy aircraft. But I came to my senses.'

After the war, Alex Cassie was employed as a psychologist in the RAF, a job that enabled him to meet and keep in contact with many of the men he had lived with behind the wire in Germany.

TONY BETHELL, like Alex Cassie, arrived back after three years of captivity spent mostly at Stalag Luft III, except for a brief interlude after his capture in the Great Escape when he was imprisoned in the Gestapo fortress of Gurditz. Dissatisfied by the treatment he received on returning home, he took matters into his own hands.

'We suffered our final indignity when we arrived back in England and the first thing that happened was that we were deloused fifteen minutes after arrival. They shoved these pipes down your trousers and all around, then pulled a trigger and blasted this white cloud that covered you inside and out. We decided that we didn't want any more of that and a few of us disappeared into London for a couple of weeks. We couldn't cash cheques so we had to borrow money from friends. One of my friends, Heather, had a very nice flat in Kensington and so we spent two weeks living there and that proved an excellent way of acclimatizing to the joys of home. It was a wonderful time.'

When Tony Bethell was demobilised in 1946, he decided to join the Middle Eastern Trading Company. Three years later, he rejoined the RAF and was posted to Washington and Germany. Sport played a big part in his life after the war and Bethell had a distinguished rugby career, playing for the Barbarians and Blackheath. In 1955 he emigrated to Canada, where he was to become President and CEO of an investment business. He retired in 1989 and now farms outside Toronto. He has a large family (14 grandchildren at the time of publication!). His hobbies include tractors and chainsaws, and travel.

DAWYCK HAIG'S period of imprisonment, first in Italy and then Germany, took a heavy personal toll, aggravated by his uncertain fate as one of the *Prominente* in Colditz, particularly in the latter stages of the war. He returned home on a low ebb both physically and mentally.

'We landed at Ampney Aerodrome, amidst the green fields of Gloucestershire. From there Charlie Hopetoun was sent to London for check-ups and dismissal. I was taken to the local hospital where I was left alone and frustrated on my first night at home. It was more than I could bear to find myself pacing around inside four walls like a caged animal, on a night to which I had so much been looking forward. My frustration was too great! I seized the telephone in the passage and rang my friend, John Cripps, who lived nearby. Luckily John was at home; he had himself recently been repatriated from a German POW camp and he knew exactly how I was feeling. He lost no time in driving to the hospital door through which I made my escape. As soon as I reached John's home I rang the hospital to tell them what I had done and where I was. They understood.

'Next morning was Sunday. I awoke to hear the chimes of the bells of the parish church and looked out to the chalk stream below my window and watched the brown trout rising to the mayfly. My sisters Doria and Rene came to fetch me. On the road to London we passed many beautiful young girls out walking with their lovers. As the reality of my return sank in, I began to weep.

'It is difficult to explain my state of mind, except perhaps to say that the whole system, physical and mental, was in a state of collapse as a result of three years of privation. On my return from Germany I still had severe attacks of dysentery. I weighed less than eight stone and my body was covered in boils.

'Readjustment to life after captivity was difficult. The effects of POW experiences had enabled me to find freedom through the inner freedom of dreams. Through them I had been taught some of the truths of my being in a world which lay far below the surface of the wartime lives of my relations and pre-war friends, many of whom found me withdrawn and changed.

'We ourselves found the outside world had changed. Relations with friends whom we had left behind had during the long six years adapted themselves in their own ways to total war. We had been cut off and had lost touch with the realities of normal life. Due to restrictions, we were only able to write the equivalent of an airmail letter every week or so. Letters from home had been mainly limited to one's family and I had very few letters from anybody else.

'We were to some extent outcasts from both the prison camp world and the world outside, so that, in times of despair, we lost the will to fight. This condition had in my case, and I am sure in the case of many others, been aggravated by an almost complete separation from women for six years at a most impressionable age, and at an age when most people are going through emotional development. Because of this emotional starvation, I did not feel as others felt who had lived a normal life. I was living a full life at an intellectual level, so that I always had a book in my hand. But I was not able to live through the animal side of my nature, which, because of its frustration, came out into the open in the form of nightmares. Many of my dreams were to do with sexual fantasies and of amputations of various parts of my body. My depressions, which were almost worse than the depression I had suffered behind the wire, seemed to come on for no particular reason. I was not happy among groups of people at parties, nor was I happy to be alone in the landscape, particularly when the sun shone brightly in summer.

'I found it difficult to come back to living life as one had lived it before. However, new aspects of my personality began to emerge which I had not known before. I became aware of new pleasures and new experiences and in my own self-awareness. I became a fuller person, able to stand on my own feet rather than be tossed around in the wake of others. I had changed. I learnt to savour life fully.'

After the war Dawyck Haig became a celebrated artist. He returned to the family estate, Bemersyde, on the banks of the River Tweed in the Borders, where he lives today. He recently published his memoirs, My Father's Son (Pen & Sword Books).

GEORGE LASCELLES, another member of the *Prominente*, had been captured on 18 June 1944. Conditions at Colditz were in stark contrast to his surroundings on arrival back in England.

'I remember few details of my return to England. My mother was in London, my father was ill at Harewood and I talked to him on the telephone. I have a feeling I slept the night at Buckingham Palace. I am fairly sure that my mother and I dined there, and I do remember smoking a cigar and being undemonstratively sick in a lavatory afterwards, I have never really liked cigars since. I was in London for VE day and, on 8 May, went home to Harewood and spent the rest of the summer there, sleeping (with some difficulty), putting back a little weight and recuperating.'

After the war, Lascelles went to Canada as an ADC to the Earl of Athlone. In 1947 he became Earl of Harewood following the death of his father, the 6th Earl. On his return he pursued his passion for opera and in a highly varied career he has been involved, strictly on the managerial side, with Covent Garden, the Edinburgh Festival and the English National Opera. His non-musical posts have included being President of the English Football Association.

MICHAEL ALEXANDER, the commando captured in the African desert, had been the first to join Giles Romilly in Colditz as one of the *Prominente*.

After the war, he joined the 2nd SAS with David Stirling. When it was disbanded he set up a visual education business for schools. He and Romilly wrote about their experiences during the war in A Privileged Nightmare. It was to be the first of nine books he published. He also undertook a number of scientific expeditions from the Himalayas to Mexico. He has additionally been a restaurateur and is a keen sailor, who annually takes part in a 500-mile race around the north coast of Scotland.

WALTER MORISON returned to England after imprisonment in Stalag Luft III and latterly at Colditz, following his daring attempt to escape by stealing a Luftwaffe aircraft.

'It was only on arrival in Oxfordshire that it really sank in that we were free and home. After being heavily dusted with DDT, which was a powerful de-louser exercise, we were led into a train and rattled off to an RAF depot at Codford near Wolverhampton. There, in a RAF mess in the small hours of the morning, I found myself eating bacon and eggs. That further brought my freedom home to me. Soon after, the anti-climax set in. Apart from a few medical examinations, nothing much happened and it wasn't long before we were sent on leave. I really didn't know what to

POWs delousing after their release. It would take several attempts to feel fully clean. SPECIAL COLLECTIONS BRANCH OF THE USAF ACADEMY LIBRARY

do with myself. Everyone was so kind, but the truth was that practically none of my friends had survived the war. Thankfully my great friend Lorne Welch rang up and asked how I was. "Fine. How are you?" I said. "Fine", he replied. Then there was a sort of pause and he came out with it, "If I stay at home a minute longer I shall go mad." I agreed and we decided to take a boat on the Norfolk Broads. The Broads were deserted and we just sailed this beautiful boat around for about three weeks. Perfect peace.

"After that, it was time to face up to what we could do next. The real crunch came when I was demobilized. In other words I ceased to be an RAF officer, which I had been for practically all of my adult life. I wept at the news because it had been a life that I had really loved. My efforts to get into civil aviation failed and I decided to commit myself to become a chartered accountant, which I hadn't the slightest desire to do but was too feeble-minded to do anything about. It was obviously a difficult transition to make. I should really have gone back to Cambridge and had a couple of years to sort myself out. I hadn't suffered in the POW camps and actually for much of the time had quite a lot of fun in them. Nevertheless I was fairly moth-eaten for a few years after the war.'

Morison thus became a reluctant chartered accountant. He did however continue to pursue his love of gliding for a number of years after the war with his great friend, Lorne Welch. He gave it up when he had children, deciding that sailing might be more family-orientated. He has managed a charitable foundation, which funds medical research, for many years.

KEN REES, the bomber pilot shot down over Norway in late October 1942, had spent the rest of the war at Stalag Luft III, where he had become a tunneller in *Harry* – the tunnel used in the Great Escape. He was one of those still in it when the Germans discovered it. During the closing stages of the war Rees had also had the misfortune to have to endure the terrible march from Sagan.

'I got home on VE day. On getting to the farm I sat down to a terrific meal of ham, eggs and home-made sausages. I was told that my wife Mary, who was in Norfolk with the Land Army, had been informed I was home. She set off straight away and travelled overnight. I met her at the station at about 5 or 6 o'clock in the morning. It was a wonderful reunion. We had only been married for three days before I became a prisoner of war and so it was fantastic to see her after three years of captivity. I could now start the fourth day of my honeymoon!

'I was so excited to be free. It was absolutely wonderful. Somehow you felt you had changed. You started the war as a young boy and returned from it more or less a mature man. A lot had happened.'

Ken Rees took a permanent commission with the RAF after the war and, at the age of thirty, became a Squadron Leader. He was to become a Wing Commander five years later and in 1963 commanded V-Bomber Squadron. A keen and talented rugby player, Rees played for the Combined Services and captained London Welsh. After retiring from the airforce in 1968, he managed a post office store, before running a private members club in Rhoseigr, Wales

Further Reading

Michael Alexander, *A Privileged Nightmare*, Weidenfeld & Nicolson, 1954 and latterly Pan, 1956.
A superb book, written with Giles Romilly, which documents their extraordinary wars. The two men were to meet in Colditz and their experiences as *Prominente* make particularly good reading.

Dawyck Haig, *My Father's Son*, Pen & Sword Books, 2000.
A fascinating and charming autobiography tracing his life from an unusual childhood, as son of the Commander-in-Chief of the British Army in the First World War, through to imprisonment at Colditz and beyond.

Lord Harewood, *The Tongs and the Bones*, Weidenfeld & Nicolson, 1981.
An honest and very readable autobiography charting an extraordinary life of royalty, war and opera.

Jimmy James, *Moonless Night*, William Kimber, 1983 and Sentinel, 1993.
A remarkable story of determination, ingenuity and daring. This is a must-read for all escape story enthusiasts.

Walter Morison, *Flak and Ferrets*, Sentinel, 1995.
A modest but highly exciting account of his war, from joining the RAF, through his daring escape attempts from Stalag Luft III, to eventual liberation.